"The Joy of Murder" is published by :

Trinity Mirror NW²

Trinity Mirror North West & North Wales
PO Box 48
Old Hall Street,
Liverpool L69 3EB

Trinity Mirror S.M. Executive Editor:
Ken Rogers

Design / production:
Daisy Dutton, Jonathan Low, Emma Smart

ISBN 978 1 905266 36 4

Acknowledgements

I would like to thank so many people, without whom this book
would not have been possible:

My sister Marilyn and brother Tony, who are great mates
and great proof-readers. My good friends Maria Allen,
Rebecca Benneyworth, Dana Braithwaite, Geri Brown,
Mal Catterall, Trudy Lowe and Mal Waring for all their help
and support. Peter Clark and Colin McKeown
for their valuable advice and encouragement.

A huge thank you to Sara Wilde, Ken Rogers,
Daisy Dutton, Emma Smart and Jonathan Low
at Trinity Mirror NW2 for all their hard work and support.

All the actors who have been involved with Murder Weekends over the
last 25 years, for their fantastic contribution to the success of Weekends and
for providing the many, many laughs that we've had over the years. Many of
them are mentioned in this book and I'd like to thank them for allowing me
to re-tell some of their funny, weird and often bizarre stories.

I'd also like to thank the guests who have made all the hard work
worthwhile and who have given us so much fun over a quarter of a century.

Most of all, I'd like to thank Chris Livesey because without him there
probably wouldn't be a book. His help, ideas, editing suggestions
and repeated chiding for me to get cracking have meant
there is a book for you to enjoy.

Lastly, I want to thank my wonderful parents, Norman and Thelma Swift,
who sadly are no longer around to read this book.
I know they would have been both amazed and enormously proud.

Cover design by Joy Swift
Front illustration by Sally Lambert
Back cover photograph by Jacqueline Kirkham

Introduction

You can't keep a good woman down

My name's Joy Swift," I said nervously, "and most weekends I kill people!". "My name's Joy Swift," said the very confident young woman sitting next to me, "and most weekends I kill people!".

Sitting next to her, an elegant older woman also claimed to be me. Although there has been many times when I sincerely thought it would be a great relief if there was more than one Joy Swift, this wasn't one of them. What I was actually thinking is unprintable – just another fine mess I'd landed myself in because of my crazy invention.

The reason this time was an appearance on a television quiz show called Tell The Truth, where a celebrity panel had to guess which out of the three of us was the "real" Joy Swift – a question that is, now I've started to think about it, probably impossible to answer.

After all, the "real" Joy Swift has, over the past 25 years, been married 134 times (frequently and repeatedly to the same man) and given birth to 230 illegitimate children. I've been battered and bruised and arrested more times than I care to remember. I've also committed (at the last count) around 3,000 murders – you'll have to excuse the vagueness because when you've been responsible for that many deaths you start to lose track after the first few hundred – something that's a bit more understandable perhaps given that I've been stabbed, poisoned, shot, strangled and drowned more times than I care to recall.

Thankfully, as I hope you've guessed, none of these things have happened to the real Joy Swift. I'm honestly nothing like any of the characters I've played over the years since I invented the idea of Murder Weekends in 1981. This isn't to say plenty of frighteningly real things haven't happened over this period – like the time I was arrested by the Anti-Terrorist Squad or when I was rushed to hospital in New York after a spectacularly innovative murder went dramatically wrong and a badly burned leg turned gangrenous – but I like to think it's possible to separate the "real me" from my invention.

And that, in a round about way, is my main reason for sitting down to write this book. I thought it would be nice, given I'm now celebrating the 25th anniversary of the original Murder Weekend, to document the highs and lows, tears and laughter of a quarter-century of murder, mayhem and a great deal of merriment. I wanted to tell the story of Murder Weekends and, echoing perhaps the words of a very good friend who once said to me "Joy, you ARE murder weekends", a bit about the story of Joy Swift into the bargain.

To do this, I've divided this book into three sections. The first tells the story of how Murder Weekends came into being, from the moment I hit upon the original idea to the first few years of their development. It also includes some material about my life, mainly because I hope it gives some insight into how and why I chose the "madness of murder" as a career.

In the second part I wanted to document some of the funny, sad and frequently downright ridiculous things that have happened on Murder Weekends – the kind of things that the guests rarely get to see.

When I started to write I began to think about how to describe "the real Joy Swift" and the best way I could think of was through what I do. So, finally, I've set you all a little challenge – a solvable murder mystery called "Love Letters Straight From My Heart" – in part three.

The Joy of Murder

Part 1

The Joy of Murder

Chapter 1

Jerry's dying and I've got no knickers

It had been a terrible week. The bad luck began on the Sunday evening when, returning home from a Murder Weekend, I crashed my car. It wasn't my fault and thankfully no one was seriously injured but it left me bruised and fed up.

It didn't help when, the next morning, there were insurance problems that left me wondering if I'd be able to hire a car for the following weekend in Salisbury (only a few hundred miles from my Liverpool home). To cap it all, the rest of the week was spent doing what Mal (my assistant and friend) and I really love doing most in the whole world – preparing the VAT return!

By Friday morning I wasn't, as you can imagine, in the happiest frame of mind as I drove down the motorway in the car I'd managed to hire at the very last minute, following some free and frank discussions with my insurer. With the events of the week still buzzing around my head, I tried to focus on the logistical details of a Weekend with 70 paying guests.

Although I was thankful to arrive at the White Hart hotel in one piece and with all the important bits of the car still attached, I had been so busy that my absent-minded packing had left me short of a vital piece of equipment.

As any of my actors will tell you, Friday night is always a little uncomfortable. I had to get into character (I'm not really the husband-abusing, child-hating, homicidal maniac I was playing that weekend), stay in character while being furiously questioned by all manner of not-quite-so-charming sleuths, all anxious to find any chink or discrepancy in my carefully constructed back story, and smile sweetly at people who would doubt not only my parentage but my parent's parentage. In addition to this, my discomfort was increased, quite literally, by the fact I'd forgotten to pack any knickers.

Thankfully, this discomfort seemed to pass off quite successfully as evidence of my character's general shiftiness and the first death of the weekend went smoothly. By the end of the evening I was beginning to relax satisfied that, whatever the troubles of the previous week, at least something was going to plan. My confidence was sadly misplaced.

The first part of Saturday morning passed smoothly enough but by lunchtime I was smack bang in the middle of a blazing row with an enraged wife, furious to the point of violence at my clandestine association with her "darling husband". This was, of course, all part of the unfolding plot.

Linda White, the actress playing the jealous wife, had just slapped me across the face pretty hard and a little too realistically. As always the guests were enjoying the scrap and encouraging Linda to new heights of violence (for someone who is a very gentle soul in real life she was certainly acting her socks off that weekend) by revealing all the juicy details they'd just read in the police incident room. It was all going swimmingly when Sheila Ackroyd, the actress playing my mother, pulled me to one side and pretended to comfort me.

Since this wasn't supposed to happen – lots of things aren't supposed to happen on Murder Weekends – I was momentarily perplexed by her behaviour. I shouldn't have been, because Sheila has been a law unto herself for many years as far as acting goes. "Expect the unexpected and you won't be disappointed" has become something of a truism as far as Sheila is concerned, but we've all learned to go with the flow and trust her judgement.

However when she whispered in my ear "Jerry's dying" I thought she had finally lost it. It crossed my mind that either she or Jerry Percy, the actor playing my lover and the errant husband, had unilaterally and inexplicably decided to change the plot. As I pushed her away to continue the argument with Linda it crossed my mind that Jerry was missing. He was supposed to have come down to lunch to get involved in the row but in all the excitement (and the unexpected pain) I hadn't realised he wasn't around. "Never mind," I thought, "I'll finish with Linda and then sort Jerry out!". As I waded back into the argument – which by now had been fuelled by a further revelation of her dear husband's double-dealing – Sheila once again stopped me in full flow, much to Linda's bemusement, in order to "comfort me" once more.

"No. Jerry really is dying," she hissed, more urgently this time.

At this point it's probably pertinent to note that Jerry, one of my actors for many years, has become known as something of a hypochondriac.

In case you think I'm exaggerating, he once 'died' on a hotel carpet that brought him out in a rash. On the way to the hospital he managed to croak (probably with what he sincerely thought was his dying breath) that we should tell the doctor it could be an allergic reaction to too much Shake 'n' Vac. He seemed genuinely upset when the two of us accompanying him in his hour of greatest need started to laugh.

With this incident in mind, once I realised he really was dying this time (I realise this makes me sound shallow but, knowing Jerry as I do, I'd say that his imminent demise was invariably much exaggerated) I pulled my thoughts together, gave Linda the (verbal) thrashing she so richly deserved and, as is the way with Murder Weekends, promptly switched to explaining the next game the guests were going to play.

Once they had been safely focused on the game, I went to Jerry's room and found Linda and a couple of the other actors hovering in the bathroom over Jerry's prone body.

His face was the same colour as the grey marble tiles and he lay, unmoving, surrounded by vomit. One of the actors joked it was a shame his Murder Weekend deaths weren't as realistic, but for some reason Jerry didn't seem to find this very funny and he begged us to call a doctor.

This being a Saturday, the doctor wasn't about to interrupt his golf by actually coming to see the body (or patient as he still was at this stage, but Jerry thought it was touch-and-go). As it turns out, Jerry was diagnosed with labyrinthitis, an ear infection that can bring on dizziness, disorientation and sickness. The doctor warned he shouldn't be moved and that he certainly could no longer act. We all probably thought it, but no one made the obvious joke as we managed to clean him up and drag him, protesting, from the bathroom to his bed.

Although we were thankful Jerry was going to be okay, this left a huge problem. One of the key suspects was now safely tucked up in his bed, snoozing softly and unable to leave his room for the rest of the weekend. To make matters worse, I had about an hour to explain his sudden disappearance before the guests reassembled for the answers to the game.

Thinking on my feet (one of the many skills I've developed over the 25 years of producing Murder Weekends) I came up with a devious scheme to dispense with Jerry's character and set about creating some clues to explain his absence to the guests as if it had always been planned that way.

An hour later, as all the guests gathered for afternoon tea and the answers to the game, a police inspector made an unscheduled call to announce to the assembled throng that Keith Collins (Jerry's character) had, as he so eloquently put it, "done a runner" as he felt the police net tighten around his neck. He had, the inspector continued, stolen a guest's car from the hotel car park but, thankfully, he deadpanned: "Mr Collins was arrested after he crashed the car on the M5 following a high-speed police chase."

This information surprised the guests, especially the regular guests who've been on numerous Weekends, since they'd never witnessed, in all their years of sleuthing, quite such an unexpected disappearance of a major suspect.

However, this information proved to be more than a little unwelcome for one guest in particular. Chris (the actor playing the inspector that weekend) had earlier gone to the car park, selected a likely vehicle at random and calmly read out the number plate of the "stolen vehicle" to the guests.

A female guest suddenly shrieked: "That's my car!", jumped up from where she was sitting and sprinted outside to the car park. She returned soon afterwards, looking a little sheepish that she had fallen for our dramatic storyline.

I was very relieved since a major crisis had been averted without the guests being any the wiser. My relief was, again, short-lived.

Later that afternoon – in what was turning out to be a very long day – we'd managed to safely position the next "dead body" on the hotel's main stairs (no mean feat given that it was in constant use by guests and led directly into the main hotel lounge). While the guests were occupied in a separate function room playing a light-hearted game, I positioned myself in the lounge out of sight of the body and waited until it was found.

The actor concerned was covered in blood and had a large, ugly gash in his chest. Blood was spewing from his mouth and, even if I do say so myself, he looked very realistic. Unfortunately, he looked too realistic because, as luck would have it, he was immediately found by the only "ordinary guest" staying in the hotel that weekend who hadn't been told he was in the middle of a Murder Weekend. To make matters worse, this guest was German. And the clincher was he had only a limited knowledge of English.

I heard the exclamation of horror as he found the body, a little earlier than I was expecting. What I really didn't expect, however, was to see someone I knew wasn't one of the Murder Weekend sleuths rush to the reception desk and, in a garbled mix of German and English, hysterically shout for the receptionist to ring for the police and an ambulance. Normally, hotel staff are more than prepared for incidents such as this; the usual procedure is to smile sweetly and then carefully explain what was happening. This particular receptionist was new to the hotel and panicked.

"No, it's alright," she blurted, looking to where the body was laying. "He'll be okay," she added to the stunned amazement of the confused guest. "But. But…you do not understand," he spluttered, gesticulating towards the body. "Dead," he said, as if this was somehow likely to spur the receptionist into some kind of activity. At this point Gunther (his name, as I later learned) gave up trying to communicate in both English and sign language, reached behind the desk, picked up the phone, waved it in the general direction of the befuddled receptionist and said in perfect English: "Call a bloody ambulance or this man will die."

At this point the deputy manager, alerted by the noise, saw what was happening and politely prised the phone from Gunther's grasp while apologising profusely and explaining what was happening, how it was "all pretend" and that the body lying on the stairs which, as Gunther later said: "The mad English were pretending wasn't there", wasn't really injured. Once he understood, he was fascinated. He went to look at the body again (which was, by now, surrounded by 70 guests, two crying actresses and an unnaturally calm police inspector), chuckled to himself, took away a brochure and has since been on a Weekend with his wife Sylvia.

Crisis averted, my thoughts turned to Jerry who was still 'dying' safely in his room. It's pleasing to record he survived, thanks in no small part to Linda who administered various medicines through the night. After being interrogated until 3am by persistent and insistent guests I eventually got to sleep, thankful that I'd managed to get through the Weekend without any more nasty surprises. By the time we said goodbye to the guests the next afternoon I'd almost forgotten what a chaotic week it had been, but then fate dealt another blow to remind me.

Tired but happy at the excellent response from the guests, we had a quick debriefing and farewell cup of coffee in the bar as we usually do.

We'd managed to prise Jerry from his deathbed, pack his belongings and bundle him across the back seat of his wife's car. Jerry didn't want to be seen by any departing guests so, true to dramatic form, he managed to pull his jacket over his head so it looked for all the world as if he were a prisoner being smuggled secretly from the building.

As we loaded up my car (you'd be surprised at the amount of baggage that has to be moved around from one weekend to the next – luckily the spare knickers I'd managed to buy in town didn't take up too much extra space...) I realised, with a resigned shrug of the shoulders, that my hire car had a flat tyre. Not surprising, as nothing seemed to be going smoothly. It was starting to rain heavily and luckily a couple of the male actors decided to take charge (we girls like to let them think they're "good in a crisis") and insisted on changing the tyre for me.

The journey home to Liverpool was long and tedious. It was now dark, with torrential rain causing accidents and traffic jams for large parts of the journey. To top it all I was being flashed by traffic behind me because, as I discovered when I pulled over, one of the hire car's tail lights was out. I arrived home at about 9pm, exhausted and very, very, fed up – a situation that wasn't helped by the fact that, having been drenched unloading all the Murder Weekend luggage, I wearily picked up the post to be faced by a large white envelope marked "On Her Majesty's Service".

After such a journey (after such a week, come to that), the last thing I needed was a tax demand or, even worse, a horrible letter from the dreaded VAT man! I opened the letter with a heavy heart.

I was a bit confused by the address at the top of the letter: "10 Downing Street". What on earth had I done now? It's not that I get a lot of letters from the Prime Minister, more the fact that, in my current brain state, it didn't register that it was in any way unusual for the PM to be personally asking that I pay my taxes promptly.

"Dear Madam," the letter began. "The Prime Minister has asked me to inform you, in strict confidence, that he has it in mind, on the occasion of the forthcoming list of New Year's Honours, to submit your name to The Queen with a recommendation that Her Majesty may be graciously pleased to approve that you be appointed a Member of the Order of the British Empire (MBE)."

The letter went on but by now it was a blur! I stood, slightly dazed, with rainwater dripping slowly from my clothes into a small puddle on the floor. "Oh. My. God!" was all I could think as I re-read the letter (which is when the bit about "You can't tell anyone about your award until it's officially announced" finally sunk in). At the end of a dreadful week something wonderful had happened to me, Joy Swift MBE.

And I couldn't tell a soul!

Chapter 2

Frozen peas and a happy New Year

It was January 1st, 2001 and I was sitting in the bar at the Whately Hall hotel with the 100 or so guests on our New Year Murder Break. Although I was happily chatting away about the Weekend as if nothing was wrong, I was actually in a great deal of discomfort – something the industrial-sized bag of frozen peas balanced indelicately on my knee was doing nothing to ease. How I'd managed to get myself into this pitiful state is another story.

The previous night, I'd planned a row between me and my deceiving husband, played by Stuart Hatcher. As soon as a guest came to me with evidence of his affair with my best friend, we had arranged that I would attack him from behind and we would both fall to the floor and grapple for a few seconds before the police pulled us apart. So far, so good we thought. The moment duly arrived when the proof of my husband's infidelity was waved in my face by an enthusiastic guest who was only too pleased to know her behaviour was about to kick off the most ungodly row. I rushed in a blind mad fury at my cheating husband and grabbed him around the throat – except, unlike every other week when we'd played out this scene, I didn't. Or at least I did, but not exactly as we'd planned. Let me explain.

I managed to get my hands around Stuart's throat and, as I did so, he grabbed my arms and we started to grapple with each other, me shouting in his face and him trying to protest his innocence. As I've said, the plan was for us both to fall (gently) to the floor, roll around for a bit and then be separated by the police. This was all happening in the middle of the room, on a wooden dance floor, so all the guests could get a good view of the action. Unfortunately, what I didn't realise was that the floor was wet – someone must have spilt their drink during the evening and it hadn't been cleared up properly. As we started to wrestle I suddenly felt my feet go from under me – this wasn't supposed to happen. As I started to fall my hands grabbed Stuart's arms and our legs became entwined. Whether we both subconsciously realised what was happening and tried to break each other's fall, or whether it just happened in the heat of the moment I don't know, but as I hit the floor I felt the most excruciating pain in my knee. I immediately knew I'd done something terrible.

Any sane person would have simply acknowledged the injury and taken it from there. But we didn't, of course. Oh no. We did what we always do on a Weekend. We carried on fighting. I continued to shout at my errant "husband", grabbed him in a headlock, pulled him roughly towards me and croaked "My knee's broken" into his ear (even now, as I'm writing this, I find it hard to believe I carried on acting even though I thought I'd dislodged my knee cap! This probably says something about Murder Weekends.

Stuart, of course, immediately disentangled himself and stormed off as though in a rage, but worried about what he was leaving behind.

I pulled myself up from the floor with the assistance of two burly coppers and, not knowing the agony I was in, they half dragged me to a chair into which I was unceremoniously dumped. I was by now crying hard and the tears rolled down my cheeks. The guests gathered round (hopefully impressed by my Oscar-winning performance) and the actors came to scold or comfort me depending on their relationship with my character. They each immediately knew there was something wrong because, as one of them told me later, they knew I could cry but they also knew I couldn't cry that well.

Oddly enough, I wasn't thinking about the pain. The only thing I could think about was how I was going to get myself to the stairs where, on the stroke of midnight, I was due to be shot!

Well, my adrenalin was working overtime and through the tears – which the guests assumed were for my marriage – I managed to drag my protesting knee to the allotted spot where I eventually met my death. And boy did I feel like I'd been shot that night. Thirty minutes later I was safely back in my room looking forlornly at a knee that was swelling by the minute. For the first and I hope last time in my life I welcomed in the New Year with champagne, painkillers and a large bag of frozen peas strapped to my knee.

The next morning, after the Weekend was officially over, I was still in absolute agony and Nick Hooker (one of the actors) persuaded me I had to go to hospital. Actually, what he said was that if I didn't get my bottom in gear (not his exact words) and get to the hospital the leg would probably get gangrene and they'd have to amputate it. Even though I knew he was joking – at least I think he was joking – this unlovely vision focused my mind somewhat and, still feeling very sorry for myself, I finally relented (as you can see, for someone who spends their whole life killing, maiming and generally drenching people in blood for a living, I have a healthy disregard for both my own safety and hospitals). It turned out I had pulled all the ligaments on my right knee. Thankfully it was as good as new after six weeks' rest.

As I was saying goodbye to Anne Edwards, one of my wonderful regular guests and someone I've known for nearly 20 years, I pointed to my knee and joked: "I'm getting too old for this malarkey, I think 'Ill have to pack it in."

Anne, bless her, looked horrified: "You can't ever stop Joy! You've got no idea how much pleasure you bring to people. We look forward to each new plot – you should get a medal for what you do."

And, although I didn't think anything of it at the time, Anne was instrumental in getting me the medal she thought I deserved. She contacted several other guests and they each wrote to Downing Street putting my name forward for the MBE. When I talked to her about it later she told me she had been contacted "in confidence" and told that it would be "looked into" and "may not be successful" but would probably take at least three years if the nomination was successful – so she was as dumbstruck as I was when I was nominated only 11 months after she had written her original letter. It's probably exaggerating a little to say my MBE all came from a broken knee, but what a wonderful, thrilling and heart-stopping surprise it proved to be.

The nomination was actually announced in the New Year's Honours List of 2001. I thought we might have a few problems because I was doing what I always seem to have been doing at New Year for most of my adult life – hosting a Murder Weekend. On this particular Weekend I was playing the role of Kate Simpson and so would not, as far as the guests were concerned, be Joy Swift at all (one of my cardinal Murder Weekend rules is that the actors never come out of character to our guests during the Weekend).

I suspected various journalists would be ringing for interviews and thought there would probably be little articles written alongside the actual newspaper lists, mainly because the reason for my receiving the award ("Services to Tourism for Murder Weekends") was a little unusual.

The New Year break starts as all Murder Weekends start – with a cocktail reception at 8pm – but I knew I would have to tell the actors beforehand. I decided to get them together, along with members of my immediate family, in the afternoon with a few glasses of champagne (but not too many of course – most of us were, after all, going to be working that evening). Later that afternoon I started getting phone calls from the Press wanting to do interviews and then Radio 4 rang to ask if I would do a live interview the following morning. It was probably the champagne talking when I enthusiastically agreed.

The next morning I, or should I say Kate, came down to breakfast to be greeted by some very odd looks from the guests. This, I have to say, is nothing unusual – especially if a character has been involved in some strange double-dealing the previous evening – but these looks were different. People winked at me, smiled at me and even patted me on the back. I, as the bitchy Kate, did of course question their sanity – and even suggested that the guests who'd developed tics and twitches would maybe like to see their doctor just in case they'd caught something nasty the night before from another of the characters I was pretending to hate. After thoroughly enjoying myself as Kate I then had to dash off, change quickly into my secret identity of Joy Swift MBE, and take part in a what turned out to be a lively debate on Radio 4 about the validity of the honours system. I was to talk in favour, against a very strident republican who was violently opposed.

Although I couldn't condone some of the behaviour carried out in the name of the British Empire in the past, I had to agree, in my total joy and surprise at receiving my own award, with the giving of honours for a job well done – although I do believe a British award for excellence is perhaps more appropriate in this day and age.

Once the interviews were out of the way it was back into character – although I must say I did find it quite difficult when, in full flow as loathsome black widow Kate, two glorious bunches of flowers were delivered to "Joy Swift" in front of the guests. I made a great play of mocking the senders for getting it wrong but I was secretly thrilled by the thoughtfulness of my guests.

However, try as I might to stay in character, I very nearly failed dismally. At the New Year's Eve Party that evening, one of the guests, John Greening, stood up at the beginning of the meal, borrowed the DJ's microphone and made a lovely announcement:

"As some of you may not know," he looked directly at me and smiled, "Joy has been awarded the MBE".

Amidst much clapping (and a few cheers which I think were ironic ones from a couple of the actors), he asked everyone to raise their glasses for a toast and handed me a large bottle of champagne. I stood there blushing for what seemed like an age but I was determined not to come out of character. Giving him the best sideways look I could muster, I took the microphone from him and said: "John, you must have finally lost your bleeding marbles. You may think I'm a Joy – and some of my ex-husbands, God rest their souls, might agree with you – but the name's Kate. And don't you ever forget it 'cos you're next on my list."

I did, of course, manage to whisper a quick "thank you" to him once the laughter had subsided. It was such a sweet gesture and to have shared it amongst friends made the moment even sweeter (even if I had to pretend I didn't have a clue what they were all on about).

That, you may think, was quite enough excitement for any one person on a New Year break, but more was to come.

At 12.30am, after we'd said a Happy New Year to all our guests, the actors (even the dead ones…) came to my room for a few glasses of champagne to toast in the New Year. We were laughing about the fun we'd had and how lovely it had been for John to make his speech and as I turned around, much to my slightly befuddled brain's incomprehension, I noticed that Stuart was sitting in an armchair. Completely naked. I shrieked "Stuart, what on earth are you doing?" and the actors all burst into laughter as I was presented with my last and most spectacular New Year surprise... the 2002 Nude Murder Weekend calendar!

As I turned the pages I nearly choked – perhaps the actors' intention all along – I was laughing so hard. For the previous three months, they had all been secretly plotting and, under Martin Payne's leadership, had carried off the most hilarious of surprises.

There was Stuart as Mr January, buck naked on a frosty lawn, with a little caption referring to his 'frozen assets' and a bullet wound in his head.

Miss February was Linda, artfully draped across a bed and shot through the heart with an arrow. Month by month I saw my actors, baring their all, murdered horribly in ways I could never show my guests. What a way to start 2002, laughing harder than I had for ages after the most wonderfully exciting New Year ever.

Chapter 3

Riots at the Palace

You are allowed to take three guests to your investiture and I invited my sister Marilyn Greenwood, my friend and colleague Mal Waring and, of course, Anne who was responsible for getting the nomination process going in the first place.

I wanted to make the day, May 2, into something really special – a lovely treat for all of us – so we went down to London the day before to savour the build-up as well.

I'd booked a West End show for the evening and we were going to have a quiet, leisurely meal together beforehand. Unfortunately, what began as a calm and relaxing day out rapidly descended into farce. My sister doesn't travel much and doesn't feel "at home" amid the hustle and bustle of the city as much as I do and she certainly didn't appreciate the extra excitement we encountered that night. And all because yours truly had completely forgotten the significance of the date. As we strolled towards Leicester Square we walked right slap bang into the May Day Riots…

Shaftsbury Avenue was filled with demonstrators and the police were desperately trying to keep the human tide that we had inadvertently joined moving. Some rioters had broken away from the main group and were lying across the street and things were starting to turn quite nasty. I remember looking at Marilyn who had turned a funny shade of grey. All the colour had drained from her face and I could tell she was definitely not a happy bunny. "Never mind," I said to her, trying frantically to put a bright spin on what was starting to look like a very ugly situation, "We'll soon be at the restaurant and you'll forget all about it."

Not a chance. As we hit Leicester Square we could hear the crowd shouting and chanting. Somehow we managed to wander straight into some sort of police barricade – five huge vans stretched across the road spewing forth what must have been 50 police officers. Not only were they all suited and helmeted with riot shields at the ready, but some of them also had very large truncheons and looked as if they knew how to use them.

Marilyn looked even more terrified but, as luck would have it, we turned down a side street and came to the restaurant and hopefully sanctuary from the storm that was starting to rage all around. Unfortunately it was completely boarded up – not an inch of glass in view and very, very, shut.

We weren't immediately sure what to do (like typical Brits abroad we stood there debating our next move while there was a riot going on all around us). All we knew was that we needed to get away from the crowd. So off we marched, wandering purposefully around some tiny back streets until we eventually found a small Italian bistro – it was only after a few glasses of wine that the colour began to return to Marilyn's face!

After a tasty meal we made our way to the show, a Morecambe and Wise tribute called The Play What I Wrote. It was hugely successful and there were a lot of celebrities in the audience and, after a night of laughs and stargazing, we retired happily to our hotel. I was exhausted after all the excitement and quickly fell asleep. With my special outfit hanging in the closet I felt like a bride – probably the only time I ever will (but that, as they say, is another story).

The next morning Marilyn, Mal and I took a taxi to Buckingham Palace (sadly Anne was, at the last minute, unable to join us) and our fantastic day really began when we handed in our invitations and walked through the palace gates. It was a breathtaking and very special moment as we trudged on the thick gravel that crunched loudly under our feet. My one regret throughout the whole day was that my wonderful mum, who had lived through all the trials and tribulations of Murder Weekends, wasn't alive to see it. She had died four years earlier and I know she would have been so proud.

The most magical moment for me was when we actually entered the palace, walking up the white marble steps I'd seen so often on television; guests were ushered one way, recipients another and I walked up the most fantastic winding gold staircase, complete with splendidly plush red carpet, all on my own. At the top stood two Coldstream Guards in their spectacular dress uniforms with red jackets, gold boots and shining golden helmets with long white trailing plumes. I was so awestruck my eyes started to well up with tears. It was just so fabulous.

I was ushered into the picture gallery with the other recipients. The room was lined with the most magnificent works of art, but I was too excited to really take them in.

Large TV screens had been placed around the room so we could watch the proceedings and, just before it was time to be called to receive our medals, Lieutenant Colonel Malcolm Rowse – a very tall, upright and distinguished gentleman – explained what we had to do.

It was difficult not to visualise him as something straight out of The Dambusters. I imagined him saying "Bandits at 11 o'clock, Dickie. Tally ho and give 'em Hell chaps" in his deliciously plummy, perfect accent. He reminded us that the men should bow and the women curtsey before and after receiving an award and under no circumstances whatsoever, he chided, should we turn our back on the Royal personage.

It was at this point that yours truly decided to ask the obvious question – the one everyone was probably thinking to ask but didn't have the nerve. "Could you show me the correct way to curtsey?" I piped up, bold as you like. He looked at me for a moment or two and said, very courteously: "Madam. I hite you, I absolitely hite you." Luckily he was laughing as he said it, as were the assembled recipients.

He then proceeded to demonstrate the correct way for a lady to curtsey in the Royal presence, as demonstrated by dancer Darcy Bussell at a previous investiture. I still treasure the moment, which thankfully was captured on the video I purchased later. It just goes to show that my big mouth doesn't always get me into trouble.

Just as he finished, the televisions came on and we saw the ballroom, with two thrones at one end on a raised dais and all our friends and families gathered waiting for our arrival. There was some wonderful music playing while we were waiting, which I assumed was taped and being piped around the rooms.

We were called up in groups of 10 and when it was our time, our names were called and we filed out of the gallery and along the beautiful corridors of the palace. As we neared the ballroom, I could see, reflected in the mirrors on the huge doors, a full band of the Coldstream Guards playing on a massive balcony at the opposite end of the room. It took my breath away for a moment or two and they must have played for about two hours all told. They were fantastic; my second magic moment of the day.

Before I had time to think I was next in line and found myself standing beside another very senior equerry wearing his finest dress uniform. As I stood waiting to be called I was "typically", according to my sister, "the only person chatting". I smiled and whispered: "I love your golden tassels," to the equerry, who grinned back and hissed: "Well you're not having them."

I was laughing as I moved forward to stand next to an enormous Yeoman of the Guard (Beefeater to the rest of us) who must have been at least seven feet tall. I felt like a very chubby hobbit as the Lord Chamberlain read out my name: "Miss Joy Swift – for Services to Tourism."

Prince Charles was waiting to give me my medal as the Queen had begun her Golden Jubilee the day before and was away on her grand UK tour. He seemed genuinely interested in what I had created and how Murder Weekends worked. Although it seemed like just seconds to me, my sister later told me I was chatting with the Prince for much longer than the other recipients. He was asking lots of questions and Marilyn laughed, saying all she could see was my big cream hat bobbing up and down as I animatedly explained about the deaths, the plots, the rows and the guests.

Finally my time was up. Prince Charles shook my hand and I remembered to curtsey without tripping, so I'm glad I had the nerve to ask about the correct way to do it, even if the equerry did "hite me".

As I turned to go I suddenly remembered I was not, under any circumstances, to turn my back on a Royal and managed to control myself sufficiently to execute what I hoped looked like a smooth reverse. Having safely negotiated the walking backwards, I was guided to an ante-room where another equerry was waiting to take the medal and place it in a leather case. As this was happening, someone came up to me and said "Miss Swift?" in a very posh, polite but stern voice. I gulped and wondered what I had done now. Did I swear? Was I rude to the Prince? Were they going to haul me off to the tower and throw away the key?

Luckily, I hadn't disgraced myself. It was the palace press officer to say that a journalist would like to do an interview with me for Associated Press. What a relief! I was ushered into another wonderful gallery room where I sat on a beautiful coral brocade and gold chaise longue to be interviewed.

My sister wondered where I'd gone as all the recipients after me had filed to the back of the ballroom and I had been missing for about for about 20 minutes. Her first thought, knowing me as well as she does, had been "Oh heck, what's she done now?".

After the ceremony was over I was clutching my medal tightly as I met up with Marilyn and Mal outside the ballroom. From there we walked down another long staircase and the video I've got of the whole thing shows me talking away to them, twenty to the dozen, about everything that had happened.

Once outside in the courtyard, we waited at the front of a very long queue to have our official photo taken. My sister had gone to the loo as we arrived, but just as we were about to have our photo taken she suddenly shrieked "My ring! Where's my ring?" and went into a flat panic. She'd left it in the loo and, as the palace was now firmly locked and bolted, there was definitely no chance of our going back in. Nothing ever goes smoothly for the Swifts!

After a quick discussion amongst ourselves we managed to find a very nice soldier who took pity on my sister. With much faffing about, including getting special orders to unlock the doors, Marilyn went back to the bathroom and found her ring. It meant we found ourselves at the back of the very long queue but eventually we were posed and photographed and crunched our way back across the gravel to meet some more friends who had come to celebrate with us. Since we were in the very last group to leave I think they'd almost given up on us, but as we walked through a huge arch we saw them all, hanging on the railings and looking like urchins, staring goggle-eyed in wonder at the posh people in the palace.

Duly reunited, we made our way over to Green Park, drank champagne and had our photos taken – not only by our friends but by several American tourists who were very excited to hear about our morning. I had arranged for afternoon tea at The Waldorf and, as we sat with our cucumber sandwiches and scones, we all agreed that it really had been a Grand Day Out. If only mum could have been there.

My sister hadn't said much all day (with the notable exception of the ring episode) but I know she was also thinking "Mum would have been so proud". Had she said it out loud, I think we would both have dissolved into tears.

Chapter 4

Ribena and goldfish – a recipe for murder?

I was reading a magazine article a little while ago about how to realise your ambitions. It was some New Age thing and I forget the exact wording but I remember being struck by the advice that if you're unhappy in your chosen career you should look back to your early childhood and remember what you really enjoyed doing then.

Perhaps my destiny had always been to invent Murder Weekends because blood, guts and gore featured large in my formative years.

I was four years old when I was sent to Mrs Hardy-Smith's private nursery and the first thing I can recall was being told to sit next to a pretty girl with a mass of flaming red hair. Her name was Carole Hornby and my first impression of her was "She's nice. We're going to be friends". In the strange way these things seem to happen, we were. In fact, although we dipped in and out of each other's lives over the years, we remained friends from the moment we met until her very sad death two years ago from a brain tumour.

When I told her I was writing my autobiography her response was: "Well, you'd better hurry up because I haven't got long and I want to see my name in print." Feisty and funny to the very end, Carole was a fabulous woman and, as she once suggested, she was probably the inspiration for my murderous career.

We were still in the first days of our friendship when Carole brought a beautiful new Dutch doll to nursery. It was dressed in national costume, had the dinkiest little wooden clogs on its feet and it was Carole's absolute pride and joy.

Completely by accident I managed to knock my beaker of Ribena all over the doll and Carole vowed to hate me forever. Did the sight of that red sticky liquid spreading across the doll's white apron trigger something in my brain? Was I destined to be a murderer?

Well, not according to my mum. She was sure I was going to be a vet mainly because when I was three-and-a-half, one of our menagerie of pets, a goldfish, died. He was fished out of his tank and we had the usual burial service in the garden. I still live in that same family home, originally owned by my grandfather, and I can't imagine how many bones there must be in the back garden from all the pets we've buried over the 90 years my family's lived there.

Three days after the burial, mum found me in the back garden sitting cross-legged on the path. I had Bubbles on a paving stone, a knife in my hand and was happily dissecting the recently departed fish. I read recently that Jeffrey Dahmer, the notorious American serial killer, started dissecting roadkill when he was only seven. It seems I had a head start on him but thankfully I chose to commit my murders on paper. Who knows what could have happened if my parents hadn't kept me on the straight and narrow?

I've always loved looking after animals but becoming a vet was never a realistic career option for me, partly because I know I'm far too soft to ever be able to deal with the emotional trauma of seeing animals or their owners suffer.

There were other possible careers I thought about during my formative years but one thing I never wanted to be was an actress (which may strike you as a little odd considering that's what I've been doing for the last 25 years). For one thing I have an appalling memory, often not remembering events from a week ago, let alone learning pages of text.

My one and only foray on stage was a disastrous and bloody one. I was five years old at the time but it clearly left a big impression. I spent every Saturday morning at Sandfield dance lessons with Miss Ruth and we'd been rehearsing a song-and-dance routine that was due to be performed at the Neptune Theatre. Anyone who knows my life-long home of Liverpool will appreciate this was quite a prestigious 'gig' for a stage debut.

To the tune of "Oh Soldier Soldier Won't You Marry Me" about 30 of us sang and danced with gangly enthusiasm and little finesse, in the costumes our parents had lovingly sewn for us. Half the girls were dressed in pretty dresses and the other half, including me (always prone towards the tomboy and loving my costume far more), were dressed as little soldiers. We must have looked very fetching in our white trousers, red jackets, shiny gold buttons and Busby hats.

Rehearsals went well but disaster struck three days before the big night. I was at home in the morning room when the telephone rang in the dining room. I answered it and called for my sister who came in, spoke briefly, then opened the French windows to go out into our garden.

Unfortunately, just as I was running out of the room as I usually did, swinging round on the door jamb, a gust of wind came through the French windows, slamming the door shut right onto my thumb. I screamed, my sister ran away (she spent several hours 'in hiding' at her best friend's house, convinced it was her fault) and my parents, who were watching the TV in the lounge, simply ignored me assuming my sister and I were playing some mad game.

There was nothing for it but to look after myself. I had to slowly lean across to push the door in order to release my thumb, the end of which was now hanging by a thread.

I'd like to say I went calmly into the lounge but that would be a lie. I ran screaming at the top of my lungs towards them, still having the presence of mind to carry the severed piece of thumb in my other hand! I clearly remember my mum looking at me and, without lifting her head to look at my dad, saying calmly: "Norman. Hospital. Now!"

Come the night of the grand performance, I was standing proudly on the stage in my neat little soldier's uniform with a massive white thumb bound up in what seemed like yards of bandage!

I was positioned at the end of the row of dancers and my proud mum and dad watched as I sang and danced my little heart out, not noticing – until I whacked it very, very, hard – the wing at the side of the stage. Mum told me later that the next she saw was yards of white bandage fluttering gently onto the stage followed by a loud scream of pain as I was yanked smartly off stage left. She rushed in a panic backstage to find me once again looking at a severely bleeding thumb. The stitches had split wide open and we ended up in casualty having my thumb stitched back together once more. It is still, to this day, a very odd shape.

Was this first and, as I thought, last terribly bloody acting experience another glimpse of what was to come?

Chapter 5

My life before murder

I have always counted myself lucky to have been born to two wonderful parents, my father Norman and my mother Thelma. My dad and his two older sisters, Mae and Dorrie, came from a comfortable middle class background.

His parents employed live-in maid Sarah and full-time gardener Bill, whose main task was to tend our small orchard and vegetable patch, something he did diligently and beautifully for many years. Coincidentally or not, he retired just around the time I was old enough to steal his carefully tended raspberries, apples, peas, beans and carrots – much to his annoyance, my parents' amusement and the general bemusement of the variety of insects I insisted on bringing back to the house as pets.

Dad was the managing director of a timber sawmill, a family business originally owned by his grandfather. From an early age I would climb the massive ladder that led to the cabin of the giant crane stationed in the mill. Once there I would "help" Jack drive the crane, lifting the huge timber logs from the yard onto a conveyor belt that guided them through the cutting saws before they emerged on the other side as perfectly sawn sheets of timber. This process produced great piles of sawdust (something I found hugely useful over the years as bedding material for my succession of hamsters) and its all-pervading smell is one that I love to this day.

When not helping with the crane I loved to sit in dad's office, answering the phone and typing important letters that probably didn't make much sense since I was only young at the time.

But the thing I really loved most about "going to work with dad" was when the mill's cats produced kittens. I remember spending many happy hours playing contentedly with them and dad always had the greatest trouble persuading me they shouldn't all come home with us, although over the years many did!

My mother, a wonderful stay-at-home mum who baked, cleaned, knitted and sewed beautifully, was a marvellous woman. Unjustifiably she always suffered from low self esteem, but everyone adored her; she was very pretty, had a fabulous smile and was the kindest and most caring of women. Mum was sure I would one day shine at tennis or music, never dreaming I would make a career in murder.

Mum's maiden name was Lake and we have managed to trace our family back to the time of the English Civil War. Edward Lake, a Cambridge-educated doctor from Lincolnshire, was born in 1600. An ardent Royalist during the English Civil War, he fought at the Battle of Edgehill against the Parliamentarian army and was eventually captured by the Roundheads after "fighting valiantly", despite being shot 26 times.

By one of those odd coincidences that seem to pop up every now and then he was actually held prisoner for a time in the small town of Great Crosby in Lancashire where, 400 years later, I now live. Given his injuries it's perhaps surprising to learn he survived and, after the Restoration of the Monarchy under Charles II, he was awarded a baronetcy for his valour.

Unfortunately I never knew my mother's father. He died at a relatively young age, a few years before I was born. He had fought in the first world war and the gassing he received in the trenches left him with severe asthma.

My maternal grandmother, Cynthia Barrow, was born in Blenheim Palace. This wasn't as grand as it first sounds because her father, my great-grandfather, was head coachman there. My great-grandmother, an Austrian, was a housekeeper at the palace. My family has always joked that perhaps it was an arranged marriage – that my great-grandmother fell pregnant by the duke and was hastily married off to prevent a scandal (well, you never know, stranger things have happened). Given my family connection to the Churchills (Blenheim is their ancestral home) my friends sometimes joke there is "something of the Churchill" in me. I can be very bossy, I say what I think to anyone and I have the requisite tummy. Of course its all quite preposterous to think I might be secretly related but its fun to speculate!

Frederick Lake was an accountant who worked for the Royal Liver Insurance company in Liverpool and, despite his ill health, was very involved in football in his spare time. He was a director of our local team (Marine) and eventually became an Everton director which perhaps goes some way to explain why they've always been our family team (as opposed to the Other Team that's rumoured to play somewhere across Stanley Park!).

A feeling for sport, particularly football and rugby, runs deep in my family. My mother, at five years old, was a mascot at Goodison Park and she retained the passion for "her team" throughout her lifetime. Much to my mum's dismay my three nephews, Mark, Robin and Andrew (my sister Marilyn and her husband Chris's children) all inexplicably became Liverpool supporters – heresy!

It was probably just as well that she liked sport because both my father and my brother Tony played club rugby, the latter being good enough to represent Lancashire Schoolboys and the Under 19 team at one time.

Both my parents were excellent tennis players and each represented Lancashire for many years. It was through tennis that they met – aged 12 and 14 – when they were drawn together in a mixed-doubles match at their club, Blundellsands.

My brother and sister were also fine players. Both were good enough to play at Junior Wimbledon and my sister was chosen as a possible candidate for the Whiteman Cup and to train with Dan Maskell, the tennis coach who achieved lasting fame as the BBC's "voice of tennis". But my mother despaired of me. Between the three of us she thought that I was the most naturally gifted player but she also knew that I was the laziest. Having said that, my formative summers were spent playing in a variety of tournaments and, when not competing, I spent much of my time at the local club.

I was a promising enough player in my teens to be coached at a special training camp by Vic Edwards, coach to the world-famous and hugely successful Australian tennis star Yvonne Goolagong, but I knew I was never going to succeed for the simple reason that I just wasn't competitive enough to play at the highest level. Unlike my sister, I never made it into the Lancashire team, mainly because at the time I was being put forward for a trial I discovered boys and they seemed, to my mind at least, far more interesting.

My brother continued to excel at sport, diverting his interest from tennis to squash – a sport at which he rapidly became so good that he played for Lancashire. My mum was always so proud when she went to watch Tony representing his county.

Both my father and brother had very competitive sporting natures and we often wondered where they got it from as my father's father was the most mild-mannered of men with a very caring, gentle and softly spoken nature. But I recently discovered that this was the case only up to a point because when my grandfather was playing croquet, his quiet Dr Jekyll was transformed into a fiendishly competitive Mr Hyde. In 1972, Tony became the first ever English National Squash Coach and, following his move to Toronto where he now manages a large sports club, the Canadian National Squash Coach in 1985. He is the world champion in doubles squash in his age range, which he won't admit to. But he's certainly the fittest over-60-year-old I know!

My sister played club tennis for many years but, unlike my brother, didn't take sport up as a profession, but decided on the much more productive role of wife and mother. She gave birth to three lovely sons (the aforementioned heretics); grandsons for my proud mum and nephews for me. They now have their own children and I find it almost inconceivable that I'm now old enough to be a great-aunt! I have to admit to being a little jealous of Marilyn because one of my big regrets is that I never had children of my own, although I do have three furry feline children – Jodi, JJ and Jinee – that I adore.

Another attribute that runs through my family is musical ability; a great uncle on my father's side was a published composer and a distant aunt on my mother's side was an organist at York Cathedral. My paternal grandfather, the aforementioned Mr Hyde, was an organist at our local Methodist Church. He was also a fantastic carpenter and, as a boy, my brother was fascinated by the beautiful tools, kept in a box "as big as a room", that grandad used to make beautiful violins – none of which, unfortunately, seem to have been passed down the family line. Coming from generations of religious relations, I'm sure they are spinning in their graves now because I am an evangelical atheist!

I seem to have inherited a talent for music from these distant relations and at 18 months I was singing pitch-perfect tunes back to my brother as he whistled them. I've played the piano by ear from the age of 3, driving my music teacher mad because no sooner had I read a piece of music than I would know it and play it ignoring the written notes. This musical ability certainly came in handy in the early days of Murder Weekends whenever we fancied a sing-song.

In my teens I went to the very respectable Merchant Taylor's School for Girls and I still feel guilty to this day that I wasted both my time and my father's hard-earned money while I was there. The ethos of the school was, and probably still is for that matter, focused on academia, with the goal of university. Although there's nothing wrong with this outlook, I never really fitted into that mould. It wasn't that I was thick; I just never applied what brains I had to my school work and I remember my parents sighing with resignation when just about every school report was sent with the words "could do better" sprinkled liberally through its pages.

They never once made me feel bad about my lack of academic application, but I know I must have disappointed them, particularly as my dad was so involved with the school (he was president of Merchant Taylors' Old Boys Association) and my brother was head boy there!

Although I was never academic in the way the school preferred, I was very creative. I adored art and English and was very good at both from an early age – I loved telling stories and had a great imagination, something I have in common with another ancestor, Gulliver's Travels author Jonathan Swift, and something I've managed to carry through to later life with the creation of numerous weird and wonderful plots to test the sleuthing abilities of many thousands of people.

At 13, however, my world was turned upside down when my father died after a long illness and I still feel guilty that I was such a torment to my mother at a time when she displayed such unbelievable strength of character. I went completely off the rails and, while I had no idea at the time, I think this was because I felt a great undirected anger at having been abandoned (as I selfishly saw it) by the most wonderful man in my life.

Dad was such a popular man. He was president of numerous groups including the Lancashire Lawn Tennis Association and chairman of various commercial organisations. I was always so proud to be seen with him. Everywhere we went people greeted him or stopped to pass the time of day in conversations frequently punctuated with gales of laughter. I realised then that one of the best feelings in the world was being liked and one of the greatest gifts was the ability to make people smile. I was his youngest child and I adored him. His passing affected me deeply and, if I'm honest, it still does at times. I'm single to this day, having had my heart broken a couple of times by men I thought were as good as my dad, but who never could be.

Every New Year's Eve mum and dad used to have huge house parties. I can remember being tucked up in bed and hearing all the laughter. They always played party games which I think were probably an early influence on the games we now play on Murder Weekends.

After leaving school I had no idea what I wanted to do. I had a provisional place at teacher training college, but my A level grades weren't really good enough and I knew my heart wasn't in teaching anyway. For a while I attended a private secretarial college but I think the only things that came out of that experience were a hatred of accounts and typing and a strong conviction that whatever work I was destined to do it wouldn't involve sitting at a desk all day.

Luckily mum came to the rescue when she noticed an advert in the local paper for tele-ad girls at the Liverpool Daily Post & Echo. I later learned they had received around 600 applications for just six jobs. They must have seen something in me because I was one of the lucky ones selected although once my initial euphoria at landing the job had subsided I quickly came to realise that I hated selling.

The job had its compensations, such as fantasic money and being able to walk out of the door at 5pm and forget about work, which it just about made it bearable. It also enabled me to buy my first car. My old friend Paul, who loved rallying and owned a small garage, persuaded me to buy an Escort RS2000, a powerful car that I adored – and so, it seems, did the thief who stole it, never to be seen again.

My fortune with cars had taken a turn for the worse, but it was around this time that my career luck began. My cousin's husband worked for a small chain of hotels and he told me about a sales co-ordinator job that was being advertised at his head office. I waved goodbye to telesales and began what was to prove a short but extremely fortuitous career in hotel sales.

Although the majority of the work involved co-ordinating the business that hotel sales executives brought in, I also got involved in the more creative and interesting side of the hotel business, the production of sales brochures and the development of ideas designed to put more 'bums in beds'.

During the 20-minute drive to work one morning I happened to be listening to the radio when I heard a report about a shooting in a hotel. My immediate reaction was "Thank heavens it isn't one of ours. What terribly bad publicity that would be". I imagined the headlines: who would stay at the "death hotel"? But then I started thinking how exciting it must have been for the guests – they wouldn't be allowed to leave, would have to give evidence to the police about what they'd seen and best of all the bar spends would be great!

It was then that I had my light bulb moment. Wouldn't it be fantastic, I thought, to be dropped into an Agatha Christie film – to be able to view the evidence, interrogate the suspects and ultimately prove whodunnit? I mulled the general idea over in my mind that morning and at a sales meeting later in the day explained it to my boss. We could create a "murder weekend" that involved guests witnessing the "death" of actors, interrogating suspects and studying carefully selected evidence that would help them identify the killer.

I was very excited at my new brainchild but the powers that be, including the company chairman, weren't so keen. One of them suggested it was a "crazy idea" but I clinched the argument by pointing out that, if nothing else, we'd get a lot of local publicity. On the basis that any publicity is good publicity, they reluctantly agreed, but with one condition: I had to organise the whole affair.

Chapter 6

Click, click... Shit!

Organising what was to be the first ever Murder Weekend proved easier than I had first supposed. Freda, a former colleague at the Liverpool Daily Post, was a member of a local amateur dramatic society and, having explained the general idea to her, she used her contacts to assemble a crew of actors.

Once they were in place I contacted a local crime writer and asked if he could write a simple plot for us to use, something he was happy to do. When it arrived it was quite unlike what I'd envisaged and certainly not something I felt would have stood up to the rigorous sleuthing from our guests. Although this was a disappointment, the setback proved to be something of a blessing in disguise because it meant I was thrown back on my own resources and, determined I wouldn't fail at the first hurdle, I arranged a couple of meetings with the actors, re-jigged the script and eventually came up with what we thought was a workable plot, though it was very simple by my current standards!

With the groundwork done, all that really remained was publicity. I placed a flier in a Murder Mystery Book Club mailshot and, six months later on Friday October 30th, 1981, Murder Weekends were officially born at the Prince of Wales Hotel in Southport, Lancashire.

Our 35 hard-bitten sleuths arrived expecting murder, mystery and mayhem. And they certainly got it. The plot was based around a small company's Annual General Meeting and dinner. The guests had received a letter explaining the theme a month before the event and they arrived prepared with a little story that explained their invitation to the AGM (they were employees, shareholders and the like). The actors played the main characters such as the managing director, his wife, the company secretary, accountant and so forth.

From the moment I came up with the idea I knew that the key to the success of a Murder Weekend would be its realism. The guests had to believe the characters were real people with creditable backgrounds and motives for behaving in the way they did. Only if this realism was created and maintained would the guests want to engage with the suspects and victims and be interested enough to want to solve the crimes.

I now regularly act on Weekends and thoroughly enjoy hosting, weeping, wailing, arguing, fighting and dying. This wasn't always the case for a couple of reasons: firstly, I had never acted in my life and secondly I wanted to run the Weekend from 'behind the scenes' to make sure everything went as planned.

On this first Weekend, therefore, I mixed with the guests so I could watch the plot unfold from their point of view.

Friday night went well and the first death, a dramatic poisoning at the dinner table, caused quite a stir among the guests. The police arrived right on cue, closely followed by an ambulance crew (a local St John's brigade booked and briefed in advance) who removed "the body" as planned. The following morning, a police incident room was set up and the guests started sleuthing in a way that was better than I could have anticipated. I knew the plot we had mapped out wouldn't take up an entire day so I had decided that we would set up a private meeting room to show a couple of Agatha Christie films on a large screen to extend the murder mystery theme. This, I soon learned, was a mistake; it destroyed the air of realism I'd worked so hard to establish. I realised a more complicated plot was needed to engage the guests for the whole weekend.

We held a fancy dress party on the Saturday night and, given the date, what else could the theme have been but Hallowe'en? Everyone played along, including my boss, his boss (the chairman of the company) and my then boyfriend, Jonathan – although looking back I'm not sure whether they were there to urge me on or to watch me fail.

Through a combination of alcohol, the anticipation of rows between the suspects and the prospect of another mysterious death, the party was in full swing. Everyone seemed to be enjoying themselves and I'd planned a very dramatic final death that would bring the evening to a satisfying conclusion.

The idea was that the victim would be happily bopping on the dance floor while the murderer lurked unseen outside the hotel. The murderer was to poke the gun they were carrying through a half-open fire exit door and shoot – the cue for the victim to throw themselves to the floor, in true western style, moaning and groaning as their life ebbed away (there were no thoughts of exploding blood bags in those days). I knew the exact time this was supposed to happen and, precisely as planned, I saw the murderous hand slip, unnoticed by the guests, from behind the curtain covering the fire exit.

I saw the trigger go back and held my breath as I waited for the explosion. All I heard was "Click". Then another "Click" and yet another followed by "Shit". Luckily the loud music masked what was happening from the guests and, after what seemed like an age of further frantic clicking, I realised I had to do something and quick.

I slipped out through the side door and ran frantically around the back of the hotel to where my near-hysterical murderer was standing. In the excitement of the moment she had completely forgotten the instructions that I'd given her about how to work the gun. I grabbed and re-cocked it, pointed it through the door and pulled the trigger. To my great relief a loud explosion ripped across the room and the victim was at last able to drop dead on the dance floor amidst some very realistic screams from the guests.

All of this frantic activity did not go unnoticed by a few of the guests and you could be forgiven for thinking this would have been my first and last Murder Weekend – strangled at birth because an actress misunderstood my instructions about how to cock and fire a gun!

Thankfully the guests were all very well behaved on this occasion (something that's not always true, as you will discover). No one tried to grab "the murderer" and no one realised that I had actually been the one that fired the fatal shot.

We then, as always happens on Murder Weekends, quickly managed to get over our shock at the grisly death of one of our group and partied the night away.

The following morning at breakfast, the sleuths had their final opportunity to interrogate the four surviving suspects before they had to submit their questionnaires detailing "whodunnit" and why. After the identity of the murderer had been revealed, the reaction from the guests was very good. Everyone I talked to said they'd had a great time and asked when were we planning another one. I didn't say so at the time but I was pretty sure this would be the first and last Murder Weekend – and probably the last time anyone at the company would allow me to run with any subsequent "bright idea".

Be that as it may, given that I'd sold the idea of a Murder Weekend to my boss on the basis of the publicity it would generate, I had arranged for a photographer and journalist from the Liverpool Daily Post to come in on the Sunday morning, take a few photos of a 'body' surrounded by some shocked guests and write a short article about my first ever Murder Weekend. Once this was out of the way and we'd waved goodbye to the guests, the actors and I had a few drinks. I travelled home exhausted, fit only for a good night's sleep.

Chapter 7

The magician's assistant

I guessed, rightly as it turned out, that I would be exhausted after the Weekend and had booked the following Monday off work. After a lovely lie-in I went for a walk to buy the Liverpool Daily Post and was really pleased with the article and the photos they printed. "Well," I remember thinking to myself, "at least the chairman will be pleased".

I arrived at work the next morning refreshed and ready to get back into the normal swing of things after the excitement and pressure of the weekend. On the way to my desk I bumped into my friend Hazel who asked me how it all went. "Pretty well, I think," I replied and we chatted for a bit about everything that had gone on. "Well" she said at length, "I'd better let you get on – I think you're going to be a very busy bee indeed today," were her parting words. I must admit to thinking this was an odd way to end the conservation but as I walked towards my desk I saw what she meant because it was covered in phone messages. As I started to sift through them I became increasingly excited. The Bournemouth Advertiser. The Manchester Evening News! The Daily Mail! The New York Times! And, to cap it all, the BBC Holiday programme! I just sat at my desk stunned, hardly able to take in the fact my crazy idea had generated worldwide interest. Not only did all they all want to interview me, they also wanted to cover the next Murder Weekend – the one that I'd given no thought to organising for the simple reason that I never thought there would be more than one.

When I eventually took it all in I told the chairman who was, as you can imagine, more than delighted at the fantastic exposure the Weekend had generated.

Later that afternoon I called Colin Strong, the series producer of The Holiday Programme and the upshot of our conversation was that he wanted to come on the next Murder Weekend as a way of getting a feel for how things worked. Not only that, he wanted to film the Weekend after that – and he wanted it to be the same plot so that he and the crew would know what they would be filming. To say I was dumbfounded and very excited would be an understatement.

To compound matters, when I spoke to the Daily Mail they wanted to send a reporter to cover the Weekend – but not a travel writer, as I'd first thought, but Bill Murray their senior crime investigative journalist. Someone at the Mail with a sense of humour thought it would be fun to see how he fared investigating a murder 'for real'! Finally, just to make things even more potentially fraught, the New York Times also wanted to send a journalist to report on the next Weekend – and if it wasn't enough that my idea had caught the media's imagination, I started to receive a steady stream of calls from people wanting to book their place on "the next Murder Weekend".

This was, of course, fantastic news – except for the minor consideration, as I've said, that there wasn't actually another Weekend planned (let alone a series of Weekends "all with the same plot").

After a bit of thought and negotiation with my superiors it was arranged that I'd put on another Weekend the following March, with four more to be added over the next six months. I contacted the actors and we met several times at my house to write a brand new plot and, on March 15th (with 60 paying guests and a smattering of the world's Press), we were ready to go. If anything, I was even more nervous than the first time. If Colin liked it we would get the kind of TV coverage that money just couldn't buy.

The theme for the second Weekend was a "Rumley School Reunion". The guests were to be ex-pupils and the actors played teachers, their partners and ex-pupils as well. I was much happier with the plot this time as it had more depth, twists and turns and included three, rather than two, murders. Having learnt from my mistake on the last one, I'd also decided there would be more clues and action to keep the guests fully occupied and intrigued across the whole Weekend.

Friday night started with a real bang. I had organised a magician as light entertainment to follow the school reunion dinner and his final trick involved a cabinet positioned at the back of the room from which his female assistant was due to disappear (or so the guests were led to believe). He led his assistant to the back of the room and when she opened the door a body dramatically slid out of the cabinet and onto the floor. This produced a great reaction from the guests (including Bill Murray who posed by the body, notebook in hand, while his accompanying photographer took the shots that would eventually appear in the Daily Mail story). The guests went into a sleuthing frenzy, the ambulance and police arrived and there was such a good buzz in the room that I knew we had a real success on our hands.

The following morning the police set up an incident room and the guests worked hard all weekend trying to work through the plethora of clues. Saturday afternoon saw a dramatic death in a lift. It was one of those old-fashioned lifts that had grilles that you could pull across and I can still hear the genuinely loud scream of surprise and panic from the guest that happened to call the lift, pull back the grille to reveal "Mrs McGregor" with multiple stab wounds.

For the final death – a little foolhardedly perhaps but undeterred by the experience of the first Weekend – I had decided on another shooting. This one occurred at the school disco, arranged for the Saturday evening, where everyone came dressed as school kids – men in shorts, caps, skew-whiff ties and with scuffed knees; girls in short skirts, suspenders and pigtails, all looking very sexy. This time the actor due to be murdered had a blood capsule in their mouth and, as the shot rang out (the gun thankfully worked first time), they bit on the capsule and spewed blood as they fell into the arms of an unsuspecting (and screaming) guest. It worked so perfectly it was almost too good to be true.

Later that night, after the guests had gone to bed, everyone – the actors, journalists, Colin, the BBC producer, even the hotel manager – piled into my room to toast a successful Weekend. We were all very excited and jabbering away as Colin sat next to me and whispered:

"Joy, when this goes out on the Holiday Programme, the response will be phenomenal. You really should go it alone, form your own company. This will be a job for life." I couldn't quite take in what he was saying – the idea of giving up my secure job and company car to go it alone wasn't in my life plan at all. I had imagined my partner Jonathan and I would get married, have babies and I'd become a happy housewife and mother... and not being a natural risk taker, I didn't give the idea too much thought at the time.

The next day the guests went away happy and promised they would return for the next new plot. We had some more photos taken and then, happily and exhaustedly (we'd only had about four hours sleep and lots of alcohol the previous night), we said our goodbyes and set off home.

The following weekend Bill Murray's article appeared in the Daily Mail – a full page, on page 3 (my one and only time as a Page 3 Girl!). Over the next few weeks the phone hardly stopped ringing and we sent out hundreds of brochures. A week or so after the Daily Mail article, the New York Times published the piece their journalist had written; it was a great article and it produced a lot of interest plus numerous enquiries and bookings from American guests all wanting to come on a Murder Weekend.

Interestingly, the two articles also generated a massive amount of further media interest from just about every corner of the globe. Newspapers and TV companies from places like America, Australia, Germany and Japan all wanted to either write about or film a Weekend – but they all had to wait their turn; the next Weekend was being filmed by Colin and his BBC team. I felt as if Murder Weekends had been truly launched on the world and I had the pleasant feeling we were destined to go into the hotel industry's history books. My life had taken a weird and unexpected turn and, although I didn't know it, was about to change forever. I had no idea this was the start of a worldwide craze that would keep me busy and employed full-time for the next 25 years!

Although a pleasant change was in the air, a much less inviting change was also occurring in my life as I heard rumours that Jonathan, my boyfriend of nine years, had been seeing someone else. I had been so busy with work that I didn't realise I was losing what I thought was the love of my life. He never even had the balls to tell me it was over, he just drifted quietly away. I was broken-hearted and threw myself into my work to cover the pain. I guess our break-up focused me even more because I now had the bit between my teeth and I was determined to make my idea work. And Colin's suggestion of "going it alone" suddenly seemed a great deal more attractive.

Chapter 8

Lights, camera, action!

My first ever TV interview took place the following week. Granada, my local TV station, had seen the piece in the Daily Mail and wanted to interview both myself and some of the actors for their local news magazine Granada Reports.

I had never been in front of cameras before and I took to it like a duck to water. I quickly realised however that the exciting and glamorous TV life we see on the screen actually hides the tedium of many hours of takes and retakes as the producer tries different camera angles, different questions and even different intonations. As my friends will tell you I am, at the best of times, an impatient person and I found the whole thing a bit frustrating – the TV life was definitely not for me. My dear mum, however, was bursting with pride when the programme was broadcast, especially when her friends rang to say they'd seen the piece and how well I'd come across – odd that I'd chosen 'murder' as a career, rather than tennis or music or something more sensible but interesting nonetheless.

We managed to get a couple more Weekends under our belt before the BBC came to film. It was a full-blown production – Colin brought two cameras, a presenter, sound and lighting engineers and a researcher. Actors and guests alike were caught up in the excitement of it all and the Weekend went superbly well exactly according to plan. Colin was very pleased and said it was going to make a fantastic film. He used the phrase I've heard time and time again from directors: "We've got so much good footage it's going to be a nightmare to edit!"

Edit it he did, however and, in March 1983, the actors all gathered at my house to celebrate what we knew would be a fantastic show and we weren't disappointed. The programme was seen by around 10 million viewers and, in anticipation of the expected public response, I'd produced our first Murder Weekend brochure and arranged 20 further Weekends on the back of the programme. As the studio presenter, Cliff Michelmore rounded off the piece I knew that Colin was right; this was going to take off in a big way and perhaps it really was the right time for me to take the plunge and go it alone.

If I had any final nagging doubts about whether this was the right thing for me, a promotion at work to a job that I really didn't want to do made me finally bite the bullet and hand in my notice. With a loan from a very kind and generous neighbour I set up my own company, Murder Weekends Ltd.

I was so glad I'd decided to take the plunge. The bookings poured in, as did the requests to write about and film Weekends. Almost every one we did for the next two years had either a journalist from a national or international newspaper or a film crew amongst the guests (something that continues to this day – it's quite rare for a plot not to have guests from the local, national or international Press).

On one particularly chaotic occasion two American companies – ABC and CBS News – wanted to film on the same weekend. We had two film crews, two presenters, two cameramen (both, of course, wanting to get the best angles and shots) two lighting and two sound engineers, complete with massive sound booms, who kept fighting each other (sometimes almost literally) for the best coverage of the rows, arguments and deaths – it truly was manic.

After the Weekend was over the CBS presenter, Martha Teichner, had a quiet word with me, just as Colin had done: "Joy," she said "you should bring Murder Weekends over to the States. They will love it there!" It was an interesting thought, of course, but since I was only just starting to establish Murder Weekends in Britain I didn't think I was ready to tackle America just yet. That, as they say, was one for the future.

Both the crews sent me videos of the pieces aired on American TV, but I didn't expect to turn on breakfast TV one morning and hear

David Frost introduce a film "…about a Murder Weekend". It was the CBS piece and I watched with amazement as it went out to millions of viewers. Frost jokily ended the piece by saying "Not the hotel I think I'd like to stay in, if that sort of thing happens," and I thought that was the kiss of death to any more Murder Weekends – but once again the phone started ringing off the hook as people clamoured to experience just the sort of thing David was so keen to avoid!

Although I've become used to having film crews around, things don't always go smoothly. The funniest (and potentially most traumatic) experience I've ever had was a Japanese crew who arrived on a Weekend without having booked an interpreter. You can imagine the hi jinx – me trying to explain to them what was happening (when and where murders and arguments were going to happen) and them trying to film them. In retrospect it was hilarious but it didn't seem quite so funny at the time.

Over the years I have had lots of requests for personal appearances and every time I've been asked I still think: "How weird. Why would they want little old me?"

Many of these appearances have, of course, been memorable – sometimes for the wrong reasons perhaps, but memorable none the less.

I was, for example, asked by the BBC to go to London to be on the panel of Midweek with Libby Purves. I was put up in a very nice hotel, collected in the morning and I arrived at the studio to be introduced to the Duke of Westminster ("call me Gerald") and Count Leo Tolstoy's nephew. I was interviewed about Murder Weekends and then asked to join in the general chat about the week's topics, which was fab. Live radio was something I found I really liked doing, mainly because it was immediate, fun and, most important of all, had no retakes.

On another occasion we were doing a Murder Weekend in Devon when I was invited by TVS to join Fern Britton "on the sofa" of their early evening magazine programme, something I once again really enjoyed because it was live. I love just being able to sit down, talk to people about what I do and then leave. This, as it turned out, was just as well because as soon as the programme finished I had to be whisked back to the Murder Weekend hotel where, half an hour later, I was sitting down at the dinner table, back in character and chatting away happily to the guests, although a few of them who had just seen me on TV as "Joy" looked at me very peculiarly when I introduced myself to them as "Sally".

Apart from taking Murder Weekends to America (about which more in a moment) I've travelled to Europe a few times for a variety of reasons – a couple of the most memorable being strange and most daunting. For the first I was invited to speak at a tourism conference in Paris and at the time hadn't really travelled much abroad. This was my first time in France and so to go on my own was quite an adventure. I was put up in a lovely hotel and a car collected me in the morning to take me to the conference centre. Everyone I met spoke brilliant English, so thankfully I didn't have to call on my very limited schoolgirl French.

I was expecting to address a small group of people in the tourism industry and had made a few bullet points to speak from, thinking I could talk "off the cuff" for the 20 minutes or so I had been allocated. I walked into the conference hall to be faced by the massed ranks of 400 delegates all ready and waiting to hear the "secret of my success". My heart, I'm not ashamed to admit, missed a few beats.

The funniest thing was that, as I started to speak, just about everyone in the audience disappeared from view as they bent down, en masse, to fiddle around under their seats. This, as you might expect, left me momentarily flummoxed, that is until everyone suddenly popped back up with headphones on. It was so hard to stop myself laughing. It felt just like I was addressing the United Nations!

My second strangest trip abroad was when I was invited to Germany to appear on a quiz show called Ja Oder Nein (Yes or No) a similar show to What's My Line?, where a panel of celebrities had to guess my line of work.

I was met at Munich airport and taken to a lovely hotel. Hardly anyone I met spoke English, which made things strange and somewhat confusing. From the hotel I was taken to the television studio where we went through various introductions and instructions. I was then taken to the make-up department where they spent what seemed like an age making me look like a middle-aged hausfrau. I looked a real fright – all my friends were doubled-up in pain when they tried to watch the video I was given. To make matters worse the panel put their questions to me in German, which was then translated through a headphone in my ear. Luckily, all I had to do was answer "Ja" or "Nein" to their questions and whether it was because I looked particularly convincing or whether they were just confused I managed to beat the celebrity panel. They hadn't a clue what I did and to cap it all, I won £2,000.

Although I've done quite a few TV quiz shows over the years, from What's My Line? to Tell The Truth ("My name's Joy Swift and most weekends I kill people!") the most interesting thing about them, from my point of view, is that I got to meet a wide variety of celebrities "up close" in the hospitality suite afterwards.

I think my favourite celebrity must be Claire Rayner, a fabulous person and a great role model for a woman starting out in business on her own. She was very encouraging and thought my idea was great – and when I explained I was thinking of taking the idea to America she said "Go for it girl". And that's exactly what I did – but not before I was literally almost stopped in my tracks.

Chapter 9

Spread-eagled at Stafford

In 1983, Murder Weekends were still very new and, despite the masses of publicity we'd received, there were still plenty of people who hadn't heard of them. Unfortunately, a good number of these seemed to be police officers – as two memorable incidents with the "uninformed uniformed" clearly demonstrate.

The first happened during a Weekend at The Royal Albion Hotel in Brighton. I'd been asleep for an hour or so following a particularly exhausting Saturday night when I was rudely awoken by a fire alarm at around 3am. As you can imagine, I was not best pleased – even more so since my long experience of staying in hotels told me it was bound to be a false alarm.

Given the fact there were also three "dead bodies" stashed away quietly in their rooms (I'd decided right from the very start of Murder Weekends that the "recently deceased" should stay that way for the duration of the Weekend – I couldn't imagine anything worse than coming down to breakfast as a guest and bumping into the person you'd just seen brutally murdered the previous day) I wasn't particularly inclined to try to get them out of the hotel.

A telephone call from one of the hotel staff – telling me in no uncertain terms there really was a fire – quickly rid me of this notion. There was nothing for it. We'd have to evacuate the bodies as best we could. Thinking on my feet as usual I rang each body, explained the situation, told them to get dressed and to come to my room. Once there we could wait until all the guests had assembled at their fire point at the front of the hotel. I would take the 'bodies' down a nearby fire escape to the back of the hotel where I was certain no guests would be.

However, to be on the safe side (I still didn't really believe the hotel was on fire and I was determined not to break one of my golden rules) I told each of the bodies to wrap themselves in a candlewick bedspread from their room. That way, if they did accidentally bump into a guest they could pull the bedspread over their head so they couldn't be recognised (okay, so it wasn't the best plan I've ever come up with and if any guest had met a dead body walking down a hotel corridor at 3am covered from head to toe in a bedspread, the thought of escaping from a fire would probably have been the least of their concerns but, what the heck, it seemed like a good idea at the time).

As we got to the bottom of the fire escape three fire engines, followed by a couple of police cars, came down the road adjoining the hotel and I thought "Blimey, there really must be a fire," and so decided to lead the bodies across the road so they'd be safely out of any possible danger. I left them huddled together on a bench on the freezing promenade, completely covered by the bedspreads in case any wandering guests happened along.

With the benefit of hindsight I realise how ridiculous (and suspicious) they must have looked but at the time my only thoughts were making sure they were safe and out of sight and then getting back to the hotel as quickly as I could to reassure the manager that three unfortunates weren't trapped inside what I felt sure was, by now, a blazing inferno (although the distinct lack of smoke in the air should have told me this wasn't the case, but since I'm rarely at my best at three in the morning I think my oversight was probably excusable).

What happened next, however, was something I couldn't have foreseen. The police, having rushed to the scene, were quickly informed by the fire crew that the hotel wasn't on fire and that the only smoke to be seen was from the cigarette being puffed by a bored member of the hotel staff.

Having been roused from whatever it was they did on the Sunday night shift, the officers decided they'd have a trawl around the promenade just to check everything was okay and, as they did so, they came across what looked liked three vagrants trying to sleep on a bench. The officers, of course, told them to "move along". The actors, still thinking the hotel was on fire, told the police they were staying at the hotel. The officers, clearly not convinced, then wanted to know why they were huddled together on a bench covered by old brown blankets, rather than standing at the hotel fire point with the other guests.

The conversation then took a turn for the worse when one of the actors, quite reasonably it must have seemed, said they were dead bodies who'd been told to hide in case they were spotted by guests.

Not surprisingly, the police took this explanation quite badly and demanded the bodies produce identification which, of course, they couldn't because they'd just thrown their clothes on before leaving the hotel, not thinking anyone would demand proof of their identity in the middle of the night on Brighton prom (which just goes to show how wrong you can be). At this point one of the actors realised the situation was starting to get out of hand and started to explain about "Murder Weekends"; all the police needed to do was "talk to Joy Swift over at the hotel" and everything would become clear.

I knew something had happened (I didn't know exactly what had gone on until the actors explained it all to me later) when a police car drew up outside the hotel and I heard my name being called. Although I was desperately trying to stay in character (another golden rule...) the officer was insistent. He got out of the car, walked over to me, pointed to the three figures huddled together on the back seat of the car desperately trying to avoid being seen by the guests and said: "Are these yours?"

For a moment or two the guests clearly thought this was part of the plot – having provided an ambulance to remove the first body on Friday night what could have been more natural than to provide a real police car, complete with two burly officers? They didn't think this for long however as I slunk off with the police to find the duty manager who verified that this really was just a case of actors taking their role a bit too seriously.

The officers thankfully saw the funny side of things and even obliged by driving the actors round to the back of the hotel where they were able once more to reach the safety and anonymity of their rooms.

Although everyone (even the dead bodies) saw the funny side of the situation the next morning, this brush with the law was as nothing to what would happen just 24 hours later.

The journey back to Liverpool is a long one from the south coast so I decided to stay overnight at the hotel. Dean, one of the actors on the Weekend, had to make the same journey so we decided that we'd go up to London together the following morning to catch the Liverpool train. Weighed down by all the luggage from the weekend, we struggled into Euston to find we'd just missed our intended train – not, we thought, that it particularly mattered because the next was due in an hour, giving us time to catch our breath and have a quiet drink in the bar while we waited.

Once we were settled I opened my briefcase to get some cigarettes (I'm a little ashamed to admit I smoked in those days) and thought no more of it as we chatted away over our drinks. A couple of minutes before the train was due to leave I glanced at my watch, looked at Dean and exclaimed loudly (giving everyone in the crowded bar – Dean included – quite a fright). We gathered our bags as quickly as we could and set off running down the concourse towards our platform at full pelt.

We arrived just as the train was leaving. And then a very strange thing happened. The train stopped to let us on! "How kind is that?" I said to Dean as we clambered aboard with our bags. "That's never happened before," he said by way of reply. I was just thankful we'd managed to catch our train and was looking forward to a nice relaxing journey to Lime Street.

Although it was an express, stopping only at Stafford, we had plenty of time to have a leisurely meal, drink and chat – which we duly did – and were just finishing a bottle of wine as the train slowed to almost a dead crawl. I looked out the window and saw we were pulling into Stafford but we weren't moving towards the main platform. Rather we were being diverted towards a siding. "How odd" I thought.

Even more oddly, as I pointed out to Dean, the siding was lined with some of the biggest, beefiest men I'd ever seen. They were wearing the same sort of huge padded jacket, the kind worn by riot police or armed police in an episode of The Bill.

I said to Dean: "I wonder what's going on?" as I watched one of the men get onto the train. He entered our carriage, walked up the aisle and, just as he got to where we were sitting, grabbed my briefcase with one hand while throwing the other around Dean's shoulders, pinning him to the seat. Before I could react I felt hands gripping my shoulder as someone I hadn't seen came up behind me and stopped me moving.

The next thing I knew we were both being dragged roughly from the train and thrown unceremoniously to the ground. As I lay spread-eagled on the platform I felt someone searching me and then a voice shouted: "Open the briefcase. The gun's in the briefcase". It was then I realised what was happening and, through a combination of fear, panic and self-preservation I immediately went into jabber mode. "Murder Weekends…blanks…not…real…decommissioned…" I spluttered, to no real avail – trust me, it's hard to make yourself speak intelligibly when your hearts coming out of your mouth and you're being held face down, with your hands locked behind you, by a very large man sitting astride your back.

Not before time, a uniformed officer managed to open the briefcase where he did, of course, find "a gun". He also found the stack of brochures, letterheads and general Murder Weekends material I happened to be carrying.

It was at this point they realised their mistake and both Dean and I were allowed to get to our feet. As I stood up I saw the siding was packed with police officers and I could see from the bulges in their jackets that some of them were definitely armed. In one of those surreal moments that you only think happens in films or on TV, I also saw several highly decorated uniformed officers standing behind the general throng. It looked like the top brass had turned out for what they thought was a big, newsworthy, operation and they were determined to look their best!

While still standing on the platform we were both questioned for a good 20 minutes, during the course of which we came to understand the chain of events that led to us both being yanked unceremoniously from the train. While we were sitting in the bar at Euston a vigilant individual had seen the gun when I'd opened my briefcase to get my cigarettes. She had reported it to British Transport police and because it was 1983, at the height of the IRA bombings, they duly contacted the Anti-Terrorist Squad who immediately went into action. After all, we were going to Liverpool, which is but a short hop over to Belfast!

After about half an hour (believe me, it seemed like much, much longer) the police satisfied themselves that we weren't actually a couple of dangerous terrorists on the loose and allowed us back on the train which was another experience in itself. During our time on the platform everyone had been peering through the train windows trying to see what was going on and, in particular, why their train journey home after a hard day's work was being delayed. When the police put us back on the very same train I nearly died from embarrassment. No one said anything to us (of course), but I could feel their eyes drilling into the back of my neck (not to mention the dirty looks we'd received on the way back to our seats) for the remainder of the journey home.

Once there I had to explain to my long-suffering mother how, not for the first time as it happens, I'd nearly ended up in jail. Not being one to look a gift horse in the mouth, I realised the publicity value the incident would have. I contacted a number of national newspapers who, the next day, were only too happy to print the story of "Another eventful day in the life of a serial murderer..."

Chapter 10

An Englishwoman in New York

B y the end of 1982 the publicity generated about the fledgling Murder Weekends in the American media meant that by the start of 1983 we had begun to see large numbers of American guests appearing on the Weekends – two of whom were Jack and Bobby Gillan, a couple of vivacious and fun New York business people.

As I was chatting away to them at the end of a Weekend, Jack turned to me and said "You know, you really should bring Murder Weekends to New York. They'd love them".

My immediate response was to talk about all the problems this would involve – travelling to a different country (you may be surprised to learn I'm not really the adventurous sort), finding somewhere to stay and, above all, finding actors who were right for Murder Weekends.

Jack jokingly replied that I "wouldn't have a problem finding actors. Every restaurant and hotel is overrun with them". At the time I wasn't totally convinced, even though he was hugely enthusiastic about the prospect. But the more I thought about it, the more interesting and exciting the idea became. So, I amazed myself when, in June 1983, I boarded a flight to New York as the first tentative step to introducing Murder Weekends to a massive new audience.

Although this was a new experience for me, my decision had been eased by Jack and Bobby encouraging me every step of the way.

Their kind offer of the loan of a small apartment they owned in

Greenwich Village certainly helped to ease any lingering apprehension at being an Englishwoman alone in New York.

I'd chatted away to the pair of them quite happily when they were in England, but I had no idea that Bobby was a party organiser and that she employed lots of actors as waiters when they were "between parts". Almost as soon as I touched down, Bobby arranged a party at their beautiful brownstone townhouse on Jane Street to introduce me to both their friends and employees, from whom I would be able to recruit actors. Hardly having had time to even catch my breath I found myself explaining at length, to a large group of friendly strangers, how the Weekends worked. To say they were enthusiastic would be an understatement; they all wanted to be involved if I could get the project off the ground.

The first priority was to find a suitable location and hotel. Two days later I went to see a hotel I'd picked out of Yellow Pages. The Vista International, owned and run by the Hilton group, was a beautiful modern hotel that had been built between the twin towers of the World Trade Centre. Sadly, it's no longer there, of course, following the tragedy of 9/11. I arranged to meet up with the hotel's sales director and, having described the concept of a Murder Weekend with the help of a few Press clippings, I left half an hour later with a contract to do three Murder Weekends at the hotel the following year. When I arrived back at Jane Street and told Bobby my news she was ecstatic and immediately decided to get all the actors together so we could celebrate.

Six months later, the week before Christmas, I arrived back in New York. The plan was to stay for a week or so at the Vista hotel, partly so I could get a feel for the location and the staff and partly so as not to impose too much on Jack and Bobby's kind hospitality. I had brought my latest plot ("The Will Reading") with me and the actors and I spent a couple of fun nights planning how we could transpose all the clues and details into "American".

On Christmas Day (the coldest day I've ever experienced in my life, with a wind-chill factor of minus 40?) I was invited to Bobby's for a xmas party as I think she and Jack felt sorry for me stuck in the hotel on my own. I got onto the subway at Corlandt Street and had six stops to travel to get to 14th Street where I would disembark for Jane Street.

As you can imagine, the New York subway on Christmas Day wasn't exactly packed with people, but I was nevertheless slightly uneasy to find I was the only person in the compartment when I caught my train.

I was, however, even more perturbed when a very unkempt middle-aged man got on at the next station. He was wearing a grubby coat, had very long, matted hair and a "Professor Dumbledore" type beard. He was also carrying a big bottle of whisky from which he proceeded to drink in large gulps. As he lurched towards me, I stared intently at something suddenly fascinating on my shoes (as you do), trying desperately not to catch his eye or give him any invitation to start a conversation. To no avail. He bent down in front of me and, with a broad smile on his face, slurred: "Have a drink with me, it's my birthday – I'm Jesus!"

At the best of times (and this certainly wasn't one of them) I don't like whisky, I don't like weird strangers and I don't like germs, but since I liked the thought of being stabbed even less I mustered what charm I could and, praying that he couldn't hear my knees knocking loudly together, politely and matter-of-factly said "Happy birthday. I'm afraid I'm a reformed alcoholic and although I'd love to have a drink with you, it would do me too much harm". I then, for some strange reason, shook his hand. This seemed to do the trick, although he then started to sing "Away in a Manger" loudly and drunkenly to me. It was after all, as he patiently explained, "his song". When he'd finished he sat down next to me and started chatting aimlessly. I think he thought he'd made a friend for life while I, for my part, was thinking I still had five stops to go and was dreading what might happen next. As luck would have it, a family stepped into the compartment at the next station and, since they were obviously much more interesting than me, "Jesus" turned his drunken attentions to them. To say I was relieved to arrive at the party is an understatement and the "reformed alcoholic" very readily accepted the offer of a few glasses of champagne (just to calm my nerves of course).

I took a few days out to recharge my batteries and flew back to England after New Year to throw myself into the production of a new plot, due to start at the end of January. The three or four weeks before each plot begins is always a mad whirl of activity where I have to produce and prepare all the things that go into making each plot special, unique and enjoyable.

Each plot is built around its own particular theme and this involves both accompanying artwork (displayed on table menus and cards, for example) and games that help to break up the action and give the guests a chance to get to know each other and indulge in a little light-hearted competition before returning to the serious work of sleuthing.

Each character has to have a believable and consistent back-story – where they live, who they're related to, how many children they have and such like – and notes for each actor have to be prepared so that, when they arrive "as a guest" on a Weekend they're immediately ready and able to answer questions (many of the regular guests start firing questions just as soon as everyone assembles for the pre-dinner cocktail party at the start of each Weekend, so the actors have to be fully prepared "from the word go").

Every plot also, of course, needs clues – not just those that lead to the identity of the murderer (or murderers) but also clues that incriminate other characters or simply serve as red herrings. Some can be fairly straightforward, such as a newspaper article or magazine cutting that highlights a particular character trait or behaviour, but others have to be more devious. One of the great favourites among sleuths is the clue that hides a code that has to be deciphered, for example. All of this preparation takes up a great deal of time before a plot even begins.

Once the new plot had been successfully launched I flew back to New York to spend a few days making the final arrangements for the American debut of Murder Weekends (including what seemed like a never-ending round of Press interviews). With the arrangements completed it was back on the plane to England once again to act on the next two Weekends of the new plot. Having hardly had time to catch my breath I was back on the plane to New York again (if only they'd had air miles in those days!) and spent the next week in a whirl of meetings, training sessions, Press interviews (including a stint on the sofa of a Good Morning-style breakfast show) and whatever else threw itself my way – to be honest I was working so hard it really is all a bit of a blur to me now.

Finally, however, the Friday of the first American Weekend was upon us, as were 80 guests (two of whom, Elaine and Marti Liston, still make the trip to England 23 years on for just about every new plot). Thankfully, after all the effort and hard work the Weekend went very well and the many journalists present seemed to absolutely love it. Without exception they each said they would write positive articles about their experience and they were all true to their word; this led to two further Weekends, scheduled for October, quickly selling out with upwards of 100 guests on each.

Following the post-Weekend party I got a taxi to Newark Airport and I was so exhausted I paid for an upgrade to a first class seat just so I could lie on the floor (no beds in those days) and sleep all the way across the Atlantic. My mother met me at Manchester Airport and she told me later how worried she had been. She thought I was heading for a nervous breakdown because I looked so terrible and was barely able to mumble a few incoherent words about how it had all gone. Looking back I can understand why she might have thought this – a combination of exhilaration, excitement and exhaustion had left me feeling the worse for wear.

There was, however, little time to put my feet up or have a well-earned rest – the next six months just flew by (metaphorically rather than literally this time) and almost before I knew it we were into another new plot, one I'd based around voodoo. Each victim was sent advance warning of their imminent demise when they received a package filled with either chicken feet or feathers. For the coup de gras, the final victim would receive a fresh, plucked chicken. Each week I bought a chicken from the local market and sliced its flesh with a knife in the exact place the victim was to be stabbed. I then painted fake blood into the cuts which looked both realistic and very scary.

Disposing of the grisly evidence after each Weekend could have been a problem (I certainly didn't want to carry it home in the car) but I came up with a simple solution. At the end of each plot I wrapped the chicken in a carrier bag, tied it tightly and then put it into another well-tied carrier bag, which I then left in the waste paper bin in my room. For the first two Weekends all went well and I left the hotel happy and confident our new plot was going nicely. Perhaps I'd counted my chickens too soon, however, because on the third Weekend things went ever-so-slightly awry.

We were sitting in the bar around midday on the Sunday, chatting with the guests about the fun they'd had and how their favourite death had been the last victim. It had been, I'm proud to admit, a pretty spectacular death, even by my standards; the victim was found in the hotel garden with his hands spread wide and tied with rope to nails hammered into the wall. The idea was to create a crucifixion-like pose and I had made cuts in clothes and applied fake blood in the same positions they had appeared on the chicken. If this wasn't enough I placed a semi-circle of hay on the ground, leaving a gap of about five feet between it and the actor. And set fire to it! The smoke and flames alerted the guests to something happening in the garden, whereupon they rushed outside and saw the most dramatic death we had staged up until that point.

Suddenly, however, we heard an almighty scream and turned to watch as a dark-haired chambermaid came hurtling down the main hotel stairs and, without pausing or looking around, ran straight for the door to the garden. I had no idea what all the fuss was about but the guests thought it was wonderful – an added bit of excitement at the end of their memorable weekend. An hour later, however, the reason for the commotion became all too clear.

The chambermaid was Italian and spoke very little English; the management staff hadn't tried to explain about Murder Weekends thinking that, firstly, she wouldn't be involved in any way and, secondly, she wouldn't have understood what they were telling her. As she cleaned the room I'd just vacated the chambermaid had lifted the waste bin and, thinking it was rather heavy, decided to investigate. Not content with simply removing the carrier bag containing the very bloody chicken, she decided to untie the carefully knotted bag and, as she did so, saw pale, pimply flesh, covered with stab wounds and awash with blood.

The poor woman thought she had found a dead baby and, dropping the bag on the floor of the room, had run screaming from the hotel, shaking like a leaf and vowing never to return.

It was only after the manager had managed to find someone who could speak enough Italian to explain the situation (and quite how he managed that on a Sunday afternoon in Southport is another mystery) that she was persuaded to return. After several cups of sweet tea and lots of TLC, she seemed to recover sufficiently to return to work (although yours truly was left to pick up the chicken pieces). I was, of course, very apologetic, but really didn't think anyone would try to unbag my double-bagged chicken!

With the two Weekends in New York fully booked and nearly upon me, I geared myself up with plenty of beauty sleep and tried to get as much of the basic organisation out of the way as I could. The weekend before I was to fly to New York we performed the "Voodoo Plot" one final time in the UK – during which the most spectacular death we'd ever attempted on a Murder Weekend went spectacularly wrong.

Initially at least everything went to plan. The victim was to be found in a small courtyard enclosed on all sides by tall walls, two of which were part of the hotel, and we managed to get him in place without arousing any suspicion amongst the guests. Once there he was successfully tied to the nails we'd pre-driven into the walls the day before and I spread the hay I was going to light a sufficient distance from his feet to make it look realistic without him being in any danger of being burnt. So far, so good. From this point on, however, things went rapidly downhill.

I struck a match and threw it into the hay. It spluttered for a second or two and went out. I tried another, then another, with exactly the same effect. I finally realised the hay was too damp to catch light.

Whenever we're putting a body in place on a Weekend we always have a couple of actors "hanging around", just in case a guest who should be somewhere else (such as playing a game or examining the incident room) comes wandering along. That way they can either intercept the guest or make enough noise to warn everyone to make themselves scarce.

On this occasion Steve, one of the actors, had a bedroom overlooking the courtyard and was hanging out of his window watching my unsuccessful attempts to start the blaze. Knowing that we were time-crucial, he suggested we get some whisky from the bar and pour it onto the hay. I trickled the alcohol around the semi-circle of hay and tried to light it – but again it wouldn't take. I was, by this point, running out of matches and was just on the point of giving it up as a bad job when one bit of hay took hold – at the exact same moment a freak gust of wind whistled around the courtyard. I say "gust" but it was more like a mini tornado that whipped around the courtyard. It was gone as quickly as it arrived, but not before it had fanned the tiny flame flicking around the actor's feet into something approaching a towering inferno.

John, the actor, panicked as the flames shot towards him and started to pull on the ropes binding his hands – which promptly tightened to such a degree he was unable to slip them free. In a moment of blinding clarity (or panic as it's sometimes known) I decided to leap over the flames and throw my body in front of his, the "thinking" being I would shield him from the flames while I untied the ropes. This, as it turned out, wasn't such a great idea since I couldn't loosen the ropes. Help, however was at hand. From his vantage point, Steve had quickly assessed the situation and shouted to me to catch a penknife which he threw from his window. I was able to cut the ropes and save John from an untimely end. As quickly as they had taken hold, the flames died away and John dropped to the floor.

I hurtled out of the courtyard just as fast as I could since I was acutely aware the guests would have seen the flames and would soon be arriving to inspect the scene. This was duly viewed and inspected by the excited guests and while the police inspector was carrying out his interrogation of the guests "the body" made his way back to my room. John was a lot calmer than he had been a few minutes beforehand. He wasn't actually hurt – just, understandably, not happy about our 30 seconds of excitement. Considering I'd been standing for a few seconds in front of a pile of blazing hay, I was okay too – or so I thought. Over the course of the evening, however, I realised my left leg felt warm and it was stinging quite a lot. It looked unnaturally pink but later that night I sat with it immersed in cold water and, believing it wasn't serious, thought it would be fine after a bit of rest.

. Over the next couple of days my leg began to hurt more and more, but I was sure that it was just a minor burn and nothing to get too excited about. I applied some cream my chemist advised would help clear it up and tried to focus on the week ahead, mainly because I was flying back to New York (once more) for the October Weekends and needed to get everything straight at this end.

Flying was the worst possible thing I could have done. When I arrived at JFK airport I was in agony. My legs had swollen, as they always do when I'm on a long haul flight, and the burnt skin was stretched and throbbing. Jack and Bobby had, once again, kindly lent me their apartment and, with only a little over a week to go before the first Weekend, I still had a lot to organise and was determined to "soldier on" despite the discomfort.

At three in the morning, two days later, I could stand it no longer. I was quite literally crying with the pain. Being alone in New York I had no one to turn to for help or advice so I picked up the phone and called a friend in England. He, as you might expect, told me in no uncertain terms that I should go to the nearest hospital, which is how I came to be in St Vincent's at four in the morning, explaining my predicament to a receptionist whose first question was to ask if I had medical insurance. Thankfully I did.

My ability to pay for treatment thus established I was ushered into ER where I lay on my own until the arrival of three burly New York cops with a very large and very angry man suffering from a gunshot wound. He was put on to the gurney next to me and had I not been in such pain I might have been frightened or excited. But at that point I was neither – I just wanted a doctor to cut my leg off and end my suffering!

I seemed to have been waiting ages before a doctor eventually arrived to see me and what he saw wasn't good. In fact, as he proceeded to tell me in a matter-of-fact way that I had the beginnings of gangrene which luckily they'd caught before it had gone too far. He said he would slice off both the infected and surrounding skin to make sure all the infection was removed. Equally casually, he sprayed my leg with something that may as well have been water for all the anaesthetic powers it had and began to slice my leg.

Although I have never known such pain it did the trick. I still have my leg, which may not have been the case had my friend not shouted down the phone at me to get myself to hospital (or if I hadn't had medical insurance…).

Once I was safely out of hospital my thoughts turned once more to the coming Weekends. Jack was convinced my idea was really going to take off in the States and, this being the case, I really ought to form my own company to handle the business side of things. He suggested I saw his lawyer (who, I later discovered, also acted for Yoko Ono) and so, swathed in bandages, I found myself in the office of a very nice American lawyer whose long grey ponytail and faded blue jeans marked him out as a child of the 60s. He advised me to form a company and move permanently to the States to protect my interests. In this way, as he said, even though there would inevitably be loads of people ready and willing to form their own murder mystery variations to jump on the bandwagon I'd created, everyone would want to go on a "Joy Swift Original English Weekend".

If I'd taken his advice I'd probably be very rich by now. But I didn't – not because I didn't think he was right but because, at heart, I'm a homebird. I love Liverpool and didn't want to leave it. Nor did I really want to live in America.

The next day I arrived at the Vista hotel ready for the first of our two Weekends. The actors were excited but not as excited as the guests, the majority of whom, I later discovered, had booked with the sole purpose of seeing and understanding how a Murder Weekend worked. They were, not put to point too fine a point on it, spies who would copy my idea and apply it in their hotels, on their trains and on their cruise ships. Within six months of debuting Murder Weekends in New York "murder breaks" were being offered everywhere across the States and I was back home in Liverpool, not minding, in truth, that I had turned down a fortune.

A year later I was persuaded, against my better judgement, to set up a Murder Weekend at another hotel in Fort Worth, near Dallas. I was accompanied to Texas by one of my English actors who helped me audition actors for the plot. Once we'd decided on the people we needed we spent a couple of weeks "training them up", during the course of which we met and got to know some lovely actors.

One pair were a gay couple who invited us to their home for dinner and they took great pride in showing us round their spacious and very brightly decorated house – so much so, in fact, they also decided to show us their "special room". This, it turned out, was a euphemism for what I can only term a dungeon. The room was painted black and it was filled with all kinds of contraptions. I must admit that, although I'm not easily shocked, I didn't hang around to see everything; that room certainly opened the eyes of a relatively innocent Scouser!

The Dallas Weekend went well but I don't think I had either the energy or inclination to make a go of Murder Weekends in the States and I vowed it would be my last 'murderous' trip to America.

Chapter 11

Murder ahoy!

Although I had decided not to do any more Weekends in America, over the next few years a number of opportunities arose to take Murder Weekends into mainland Europe and beyond.

Initially these arose from requests to do corporate events – one of the first of which saw the Murder Weekend crew travelling in a private jet to Germany to commit a hijacking (something we would never be able to do nowadays) and several murders on Rhine cruise ships and in German castles. On another occasion, again for a very large corporate event, I was flown to Oslo to perform a special plot I'd written that took us around the city sights and incorporated a number of Norwegian customs (although, being a vegetarian, I managed to ensure I was safely killed off in order to avoid having to sample the delights of reindeer and seal).

These "trial runs" should have prepared me for my next big Murder Weekend leap into the unknown when I was contracted by P&O to produce Murder Cruises for some of their ships. The first of these took place in May 1989 when we set sail for a cruise around the Mediterranean, performing four specially prepared plots over a two-week period (something I'd worked so hard to create in the preceding weeks that I was exhausted before I even set foot on the boat).

Although the cruise promised to be a lot of fun for everyone involved, as it got underway I immediately became aware of a fundamental problem that made this – and subsequent – cruises a frustrating experience at times. The problem, from my viewpoint, was that these weren't Murder Weekends, as such. What I mean by this is that the guests had, first and foremost, booked a cruise and the Murder games were just something they signed up for once they were aboard, much as they could sign up for all the other activities on offer. The Murder Break was, from the guests' point of view, just one extra form of onboard entertainment.

This was fine at the start of the cruise when lots of guests signed up and participated in the fun and games as we sailed across the channel and battled our way through the Bay of Biscay, but as soon as we arrived in the Mediterranean we lost the majority of our audience as they were too busy sunbathing to keep up the necessary level of involvement in the Murder Cruise to make it understandable and enjoyable. To add further to the confusion (for both the actors and the guests), we were only "in character" at certain times during the cruise (as opposed to the "always in character" routine I insist upon during normal Weekends). This meant that one minute I was "Fenella Barchester", a psychopathic nymphomaniac from Crewe and the next I was sitting at the dinner table or tramping round Pompeii and talking to people quite normally as Joy Swift.

This was not, I felt, a very satisfactory way to run a Murder Break and although we carried on with the cruises for a few years (I eventually decided to quietly and gracefully decline further contracts in 1991) it was obvious to me, if not the bosses at P&O, that although the format could work it had to be organised differently. The Murder Break had to be an integral part of the cruise, not something bolted on as an "optional extra".

Although the cruises involved a lot of hard work for both me and my crew of actors, looking back on the experience there were some fabulous moments and some ridiculously funny incidents, the first of which happened on the SS Canberra.

Although the entire ship's company had been briefed beforehand about what to expect in terms of deaths, fights and arguments (much to the amusement of the lovely Philippino stewards), this didn't extend to the ship's passengers (some of whom were blissfully unaware of the murderous games going on around them. For this particular plot I was playing a none-too-bright girl called Tracy; she was madly in love with a sophisticated film star and had been stalking him since the start of the cruise. We had arranged that I would pester him once more by an outside swimming pool and, in his understandable desire to be rid of Tracy's unwanted attentions, he would push me into the water. The "ordinary guests" sunbathing around the pool were supposed to have been warned by one of the stewards about the argument to prevent them thinking that what was about to kick off was for real.

Come the allotted moment for the argument and drenching we were all mingling around the pool, the various characters being interrogated by Murder Break guests and the film star standing aloof to one side preening himself and basking in the attention of his adoring public. After a few minutes Tracy approached him and, for what must have been the thousandth time, professed her undying love. If only he would give her one little kiss her life would be complete...

The outraged film star let Tracy know in no uncertain terms that he wasn't about to kiss a mad stalker and, with a violent shove of his arms, he pushed me backwards with such force that I flew horizontally into the pool. In one of those mysterious moments of perfect clarity, where everything seems to happen in slow motion, I could see – in what must have been no more than a split second – the expressions on the faces of the sunbathing passengers as I flew through the air. They had absolutely no idea what was going on.

When she hit the water Tracy began splashing frantically around, screaming that she couldn't swim (being a strong swimmer, I wasn't actually in any danger) but Tracy was sinking and rising and then sinking once again as if her life really was ebbing away. A couple of guests threw a life buoy into the pool, but Tracy was panicking too much to either see or grab it as she aimlessly flapped her arms in a vain attempt to stay afloat.

And then, much to my surprise, a steward decided he would jump, fully clothed, into the pool to effect a gallant rescue. I don't know who was more surprised – me to find myself suddenly being grabbed from behind by a pair of very strong hands that were determined, despite my best efforts to the contrary, to "save" me, or him to find me trying desperately to fight him off.

Either way the whole episode must have looked fantastic. As I was eventually "rescued" everyone – the actors included – seemed to find the whole episode hilarious. Everyone, that is, apart from the sunbathing passengers. They were not amused to find the whole thing was just an act. This was my first lesson learned; always make sure that all passengers – those playing the game and those not – have written explanations about what to expect from a Murder Afloat.

If the "innocent bystander" is sometimes a problem for actors (and corpses in particular, as I've already described), "corpsing" (when another actor says or does something that makes you respond in a completely inappropriate way, such as being unable to stop yourself laughing when you're supposed to be responding angrily) is a much more frequent problem.

Corpsing is an ever-present possibility on Murder Weekends because not only is the action "live" (if you don't do it right first time you don't get a second, third or fourth "take") but it's also largely unscripted, by which I mean the actors aren't given lines to learn, only situations to interpret. This means, of course, that actors can sometimes say or do things that are so unexpected – or so open to misinterpretation – that the poor recipient finds it next to impossible to stay in character, at least for a few moments until they regain their composure.

Corpsing another actor is generally frowned upon (it breaks the illusion of realism) but there are times (some of which I'll describe in more detail in Part Two) when an actor, despite their best endeavours, just can't help themselves – one such instance being on a cruise as we were crossing the Bay of Biscay. As I've already suggested, we take our "dead bodies" very seriously on Murder Weekends and try to make them as realistic as possible, both in terms of how they look and how they behave. We learn, for example, how to "shallow breathe" so that as far as is humanly possible it doesn't look as though a "dead body" has just run a four minute mile. A body is never allowed to move (another actor always holds their hand, for example, so that if a body ever needs to sneeze or cough a gentle squeeze of the hand is enough to alert the hand-holder to do something that creates a temporary distraction). When all of the guests have viewed the body the actor is then spirited away to their hotel room or cabin where they remain out of sight for the duration of the Weekend. Touch wood, it's quite rare for a corpse to be obviously "alive", but there have been times when circumstances have conspired to ruin the best laid plans...

This particular crossing was very, very rough; the ship was rolling and listing with such violence that crockery was flying everywhere and many of the passengers were forced to retire to their cabins suffering from severe seasickness. Although a couple of the actors said they felt a little queasy, none were forced to take to their beds and it seemed that those passengers who had signed up for the Break were generally a hardy bunch too.

So there we were, acting our socks off on the high seas in the middle of a raging storm, rowing and arguing as if our lives depended on it. Suddenly one of the characters took a sip of wine, spluttered and choked violently and staggered slowly across the floor before collapsing dramatically at the feet of the detective who just happened to be a passenger on the cruise.

All the guests and actors crowded around the prostrate body, his wife crying loudly and his apparently distraught brother bemoaning the fact the victim had promised him a share of his fortune but hadn't had time to change his will. The detective searched frantically for a pulse but, unable to find one, pronounced the character dead (cue further tears from even more distraught wife).

The lifeless corpse had, at this point, been lying on the floor with his eyes closed for a good few minutes and the motion of the violently swaying ship finally got to him. Without even moving a muscle, he projectile vomited across the room. The impressive spray flew over shoes, handbags and whatever else was unlucky enough to be in its path – including his erstwhile wife who had been unfortunate enough to be hugging the body at exactly the wrong moment. In an equally impressive display of acting talent, the dead actor showed absolutely no emotion whatsoever – his eyes remained tightly closed, his body prone – and no one could quite believe what they'd just seen – a true professional if ever I've seen one.

Although the Bay of Biscay quickly became notorious among the actors for sickness (even those with strong stomachs were sometimes affected by the inevitable rough seas), on one particular cruise it was a virulent stomach bug, rather than the sea, that was responsible for a terrible outbreak of vomiting. Just about everyone was affected at some point in the voyage – it was so bad it actually made the national newspapers – but since, like the dancers and singers, we were there to entertain the passengers we had to carry on as best we could.

At times it really was like something out of a Carry On film – a quick argument or fight before an actor would dash outside to be sick. Worst of all were the lengthy sessions spent sitting on the loo, but at least the actors all recovered. The same, unfortunately, could not be said of some of the other people on board. In the ship's foyer there was a list of passengers and when one of them died, their name was crossed out in red. During the cruise we saw five such lines appear and, on our arrival back at Southampton, four hearses were waiting on the dockside. The fifth passenger was buried at sea.

On a less solemn note, one of the nice things about the cruises was that as well as performing the plots we had some free time to look around the places we visited. On one such occasion John Shepherd, one of the actors, and I decided we'd like to explore a small Italian island at which we'd docked and we hired a jeep so we could drive around with relative freedom. Since John didn't have his driving licence with him, I got to do the driving.

We set off on our journey with me initially trying to get used to both driving on the right hand side of the road and the fact the completely open jeep meant that to my left I had nothing but road. I'd started to get the hang of things when the road started to narrow as we came to a small village.

As we passed through it a very large dog ran out into the road alongside the jeep and started to bark loudly at me, his rather fierce teeth only inches from my ankles. I was a little panic stricken by the dog's behaviour and, being an animal lover, I was concentrating so hard to avoid hitting and injuring it that I didn't, at first, hear John shrieking "Joy! Joy! Joy!" at the top of his voice.

By the time I heard him it was too late. There was a loud grating sound as I turned the wheel to avoid the dog and then a "thud" as we crashed to a halt. It probably says something that I was so concerned about the dog's welfare that it took me a few seconds to realise what had happened. I looked to my right and saw that in swerving to avoid the dog I'd driven into a small concealed ditch.

The jeep was tilted at a very odd 45% angle and the right-hand side was resting against a low wall. Oddly enough I neither swore nor cried at this unfortunate turn of events; rather, I burst into hysterical laughter, the reason for which was John. He was sitting beside me with a bright red face covered in scratches. He was also encased in what looked like a hay stack of green leaves, with just his upper body poking out of the top.

All the time I'd been focusing on the snarling teeth of a no-doubt rabid dog, John was being whipped by the low lying bushes on his side of the road. As the leaves came off they simply collected around him in the jeep. He looked so funny perched amidst the leaves I just couldn't control my laughter and although John wasn't laughing much (actually, he wasn't laughing at all) I was uncontrollable for about half an hour.

As luck would have it the village housed a small hotel and four burly German tourists came rushing to the scene and effortlessly lifted the trashed jeep from the ditch. I think, at first, they thought I was injured as I crouched by the ditch holding my sides and apparently sobbing. They soon realised, however, that I was crying with laughter rather than pain.

Being foolhardy (and John, apparently, fearless), as soon as we realised the jeep was relatively undamaged we decided to carry on with our exploration of the island. The small road we'd been travelling continued up what turned out to be quite a large hill and as we drove the road got progressively narrower until it eventually became a dirt track. I was sure it would widen again, but if anything it became even narrower.

Then, as we rounded a blind bend, I had to slam on the brakes as the jeep came to a shuddering halt literally three inches from a long dining room table. Seated around the table were about 20 members of an Italian family who scattered rapidly in all directions, justifiably terrified they were about to be mown down by a dirty old jeep driven by a mad woman and her battered companion. I think, from the general expressions on their faces, they thought their time was up.

It didn't help that, being in an already very giggly mood, I started to guffaw loudly once again and their terrified expressions turned to anger. Once they realised the danger was over they, almost as one, started to hurl abuse at us and even as I reversed down the track (and we were thankfully well out of sight and reach) I could hear what sounded like very, very rude language!

At this point most people would have probably given everything up as a bad job and just returned to the ship. We, however, were determined to be different and decided we would find a beach so we could relax and sunbathe. It was, however, not to be because we proceeded to get hopelessly lost among the winding roads and tracks of the island, eventually managing, more by luck than judgement, to find our way back to where we began our "adventure" many hours earlier.

By the time we arrived at the car hire shop to return the jeep we only had about 10 minutes left before the ship was due to sail. Given that one of the first things we had been told on boarding the ship was that "You must never be late because the ship always sails on time, come what may," we were both seriously worried about being left stranded on the island.

While I'd be the first to admit that, yes, the beaten up old jeep was slightly more beaten and battered than when it had first been handed it over to me seven hours earlier, the Italian shop assistant seemed to want me arrested for all the wrongs in the world. He was certainly not listening to my garbled explanation about the mad dog and how my fears had caused an understandable accident. Even the considerable number of lacerations around John's face didn't seem to evoke a sympathetic response.

My initial pleadings for him to allow us to return to the ship fell on deaf ears and there was nothing for it but to offer him a not too shabby bribe. He accepted this ungraciously and spat at John as we left the shop.

We ran for all we were worth back to the ship, sprinting up the gangplank just as the stewards had started to release the ropes. Strangely, John didn't want to come out with me on any other trips after that, but I've dined off the tale of the rabid dog and his hedge-trimming exploits ever since.

Another cruise, another John – Pendleton this time (a very funny actor with a wicked sense of humour) – was playing my husband and we had such fun.

For the purpose of the plot we were playing a family of "country bumpkins" (the Tibbs) who'd won the lottery and booked the cruise as a treat. As a way of introducing the plot to the guests John and I were asked to do an interview for the ship's radio that would explain all about our characters and the lottery win. I'm not quite sure how it happened but as the interview began John and I went straight into character. Instead of us chatting generally about Murder Weekend plots and characters "as Joy and John" we immediately became Billy and Maisey Tibbs who were not, as they say, the brightest stars in the night sky.

It all began quietly enough, but chaos rapidly ensued as John and I got deeper and deeper into our practised characters. The DJ began by asking us what we thought of the posh food and John (in his best West Country accent) immediately became very agitated and said that he had a very pooey bottom because the food was too rich and they didn't have the McDonalds and Kentucky Fried Chicken he usually ate.

Maisey then complained long and loud (again in my best country bumpkin accent) about the stupid clothing rules they had on the ship; in particular she was most put out she wasn't allowed into the restaurant in her Doc Marten boots. Both John and I were having a ball and the DJ was quick to realise what we were doing and let us run with it. Somewhat surprisingly, we didn't corpse each other until I said that I thought all the guests were a bit quiet. Billy promptly retorted, "Yes, they're as quiet as a carrot" and I then leapt in with,"They're as quiet as a carrot in a wheelbarrow". John, who always refused to let me have the last word, responded with, "As quiet as a carrot in a wheelbarrow that's been left in the bunker at the bottom of the garden". By this time we'd all had enough and the DJ burst out laughing, as did John and I as we fell out of the radio room.

Occasionally actors say that their characters "take on a life of their own" and this was certainly true on that particular cruise for Maisey

Tibbs, the vegetarian animal-lover with a mile-wide gullibility streak. Picking up on this, one of the guests informed Maisey that the magician currently performing in the ship's theatre was very cruel.

"Why?" Maisey innocently asked.

"Well" came the reply, "He's got lots of doves shoved down his jacket and to keep them quiet until they're needed in the act they have wires embedded in their chest. When he presses the wires the birds become paralysed".

Maisey was, of course, outraged by this news and immediately resolved to do something about it. What that "something" actually was wasn't totally clear, but a petition signed by all the guests decrying this blatant example of animal cruelty seemed to be as good a place as any to start. Egged on by Billy, Maisey also hit upon a plan of further action; after dinner that night we would all march to the theatre and protest!

The guests, knowing that these two characters were going to cause chaos, loved this idea but I wasn't so sure. "How are we going to get out of this one?" I said to John later when we were discussing the afternoon's excitement. He just smiled and said: "You can get yourself out of it. It was your idea and you're the one who got carried away." He was being devilish, of course, but I had no idea that he was already planning something that would dig me deeper into the hole I'd started to dig for myself.

After dinner I met the guests who were up for the protest at the arranged time and place, still having no real idea about what we would do or even whether someone would say it wasn't actually a very good idea and perhaps we should call the whole thing off (as I was secretly hoping). John, however, was revelling in my discomfort and had decided that if (when?) I got cold feet he had prepared a little something that would stop me backing down. He had found a large brown paper bin bag, cut a hole in the top for my head and two holes either side for my arms. He had then written on the front of the bag in very large capital letters, deliberately misspelt to emphasize his lack of education, "SAFE THE DOVES!!".

I was, of course, mortified. Maisey, on the other hand, was thrilled and immediately donned the bag, thanking him for his thoughtfulness while desperately thinking about how on earth I could get out of the mess I'd helped to create. For some reason, once fully bagged I began to very quietly chant,"Safe the Doves" and the 50 or so guests who had been brave enough to accompany us on the "demo" joined in.

I began to feel sick as I found myself marching down the ship's corridors at the head of a gaggle of guests all chanting "Safe the Doves! Safe the Doves!".

If this wasn't bad enough, to get from our starting point to the theatre was quite a long walk, through a large number of corridors and up and down a few flights of stairs. I was frantically hoping that as we marched people would gradually lose interest and that by the time I arrived at the theatre I'd be on my own. But no. As we marched and chanted cabin doors started opening to see what the commotion was all about and more and more people decided they would join in the fun. By the time we approached the theatre it was as though the ship had announced they were giving away free Ferraris – our little demo had ballooned to a full blown "poll tax" type rebellion.

John, being a complete swine, was hanging back and enjoying every second of my extreme discomfort, but a few yards from the theatre he finally decided that enough was enough. I heard a familiar voice behind me and the next thing I knew I was on the floor. John had pushed past the guests to be with his wife and as he got next to me pretended to trip over his massive Doc Marten boots. As he fell he lunged out to save himself, ripping the bag off my back and falling in a heap on top of me. Seizing my chance I protested that I'd hurt my leg and that, unfortunately, I wouldn't be able to make it to the theatre. The guests that were "in the know" were laughing hysterically (partly, I suspect, because they were more than a little relieved that they didn't have to march into the theatre shouting "Safe the Doves") while the people we'd picked up on route looked totally confused. I, however, was faint with relief that I didn't have to climb on stage and accost the innocent and confused magician!

Although I'm not usually one for playing practical jokes, I have to admit that on one cruise I did manage to pull off a pretty spectacular effort – one that lasted an entire week. All of the actors were having a fantastic time, getting on together brilliantly and having lots of laughs amongst ourselves in our free time. Part of our team were a lovely couple, Dave and Marg, who'd been acting on Weekends with me for many years – but it was only on the cruise that I began to realise they were a little gullible.

Shortly before the start of the trip there had been a lot of media coverage about a hurricane off the coast of Florida and, since we were heading in that direction, I blithely announced to the actors as we were sat around the dinner table: "Don't tell any of the guests but I've just been told that we're heading for a hurricane."

Everyone's face dropped, but Grant, my partner in crime and dear friend, immediately caught on. "I've heard that too," he said. "Sometime around the end of the cruise. About five days I think."

Realising I had an accomplice, I was on a roll. I explained that the crew were really worried. It was unlikely that the ship would go down, of course, but they had to be prepared and this included having to take "special medication" so they wouldn't be seasick if the worst came to the worst and they had to abandon ship. The medication would ensure they could all be on hand to help guests into the lifeboats. Everyone looked very worried, including Grant's mother Sheila, also a very dear friend, who I was willing to catch on. They looked even more worried when I described how the medication was given – through an apparently excruciatingly painful injection administered using a long syringe.

What I thought at the time was a relatively harmless little bit of fun then took on a life of its own. The following day I casually mentioned to the actors at dinner that, because I was technically the organiser of the Murder Weekend part of the cruise I'd been told I was the contact between the captain, his medical staff and the actors. In this capacity I had to attend a meeting later that evening where I'd be given all the details about the hurricane and any precautions we had to take. Because of the sensitive nature of the information, whatever I told my actors was confidential and they weren't allowed to pass any of it on to the passengers since, if they did, it might cause a mass panic. Everyone around the table listened quietly and sensibly and pretended to be very brave and keen to help in any way they could.

Sheila, Grant, Dana and Mark (two more of the actors who had by now cottoned on), were amazing. How they stopped themselves from laughing I'll never know.

The only two actors who hadn't realised it was a wind-up were Dave and Marg. They looked mortified when, a little later, I reported back to everyone the results of my "meeting". The captain and medical staff had informed me, I lied, that since the actors were technically not passengers they were classified as "crew" and would also need to have the horrendously painful injection to ensure they wouldn't be seasick. Lowering my voice I also informed them that if we had to abandon ship we would have to go with the rest of the crew in one of the last lifeboats. I don't know how we managed to keep a straight face when I added, for further effect, that, like the musicians on the Titanic, we would be responsible for keeping up the morale of the guests as they waited on deck to get into the lifeboats.

Over the next couple of days I took every opportunity to reassure Dave and Marg that it was very unlikely that anything would actually happen – it was, after all, a huge modern ship. The fact we hadn't encountered any particularly rough seas or high winds was explained by the fact the captain was trying to steer a course to avoid the hurricane – the mere mention of which was by now guaranteed to render Dave and Marg even more ashen-faced.

I did, at this point, start to feel a little guilty about the whole thing, but it had all gone too far to stop, especially since we had, by this time, let both our dinner waitress and steward in on the joke. Come dinner on the 'night of the hurricane' they both played their part to perfection by letting it be known they'd both had their injection ("very painful") and casually asking when we were due to have ours.

At this stage everyone at the table except Dave and Marg (who, unbelievably, still hadn't realised it was a practical joke, even though I was desperate for them to finally catch on to the scam), was nearly uncontrollable; they kept having to leave the table to guffaw outside without being seen. I told the actors I had to go to the hospital to be given our times and that I'd meet them in our favourite bar for a 'final' bottle or two of champagne which, as the person responsible for them all being in this situation, I felt duty-bound to provide.

I went back to my cabin for what I thought would be a suitable amount of time and returned to the bar. I then informed everyone of the time for their injection but there was just one more little bit of information to give them. I said that because the hospital was extremely busy, filling up with those crew members suffering the painful after effects of the jab, the ship's doctor would visit each of us in our cabin.

As a couple, and effectively dealing with two for the time of one, Dave and Marg would be the first to go and the doctor would be with them at midnight. To calm their nerves (and explain the deceptively calm sea) I stressed the hurricane was highly unlikely to hit us, but the captain had said that we had to take these precautions.

After a few minutes of excited chatter things settled down and we were having a lovely drink when Dave suddenly shouted: "Oh my God! Did you see that?" Everyone looked puzzled because no one except Dave had seen anything untoward. "See what?" someone said. "A huge flash of lightning," Dave exclaimed. A couple of the actors tried to laugh it off (mainly because as soon as he said it we were all really trying hard, unsuccessfully, not to laugh).

How Dave and Marg didn't twig at that point I'll never know. Perhaps they thought we were all trying to put a brave face on things? I turned to Grant and said we should go outside to see what the weather was like and as soon as we closed the door and were on deck we both pretended to fight a losing battle against a very strong wind. We were obviously better actors than we thought because even this pantomime performance didn't alert the worried couple to the magnificent hoax!

You may find what I have to say next totally unbelievable, but I swear it's the truth. Dave and Marg had brought a video camera with them on the cruise and while Dave busied himself videoing all our arrivals, trips and departures at various beautiful ports of call, Marg had amused us by providing a running commentary to Dave's filming. When we returned to the bar Marg turned to me and said that, as she had her video camera with her, would we record them saying their last farewells! Call me evil and tell me that bad karma will follow me all my life, but even then we didn't crack. On the contrary, everyone quickly agreed this was such a great idea that they'd all like to record a "last message" for their loved ones, "just in case the worst happened". One by one we solemnly took our turns in front of the camera, turning our loving farewells into stilted, stumbling, tearful affairs, just so we could cover our faces and hide our laughter.

Marg thought it would be a good idea to wrap the video in a black bin liner, to protect it, when divers eventually uncovered the wreckage many years later, like the Titanic! At a quarter to midnight we said our goodbyes and everyone except Dave and Marg retired to my room.

At exactly midnight I called Marg's room and asked if the doctor had been and if it was really as painful as we'd been led to believe. Marg told me they'd just had a call from the hospital (Dana putting on a great accent) to say they were running five minutes late (she still hadn't twigged that if they really were in the middle of an emergency inoculation they wouldn't have the time or inclination for such courtesies!).

The group of us then slipped out of my cabin and tiptoed along Dave and Marg's corridor until we were standing outside their cabin. With Grant at the front pointing his video camera at their door, we tentatively knocked and after a few moments Dave slowly opened the door. With Grant in the lead and laughing uncontrollably we pushed past him into the room, where we saw Marg face down on the bed, her bottom bared, ready and waiting for the dreaded injection.

Even when faced with a bunch of shrieking actors complete with video camera, Dave still didn't quite get what had happened, but Marg did. She leapt from the bed and gave me a damn good slapping and well deserved it was too!

Although it's now been 15 years since we did our last Murder Cruise I always believed, as I said earlier, that the problems we experienced were not because of the format – a Murder Weekend can, I think, be made to work just about anywhere if the organisation is right. The crucial thing about Murder Cruises, all those years ago, was that we didn't have a dedicated audience – a group of people whose main interest was sleuthing and who just happened to be doing what they loved in a very beautiful location. What we had instead was a group of people on a cruise, some of whom also happened to sign up for a Murder Weekend.

I remember thinking "Never again" when the cruises ended but, as Sean Connery once said, "Never say never again" because, as I'm writing these words, I'm sitting on my bed in the cabin I'm occupying for the next seven nights. I think this is probably as close as I'm ever going to get to heaven: Doing something I love (writing) while listening to Mozart on my ipod and looking out over the banks of the River Nile, as we sail gently down towards the famous temples at Abu Simbel.

Although it's hard to believe, I am actually working (and not just on this book). I'm here to check out the logistics for what I think, in 2007, will be one of my most exciting projects ever. "Death on the Nile" involves seven-day cruises that include two Murder Weekend plots, one for the cruise down to Aswan and another for the return journey to Luxor.

I've always said that if I was going to do Murder Cruises again, the thing I'd do differently would be to produce a Murder Break on a ship, rather than sailing on a ship with an optional Murder Mystery to solve. This time it will indeed be different as we're taking over the whole ship – and the wonderful Egyptian management and staff who've been so friendly and helpful in making it happen are in for a real treat.

Six months later I find myself "back on the Nile" – performing the very same cruise I've just described, while also checking through the proofs of the book you're now reading. I'd had a good feeling about the cruise (as you can probably tell from the previous paragraph) and I'm glad – and a little relieved – to say my predictions were right; it's been one of the most exciting, exhilarating and exhausting of any of my murderous adventures.

Each morning the guests disembarked to visit such amazing temples as Karnak, Edfu, Komombo and, of course, the wonderful Abu Simbel; on their return we've lied, argued, died and generally caused chaos on the ship – much to the amusement of the staff.

Last night, for example, I expired in the ship's reception area and had the luxury of being able to dramatically spew blood everywhere, knowing that it wouldn't stain the marble flooring. After the guests had been ushered into the restaurant for interrogation, I opened my eyes to see a wall lined with the ship's staff – from waiters through to those who worked in the bowels of the engine room. Stood in front of them all was Saleh, the boat manager, taking a huge number of photos and loving every single minute of the action (he told me later that his crew were "very upset" that in a couple of days we'd be leaving and the cruises would be "back to normal").

During the cruise we had so many laughs that I can't even begin to relate – there's almost been enough material for another book! To give you a flavour of what it's been like, however, I can't resist retelling two of my favourite moments on the trip. The first occurred when Maria Allen (an actress and good friend who's been with Murder Weekends for many years) shocked everyone to the core.

It was the third night – the traditional "meet the staff" night – and all of the guests were assembled in the lounge bar where Sherry our wonderful tour guide, was introducing everyone to the crew – from the boat manager, head chef, captain and chief engineer down to the restaurant waiters. They were all neatly lined up and ready to take a bow when a very loud (pre-planned) row erupted between Lulah (a bi-polar, erotomaniacal, schizophrenic, beautifully – and perhaps just a little too realistically – played by Maria) and BD Baxter, a screenwriter and the focus of Lulah's mad desires. Lulah had just discovered BD was engaged to be married to Gwyneth and went completely and utterly ballistic. She started to rant, rave and shout at him, a torrent of blind aggression that ended with her screeching and screaming "You don't know what you're missing" at the bemused BD.

It was at this point that the red mist seemed to descend and something in Maria's mind told her that not only would she tell him what he was "missing" she would, for some unaccountable reason, also show him (and the guests, crew and other actors…). Maria (who I jealously admit has a wonderful figure and fantastic boobs) suddenly removed her blouse and thrust her ample chest in BD's general direction. As if this wasn't enough she then started to slowly and suggestively move her hands down to the zip of her jeans. At this juncture the guests were shrieking with excitement – but not solely at Maria's rude antics; they were falling around with laughter at the sight of the Egyptian crew, still standing neatly in line (all except the captain who had run out of the room in embarrassment) but with their eyes bulging as if on stalks. Saleh, the boat manager, just did what he seemed to do all week – take as many photos as was humanly possible in the time available. Maria, for her part, was professional to the end; she calmly picked up her blouse, walked deliberately across the room, slapped BD hard across the face, fluttered her eyelashes and flounced out of the door – to loud applause and gales of laughter.

The second incident involved Dana, who was playing a really daft character called Petula – a psychic who, at various appropriate and totally inappropriate points in the plot (with Dana it was actually any time that it took her fancy) would stop everyone in their tracks (guests and actors alike) by suddenly exclaiming: "Ooooooooooooohhhhhhh" and then going into a long, rambling, conversation with her "spirit guide". As usual when Dana's playing this type of character most of what she said was just made-up garbage – but there were times, when something dramatic like an argument or death had happened, that she would turn to guests, wink conspiratorially, nod sagely and say: "I knew that would happen!!".

On the morning the guests and cast went out to Karnak Temple in Luxor, Dana (still in character as Petula) was suddenly "overcome by the heat" and slumped herself into a corner, much to the consternation of a group of Japanese tourists who were also visiting the temple. She managed to drag herself to her feet and, to the bemusement of Sherry the guests and possibly any stray tourists, began to strike up a lively conversation with Ramesses the Second! I don't think she learnt anything that will change history, but Dana certainly had a lot of fun, having become completely taken over by her wonderful creation (either that or she really was suffering from heat stroke – with Dana it's often difficult to tell…).

Chapter 12

A little bit of magic

P art of my reason for writing this book has been to document some of the funny, frivolous and just plain daft things that have happened "behind the scenes" on Murder Weekends.

I also wanted to write a little about some of the magical and often quite profound moments that have occurred over the years. Such "magic moments" are, I like to think, based on the fact that I've always done my very best to make Murder Weekends inclusive; no one is ever made to feel "out of place" and everyone is encouraged to get into the swing of things from the moment they arrive at a hotel to the time that they leave.

Part of the secret of bringing people together is not being afraid to have a joke and a laugh; I've lost count of the number of times guests have said to me that "they haven't laughed so much for a long time" – laughter is, after all, the best medicine (although the guest who suggested that "You should be on the National Health!" was probably being a little unrealistic).

Also part of the magic is that, because each Weekend is packed so full of games, incidents, arguments and just plain sleuthing, guests feel they've been away for a lot longer than just a couple of days. At the end of the Weekend they can be totally exhausted while at the same time totally relaxed and rested.

Something about the atmosphere on Murder Weekends is, I believe, very special and one of the things new guests frequently say to me when we're chatting away together at the end of a Weekend is that they are amazed at how sociable the whole event has been – how they can sit down to dinner with total strangers on the Friday night, talk to them as equals (whatever their age, sex, race or creed) and end up, by Sunday lunchtime, feeling like they've known each other for years.

For example, a guest on a Murder Weekend in Chester, who had come on her own and who told me she had saved up for ages to be able to attend, found herself seated at a table with a very attractive, very tall, Texan gentleman and his extremely glamorous wife. The three of them immediately got on famously, decided to team up and sleuthed together like mad all weekend.

On the Sunday we were all together in the bar and as part of the general chit-chat I happened to ask the Texan what he did for a living. "I work for Kellogg," he said matter-of-factly, "Actually, I'm the president of the company," he added equally nonchalantly. I saw the face of his new found friend freeze and for the rest of our conversation she didn't say a word – she'd suddenly realised the huge social gulf between them. Murder Weekends had brought them together and made them the same; because they'd role-played the whole weekend neither knew the other's real status. They'd chatted and laughed together as equals. If only we could translate that magic to world politics and religion – wow!

Murder Weekends don't just bring strangers together; sometimes the excitement and sense of working as a group helps to bring families together, "across the age divide". By way of example, within my own family not so long ago 15 of my cousins, having not seen each other for a while, all came on a Weekend and had a fabulous time. Their enjoyment was particularly fuelled by John, the husband of one of my cousins, who couldn't grasp the concept of role-playing at all. He kept calling me "Joy" throughout, much to the amusement of regular guests since on that particular Weekend I was playing a character called Rachel.

John is a gentleman from the top of his head to the tip of his toes and his finest hour came when he was ready to "fight for my honour" as, during a row with another actress, she tipped a jug of ice-cold water over my head, calling me a slut!

On another occasion, we had eight members of the same family –

grandparents, parents and grandchildren – all playing together and having a fantastic time. Apart from the fact there's a minimum age limit of 16 (because of the adult nature of much of the plot content) I believe that one of the really magical parts of Murder Weekends is that age itself is no barrier to letting your hair down and having fun.

Being part of a large group, all single-mindedly focused on trying to unravel and make sense of the twists and turns of a devious mystery, also seems to help people forget, at least temporarily, any worries they may have, whether it be about their family, friends, work or health.

From the moment they arrive at the champagne reception we seem to keep them so absorbed in the events taking place around them they don't have time to think of anything else – something that was first pointed out to me on the third Weekend I ever did. A psychiatrist from Beverly Hills said to me, in all seriousness, "You make people forget their worries" (although he was probably joking when he added "You'll be putting me out of business!").

A good example of this occurred at the time of the 1987 hurricane that struck Britain with such huge effect. It was a Thursday evening when the BBC weatherman Michael Fish famously said on national television "I can assure you there will be no hurricane" – just hours before one of the fiercest storms ever to hit Britain arrived!

Having seen the warnings on the news that the south of England was going to be badly hit by very high winds, I was concerned that, as we were performing in Devon, we wouldn't have a hotel to stay in. By Friday morning, having seen on the news the total devastation caused across the country by the hurricane-force winds, I rang the hotel to check that everything was alright and whether many guests had called to cancel. Everything seemed to be okay, however, and so I set off on the long drive from Liverpool.

No sooner had I arrived, after a five-hour drive, I bumped into a very disconsolate looking couple sitting in the hotel lounge. I said "Hello", asked if they were there for the Murder Weekend and, when they said they were, I asked if they were both alright. "Not really," the man replied and proceeded to explain that he owned a nursery and that during the night his 10 greenhouses had been flattened by the wind. His nursery was in ruins and he'd said to his wife that they shouldn't go away for the weekend. She, however, had convinced him they should since there was nothing they could usefully do at home – the insurance assessors couldn't get to them until Monday at the earliest. He had reluctantly agreed, but apologised in advance to me for the fact that he didn't think he would be participating on the Weekend. He would be too upset, worrying about his business.

But by Saturday evening the Murder Weekend had worked its magic. He was totally engrossed in the plot and, on the Sunday morning when I asked how he was feeling, he laughed and said: "I've only thought about the nursery twice all weekend." The Weekend, he added, had been a real tonic and just what he'd needed at that particular moment.

Thinking back to what the Beverly Hills psychiatrist had said all those years ago, there have been several other occasions when Weekends have acted as a form of therapy for guests. But the most profound was probably when one guest found the content of one of my plots almost too painful to bear.

On the Saturday lunchtime there was a fierce argument between two of the characters that culminated with one of them revealing she had been raped by the other. As she burst into tears and was comforted by some of the guests she sobbed that her life had been ruined.

As with any contentious storyline I endeavour to counteract "the bad" by having the perpetrator pay for their crime in some way. I also strive to include other sympathetic characters to counterbalance the argument and comfort the characters who have been wronged. In this respect I take some pride in the fact I write plots where the people killed always have a nasty past. The murderer is frequently killing for revenge or to prevent evil.

A little later a young female guest took me to one side and asked if she could talk to me "out of character" (as Joy Swift in other words). Normally this is something I would never do, but on this occasion I could see that something was very wrong. I asked her what the problem was and she tearfully explained that she had been raped a year ago. She had never talked about it to anyone, found the storyline very distressing and wanted to go home.

I was very upset for her and for any distress that we may have caused, but knowing that that particular line of interrogation was over and that we were about to change the mood with a light-hearted game over afternoon tea, I managed to persuade her to stay.

I was also able to reassure her that there were no more discussions or rows about rape as the rapist was about to be killed and the main plot details, involving a completely different storyline and motive, were still to be revealed. She agreed to stay for a while, but said she would probably still go home. During the game I kept a careful eye on her and I could see her gradually relaxing and laughing. Happily, she decided to stay and see the Weekend through.

The next day I made a point of looking for her and as we were chatting in the bar she told me she had stayed up late the previous night and, with a few drinks inside her for courage, explained to her friends exactly why she had been so upset. She then told me that the plot had been an outlet for her bottled-up emotions and she was so pleased she'd stayed and finally talked about her terrible experience.

We often get groups of middle-aged ladies who come on a Weekend (leaving their husbands at home to football and fishing) to spend a little time away from the children and the housework. They seem to have a ball, laughing non-stop, dancing like demons at the Saturday night disco and going away revived and very happy.

The six ladies who joined us at Gisborough Hall in Yorkshire were no exception. They were lovely, joined in all the games with great gusto and were great fun to be around.

On Sunday they all said they'd had a wonderful time, hadn't laughed so much for years and would definitely be back for another Weekend. I was thrilled and said I would love to see them all again because they had been such fun.

One of the group took me to one side and said that, unfortunately, they probably wouldn't all be here next time. "Oh dear," I exclaimed, "Why not?" (thinking that one of the group hadn't had such a good a time as I'd thought). She then explained how they had all originally met at a breast cancer support group – they all had breast cancer and one of their group was terminal. She had only been given a month to live. I was floored. I couldn't believe that someone, told they were terminally ill, could be so strong and have such a super time, laughing so hard and spreading such happiness. It made me so proud of my actors and my idea!

One final bit of magic springs to mind which, funnily enough, also happened at Gisborough Hall, involving a very attractive young woman and her husband. She had been in a serious car crash and had been hospitalised for months. It had, at one time, been touch-and-go as to whether she would survive and she was still finding it difficult to walk, even with the aid of crutches. This was their first weekend away from home since she had started her slow recovery back to full health.

As regular guests know, on Saturday afternoon we often play a music game (it usually involves playing snippets of famous tunes with the guests having to guess the song, the year it was a hit and the singer). When we come to do the answers I often get the guests to sing the choruses, which frequently results in people getting carried away with singing and dancing. It is chaotic, but enormous fun for all.

On this particular occasion I was watching everyone having a great time when, much to my surprise, this young lady suddenly shakily stood up, threw down her crutches and started to sing the chorus to the Village People's "YMCA" at the top of her voice. Everyone cheered and clapped, but none as loudly as her husband, who was clearly very moved by his wife's actions.

When I talked to her later about what she'd done she said she had been having such a great time that she completely forgot her pain – and her crutches. She had just felt so wonderful, it was like being her old self, the person she had been before her dreadful accident. Her husband laughed and said: "We're definitely coming back and from now on I'm just going to call you Jesus!"

I've been called many things over the past 25 years but two more really stick in my mind. The first was a comment by a travel journalist for the Independent on Sunday. He started both the Weekend and his subsequent article by saying he didn't like joining in with things but was amazed to find himself completely sucked in by the realism and captivated by the complexity of the plot. He even enjoyed playing the games, describing the way I hosted them as being like "a Girl Guide on speed".

Much as I like this image – mainly because it seems to capture something of the energy I try to put into whatever I do – I have to say that the description I loved the most was penned by another journalist, Maria Harding, in an article for the Sunday Express. There's something about being described as "an evil genius" that really appeals to my sense of the dramatic!

I searched high and low for a photo of mum, dad and I but realised as my brother and sister were both grown up we more often than not went out as a threesome. These two pictures, above, best represent the memories of my childhood: picnics, fun and lots of laughs

One of my favourite photos of my brother Tony, mum, my sister Marilyn and I at Marilyn's 40th birthday party

I took up tennis at the same time I was dissecting my pet goldfish Bubbles but mum was reassured that I wouldn't follow a life of crime when I was made captain of the First Team at Merchant Taylors school (front, centre)

My first days at nursery (centre, back row) when I met Carol Hornby (second row, third from left) who set me on my murderous course when I 'killed' her Dutch doll with Ribena

Above: The fancy dress party on the very first Murder Weekend. I was the bat (right) and the devil's tail was ironically pointed at my ex's heart!

Right: A very drunken schoolgirl with Colin Strong, the producer of the Holiday Programme who changed my life in 1982 when he said: "This is going to be big, you should go it alone."

Left: Another fancy dress, another glam role as Dracula's bride, this time at the first Murder Weekend in New York with Bobby Gillan (standing next to Dracula) and the fabulous American actors

Below: In 1989, I wrote a special Murder Weekend for ITV. Here I am with the presenter Michael Aspel and actors Brian Hall and Simon Oates

Murder Ahoy! This is the jeep that missed the dog, that hit the hedge, that landed in the ditch. Photo taken by the bloodied and not very amused John

Above: The cast of 'Hurricane Hancocks'

Left: Grant and I battling 'the wind' on the night the 'hurricane' arrived

With Mal and Marilyn on my Grand Day Out at the Palace in May 2002

My parachute jump in 2005 for my three favourite charities, Breakthrough Breat Cancer, Roy Castle Lung Cancer Foundation and Born Free. 2007's challenge is doing the London Maraton, for Breakthrough Breast Cancer – note I don't say running! Even if I crawl, as long as I finish I don't mind!

The Swift siblings celebrating at Murder Weekends' 25th Anniversary Ball in October 2006

Here I am with several birthday cakes, many guests and some of my terrific actors on our Silver Jubilee weekend

'Never say never again'. My first murderous cruise for 15 years. The cast, crew and actors of the highly successful and hugely enjoyable Death On The Nile, February 2007

Part 2
Carry on Murder

Chapter 1

Early learning

The running of a Murder Weekend is quite a complex business, one that involves a lot of preparation (developing a plot and assigning actors to different roles for example) as well as a lot of organisation during the Weekend itself (things like the time and place of arguments between the characters, where bodies will be found and so forth).

The preparation and planning is done to ensure that every single guest on a Weekend has the best possible experience, both in terms of their level of satisfaction with the hotel and with the Weekend itself – guests need to feel the plot is logical and solvable, for example. Everything that goes on before and during a Weekend should be transparent to the guests. In other words, within reason (and some suspension of disbelief – it's hardly likely, for example, a group of people would play a game of charades or a quiz minutes after one of their number has been brutally murdered) guests shouldn't be distracted from both having a good time and trying to solve the puzzle.

I decided right from the start of Murder Weekends that the best way to get the total involvement of guests was to make the whole scenario as realistic as possible. The characters should be the people they were playing, rather than acting out parts as if they were on a stage, and the plots should be gritty, true to life and modern. Part of the realism, I decided, would be to make the deaths look as authentic as possible – although I obviously had to take into account the fact that hotel managers wouldn't be too happy if we trashed their rooms by spraying fake blood all over the walls, beds and carpets. The blood we use is hugely expensive (it has to be imported from Germany) so you can probably imagine how upset I get when a guest – even if they're joking – asks if I've used tomato ketchup! For this reason I decided it was important that the bodies had to be 'dead' – once they'd shuffled off this mortal coil they couldn't be seen by the guests again until the Weekend was over – they were, as far as the guests were concerned, lying stiff and cold in the local morgue.

Although I've referred throughout to "my actors", a better way to describe what we do is role-playing – the basic idea being that each actor becomes the character they're playing. They stay in that character throughout the Weekend so that even if guests bump into them in the street or a shop they are still, to all intents and purposes, that character.

Although we have a general "script" for each plot – how the characters are related to each other, their personal details and the like – but the actors don't have lines to say as they do in a conventional play. From the start I decided the actors shouldn't work from this kind of a script for a couple of reasons; firstly, it wouldn't be very realistic to have people suddenly start spouting lines in the middle of a crowded room and secondly, probably more importantly I think, there would inevitably be times they would be asked a question that "wasn't in the script" and if they couldn't provide a satisfactory answer the realism of the character would be completely lost.

By playing a role, rather than learning a script, the actors are free to think about questions and answer them in the way they think their character would answer. If a guest asks a rude or personal question, for example, the actor is free to answer them in whatever way they think the character would answer.

All things considered, it's a pretty simple concept but this isn't to say that things don't go wrong – sometimes through no fault of our own (the people we rely on to do our job properly sometimes fail to deliver – or, as in the case of the ambulance crews in some of the early plots, take away), sometimes through the behaviour of guests and sometimes, although thankfully rarely, through the fault of the actors who, like everyone else I suppose, can do daft things for daft reasons.

In the early days of Murder Weekends, for example, I developed a relationship with the St. John's Ambulance service in each town we visited. In return for a charitable donation on my part they would arrange for an ambulance to arrive at the hotel to take away the 'corpse'. Guests were always very impressed when they heard a siren, saw blue flashing lights and then watched as a couple of burly men efficiently removed the dead body from wherever it happened to be lying. More often than not the ambulance crew did a fantastic job, but this wasn't always the case.

On some occasions the crew consisted of volunteers who looked as if they were too frail, too old or too young to lift a child let alone some of the fairly hefty male bodies they were required to remove. On other occasions they would get the instructions wrong, sometimes arriving too late (which we could just about cope with) and sometimes too early (which took a lot of frantic explanation on my part). To be fair, however, most of the time they were "just right", which considering the logistics involved was pretty impressive.

My instructions to the crew before the Weekend were always that they should arrive about 15 minutes before the murder was due to be committed and park the ambulance in a side street out of view from the hotel. When the victim was discovered one actor would rush to reception to pretend to ring for an ambulance (they would actually be calling the room in which the detective was staying to alert them to the fact they were needed). Because this was long before the invention of mobile phones another actor would slip out of the hotel without being seen by the guests and run to where the ambulance crew were parked to let them know they were required to go into action and screech up to the hotel forecourt with all lights blazing.

This system generally, as I say, worked well but I remember one occasion when I just happened to walk down to reception about half an hour before the crime had been committed and saw two ambulance men in the hotel lobby. I rushed up to them and, aware that guests were around, whispered frantically to them that they were much too early and that they needed to leave the hotel quickly and hide round the corner. They looked at me as if they thought I was mad, drunk or possibly both – the reason for which was quickly revealed. One of the hotel staff saw our one-sided conversation, dashed over and asked the crew to follow her – the hotel were hosting another function in their ballroom and a very drunk lady guest had been doing the hokey cokey when she tripped and put more than her left leg out – she'd broken it.

Despite my best (or maybe it was worst) efforts a guest saw me talking animatedly to the ambulance crew and decided, of course, to alert other guests who all dashed out to find out what was going on just as the poor lady was being carried to the ambulance. The guests, at this point, all started to make notes about the incident "just in case" it turned out to be anything to do with the plot.

One of my biggest nightmares is that one day a guest will actually die on a Weekend. I feel sure that, not only would the other guests be totally unsympathetic, they would then proceed to interrogate the victim's wife, sister or friends because they were convinced it was somehow part of the plot.

A couple of further incidents with ambulance crews finally made me decide that, realistic as it may be to have the body physically removed from a hotel, they were becoming more of a hindrance than a help.

On the first occasion we were on a Weekend in a hotel deep in the English countryside that could only be approached by navigating a long, narrow, drive. As I was briefing the elderly driver it quickly became clear he didn't think he was up to turning in such a tight spot, but decided he'd give it a go nonetheless. His co-driver was an elderly lady and when they had eventually managed, after a bit of huffing and puffing, to lift the thankfully small and rather light actress on to the stretcher and into the ambulance they decided they couldn't, after all, turn in the tight drive. They then took the decision that it would be best to reverse the 200-odd yards along the drive until they reached the main road where they could turn.

This, I suppose, would have been okay if the watching guests had then witnessed the ambulance reverse away at a decent rates of knots. What they actually saw was the lady walk to the back of the ambulance and start shouting instructions to her co-driver. Again, if there had been a sense of purpose and urgency in her voice and actions they could probably have just about carried it off. Unfortunately her instructions were so bad that the guests watched the ambulance crawl at a snail's pace away from the hotel, twisting and weaving all over the place as the driver struggled to make sense of his partner's directions (it was probably just as well the driver didn't manage to put his foot down because if he had he would surely have run his colleague over; she insisted on walking directly behind the vehicle so he couldn't actually see her...). As the guests watched open-mouthed in disbelief one started laughing and this set the rest of them off (including, I have to confess, a number of the actors). The whole fiasco ended up like something out of a Morecambe and Wise sketch rather than the solemn spectacle of a murder victim being taken to the morgue.

The second incident, oddly enough, happened on the very next Weekend. When the ambulance arrived for my usual briefing and the two crew members jumped (a word I use very loosely) out I was immediately worried by what I saw. The man had a very slight build and couldn't have weighed more than 8 stone fully clothed; he was accompanied by a middle-aged lady of similarly small stature. I explained, almost in horror, that the actor they were due to remove was over six feet tall and very well built. This was not a problem, they confidently assured me – they'd been doing the job for years and they'd dealt successfully with many similar situations so everything would be fine. Although I seriously had my doubts about this I decided that, since they seemed to have such calm confidence in their abilities, I'd have to let them carry on. Besides, it was much too late to find a replacement.

I really should have stuck to my guns because, as it turned out, I was right and they were wrong. The dead body was positioned in a room at the top of a reasonably long set of wide, red-carpeted stairs and I must admit to being impressed when they managed to lift him efficiently onto the stretcher from his prone position.

Unfortunately this is where my admiration began and ended because, as they tried to manoeuvre the stretcher plus heavy body downstairs the leading bearer couldn't handle the weight and let go of the handles – which meant the dead body promptly shot off the end of the stretcher and down the stairs, landing in a heap at the bottom. The actor concerned managed to break two fingers in the fall but, incredibly, he didn't even flinch. It was only after he'd been put back on the stretcher and deposited in the back of the ambulance that he let out an almighty scream of pain and instead of depositing the body by his car parked a few streets away, they actually drove him to the local A&E! This incident made me decide that enough was enough – asking my actors to play dead was one thing, to actually kill them off would be going a little too far!

Murder Weekend guests, as a general rule, are a well-behaved bunch and one of the things they are asked to do, in the instruction pack on "How to Play the Game" they're sent prior to any Weekend, is not to follow actors when they leave a room.

The main reason for this is that whenever a killing is about to be committed both the person to be murdered and all the possible suspects have to be out of the room at roughly the same time – it's integral to every plot that each suspect has to have had the opportunity to deliver the fatal blow. In the meetings we hold throughout a Weekend one of the most important things to clarify and coordinate is the exact time and place for a body to be discovered; each suspect has to have this information so that they can not only "go missing" for a few minutes prior to the death but also so they can be somewhere (usually their room) without any guests. This is vital because each suspect must avoid having "an alibi" for any of the deaths.

Some guests do, for whatever reason, occasionally try to follow actors to see if they can discover the murderer "in the flesh" but since actors are generally aware they're being followed – when it happens it's invariably a largish group of guests all giggling and shushing each other and even the dimmest murderer is hardly likely to carry out their plan with half-a-dozen people "hidden" behind a pillar a few feet away (I always find it amazing to think how people imagine they're hidden by a six-inch pillar) – all that usually happens is they will go to their room and telephone me to say they haven't been able to get away. We then have to delay the death and the action until the "all-clear" is given, something that usually happens after a few minutes when the guests in question realise that nothing's going to happen while they're trailing a suspect or camping outside their room.

There have been times, however, when someone has been unable to shake off a group of guests and one that particularly comes to mind was again in the early days when an actor called Freda was desperate to get away from a very persistent group of five guests who were determined to follow her, no matter where she led them. As a major suspect she was desperate to be on her own at the allotted time of the next death (which was rapidly approaching) and, finding herself on the second floor of the hotel after several unsuccessful attempts to lose her followers, she suddenly realised the corridor she was in was a dead end. Thinking on her feet she darted into the first unlocked door that wasn't a bedroom she could find, which happened to be a public toilet that was in the process of being renovated. Once inside she saw there was nowhere to hide and knew she'd only have a few moments breathing space before the guests cottoned on to what she had done. In a mild panic she opened the small window at the back of the room and saw that the workman who'd been doing the room up had, for some unknown reason, placed a plank from the window ledge to the balcony of the bedroom next door.

Being a very athletic individual – not to mention totally mad – she immediately decided to shimmy onto the plank, closing the window behind her. And there she stayed, perched precariously on a plank two floors up from the concrete ground below, and thoroughly enjoying hearing the guests in the loo expressing their amazement at how the prime suspect had vanished into thin air. Once the guests had gone Freda calmly returned to the room and couldn't wait to tell us all about her great escape and how she had achieved her objective to be missing at the time of the murder. Although I marvelled at her resourcefulness and athleticism I wasn't best pleased and told her so in no uncertain terms – she could have been killed in the process!

If guests can sometimes do things they know they really shouldn't, the same is also true of actors. Again, most of them are professional and totally on the ball, but there have been times when I've wondered why I bother to issue guidelines about how to behave during a Weekend.

On one of the very early Weekends, for example, I needed an older man to die on Friday night ("Friday night deaths" usually involve the actor in question only being around with the guests for a couple of hours before they're dispatched so their role doesn't involve a great deal of acting) and Shirley, an excellent and very witty actress who was subsequently with Murder Weekends for 20 years, said her cousin would be able to do it. When I met him before the Weekend he looked just right, understood what I needed him to do and, having been well briefed by Shirley, knew his character details inside out.

On the Friday night everything seemed to go well and Dennis, the actor in question, played his role perfectly. Unfortunately it was only after he was duly despatched that things went horribly wrong. I made sure that Dennis was safely delivered to his room, gave him instructions about how to order his breakfast in the morning, wished him goodnight and returned to the guests who were eager to interrogate me to see what they could learn about the deceased and any possible skeletons he'd kept in his cupboard.

I was actually quite relieved things had gone so well because I always worry a little about whether "first timers" will say or do something they shouldn't that will disclose something about the plot or characters that shouldn't be revealed until much later in the Weekend. Dennis, however, had been perfect and all was going swimmingly until a guest rushed into the room and announced loudly to everyone that they needn't worry because: "The body's okay! I've just seen him out in the car park in his pyjamas. I asked him if he was feeling alright because we all thought he was dead and he said he was fine, was just off to bed and needed to get to his car because he'd forgotten his toothbrush!"

I nearly had a stroke!

If something goes wrong on a Weekend there's usually some way we can get around it, to explain it to the satisfaction of the guests within the context of the plot – but there was definitely no way to explain the fact that someone pronounced dead ten minutes ago was now apparently wandering around the car park in his pyjamas looking for his toothbrush. The best I could think of on the spur of the moment was to leap to my feet and shout loudly enough for everyone to hear: "That's my father you're talking about."

For added impact I started to sob and added softly: "and I left him cold and dead in the hospital not 20 minutes ago." For a moment or two the guest looked shocked, but suddenly the realisation dawned that he really had seen something he shouldn't. "I'm so sorry, my dear," he said softly, "I must have been seeing things. I really think I've had a little too much to drink!"

Thankfully such blatant examples of resurrected corpses are very few and very far between on Murder Weekends, although an incident from our recent trip to Northern Italy just goes to show that even on those rare occasions when the dead do walk among us it's not necessarily the case that anyone notices!

As part of our 25th anniversary celebrations in 2006 we took Murder Weekends to the tiny medieval village of Triora, situated high in the Maritime Alps on the border between France and Italy, where we performed two three-day, Murder Breaks each attended by 60 regular guests. With its tiny cobbled streets set in wonderful countryside with extensive views across the surrounding mountains, Triora was a perfect location for a Murder Break. The fact it is known throughout Italy as "the town of the witches" simply added to the fabulous atmosphere. Everywhere you went there were constant reminders of the infamous 1588 trial of local women for witchcraft.

The original idea to go to Triora was Anita Watson's, a Murder Weekend regular and very talented events organiser (her "Incredible Event Company" has, for many years, successfully created special events for companies as diverse as Shell, NTL and Manchester United). The plot we used was the one we were currently running in the UK and it included a body being discovered at the welcome reception right at the very start of the Weekend. Since I didn't think it would be fair to ask one of my actors to fly all the way to Italy just to die almost before the Weekend had started, Anita suggested we use someone she knew from a neighbouring village. I readily agreed and a lovely woman called Alex was duly roped in to be horribly stabbed. She proved to be great fun, understood what was required of her perfectly, followed my instructions to the letter and died dramatically right on cue. She was faultless and we were all – actors and guests alike – suitably impressed.

The following day we all went sightseeing (with the actors staying in character throughout, of course) and ended up having lunch at a small pizzeria in the next village, after which everyone nipped across the road to a small souvenir shop to buy their own little witch as a memento of their visit, something I mention only because the woman who served the guests was none other than Alex, last seen the previous evening covered in blood with a long serrated knife sticking out of her stomach.

The really odd thing was that not one of the guests seemed to recognise her, even though they'd all stared at her lying dead for a good 10 minutes, taken pictures of her on their cameras and mobile phones and seen pictures of her dead body posted in the incident room that morning. Either they were a remarkably unobservant lot or, as I prefer to think, much too polite to point out the blatantly obvious!

While it's one thing to explain away the apparently miraculous resurrection of the recently deceased with the help of a cooperative guest, it's quite another to explain how, if actors get their timings wrong, a murderer can be happily sitting in the same room with 60 or 70 guests as his victim suddenly bites the bullet – quite literally in the following case.

In this particular instance the victim was to be shot as he enjoyed his afternoon tea and scones. The actor in question had been fitted with a blood bag just before he went down to be with the guests and this would dramatically burst as the gunshot that was to kill him rang out across the room.

At the actors' meeting (where we finalise the necessary timings for the next few hours actions and run through the clues that each particular actor needs to be aware of) just prior to this we'd decided that all the suspects would leave the room at 4.10pm and we all synchronised our watches. As you will appreciate it's imperative that when there is a shooting every suspect has to be out of the room because clearly they couldn't have pulled the trigger if they were still chatting away with guests.

On the stroke of 4.15pm a gloved hand and gun poked through an open service door, a shot rang out and John (the hedge-trimmer!) who was playing the victim dramatically dropped to the floor with blood oozing from a gaping gunshot wound. This much was planned. What hadn't been planned was that the other person to drop to the floor was Wes. This was unfortunate, to say the least, since Wes was playing the killer that weekend. Instead of his fingers being the ones that pulled the trigger to fire the fatal shot he had been using them to happily tuck into a delicious plate of scones and cream. So irresistible had he found them that he'd completely forgotten to leave the room and was munching away obliviously when the shot rang out.

To give him credit, Wes immediately knew he was definitely in the wrong place at the right time and in his panic at this sudden realisation the only thing he could think to do was drop to the floor and then 'subtly' scurry out of the room on all fours. I was absolutely livid when a couple of minutes later he described to me what had just happened. I would now have to completely rewrite the entire plot "on the hoof" and somehow create new clues to make another character the killer. Or so I thought.

Unbelievably, however, as the inspector was doing his interrogation after the body had been removed and he asked the obvious question "Did anyone see Mr Brown (the character Wes was playing) as the shot was fired" no one said a word. Even the guests sitting at the same table as Wes all swore blind that he was out of the room at the time. Ever since this particular incident I've dreaded the thought of being wrongly identified in a real police line up (not, of course, that I ever intend getting into a situation where one would be necessary for me). The number of times guests have described things they've just witnessed a few moments ago totally inaccurately is really very scary indeed! A room full of people can see totally different things and have completely opposite views on the times people were out of the room. Green clothes become red, long dark brown hair becomes short and blonde – my advice is never, ever look vaguely like a wanted fugitive!

Having said that, even coppers sometimes get it wrong. We had, for example, an ex-chief superintendent on a plot where there was a kidnapping early on the Friday night. Just as the guests had finished their starter the lights suddenly went out and two people ran into the dining room, loudly demanding their intended victim make themselves known and firing guns into the air. They both wore large, bulky jackets and black balaclavas that completely obscured their faces.

Impressively the ex-detective very accurately described the height and build of the kidnappers, even though it all happened in an instant and in almost complete darkness. Less impressively, however, he was certain it was two men who had run into the room, describing their physiques very accurately, even down to shoe size. In reality, both kidnappers had shouted and one was actually a woman!

Chapter 2

Disastrous deaths and bothersome bodies

The successful staging of a Murder Weekend, as I've tried to convey in the previous chapters, involves a combination of a strong central plot with supporting clues, scripted "incidents" (such as arguments) that develop at certain times during the Weekend and which rely for their realism on the ability of the actors to improvise around a particular theme (such as an illegitimate child or bigamous relationship) and, of course, death.

Although outlined in script form, the incidents and deaths are effectively "live" each time they're performed and this means that when things go wrong, as they surely do, they can only be "put right" through the initiative of the actors. Most times it's not too difficult to paper over the crack that's just appeared. But it's a bit more difficult if the actors involved decide to demonstrate a talent for misplaced initiative (they decide to "wing it" as we say). As I'll describe in a moment, it's not just actors who sometimes ad lib – we occasionally have to deal with tricky interventions from people who are not part of a Weekend (as in the case of Gunther that I related earlier) and to understand why these happen I need to explain a little bit about bodies and their preparation.

In theory the actor who's about to become a body leaves the guests at an allotted time and goes to the organiser's room to be made-up (or "blooded" as we call it). The organiser is always someone on the Weekend who has overall control of everything that happens; this can range from liaising with hotel staff to ensure that guest places at dinner tables are correctly labelled and the actors are seated in the correct position, to chairing the actors' meetings where we run through character details and relationships and establish times and places for arguments and deaths. Because every hotel is different in terms of room numbers, size and layout we can't easily decide these things in advance of a Weekend – hence the need for meetings.

"Blooding" involves things like attaching a blood bag or knife, creating a stab or gunshot wound and the like. Once made-up, the body is then 'topped and tailed' – two actors, one leading and the other following, help get the body into position unseen by the guests. Sometimes, if the wound will allow, the victim can stagger into a crowd of guests and we occasionally manage to stage it so a victim can be shot in front of guests. From our perspective the most effortless death is when the victim is poisoned; they can take a drink, start to choke and then collapse into the arms of a nearby guest. There are only so many ways to dispatch a victim, but I have endeavoured over the years to make them as varied and interesting as possible. In the main, however, once in position bodies are usually left to their own devices. If we have actors loitering around the vicinity of a body it simply casts suspicion on them.

While this adds to the realism (a real murderer would hardly hang around their victim, waiting to be caught and questioned) the downside, of course, is that it can cause problems if a guest at a hotel who's not part of the Weekend stumbles upon the body. On one occasion, for example, a victim who had supposedly been gutted like a fish (it sounds revolting but it was pertinent to the plot – the make-up had taken a long time to apply and I was rather proud of my handy work) was in situ lying on the stairs ready to be found by guests as they went to their room in the early evening to prepare for the Saturday night fancy dress party.

Unfortunately, at this exact moment a guest was checked into the hotel by a new receptionist who hadn't informed him what was going on. As he started up the stairs to his room he was the first person to stumble across the macabre scene.

In one of those odd coincidences that occur from time to time this particular guest happened to be a doctor and, on seeing the body, immediately went into life-saving mode. He dived into his suitcase and pulled out a shirt that he then used to staunch the "blood".

When we arrived on the scene the doctor was doing a fine job. He was, however, extremely cross to discover it was all just part of a complicated game.

Once the guests had been cleared and the body removed I took him to the bar and, over a drink, apologised profusely for his embarrassment. Luckily he saw the funny side of things and paid me what I though was a huge compliment; the make-up was so realistic that he hadn't given it a second thought: "I just saw the blood and went into action."

You might, at this stage, be thinking why didn't "the body" say something to the doctor and there are two main reasons for this. Firstly, when you're lying on the floor "playing dead" the next thing you're expecting is for a guest to find you – you steel yourself not to move or react in anyway since, with your eyes tightly shut, you have no idea who the person standing over you actually is. It's also quite traumatic to play a body – all your efforts go into trying not to obviously breathe, something that can be a real trial. A body may spend 5-10 minutes lying dead while all the guests shuffle around trying to see it, taking photos and so forth, so holding your breath isn't really an option. We try to shallow breathe, but it's very difficult not to be seen.

Secondly, it's actually quite weird when you're playing a victim, because you do almost become disembodied. You can hear everything that's going on, but it's almost as if it's not happening to you. It's probably something to do with having to concentrate so hard on staying motionless and not reacting to anything anyone says or does (actors as well as guests) that makes it all seem a little unreal. Over the years I've been kicked, poked, prodded and slapped while 'dead' but I've never once reacted. It's not so much the physical stuff that's difficult to cope with. The worst is when someone makes a funny comment, intentionally or otherwise; then you just have to bite your cheek and pray a smile doesn't appear on your lips.

Once all the guests have viewed the victim the police shepherd them to a room as far away from the body as possible for an "interrogation", asking questions about whether anyone saw anything, where the prime suspects were at the time of the attack and so forth. This is just a diversion to allow a couple of actors time to photograph the body in situ (for display in the incident room) and then help the corpse back to their room where they're holed up for the rest of the weekend, never to be seen again (unless, of course, they're discovered in their pyjamas wandering around a car park in the middle of the night looking for a toothbrush!).

A good example of an actor deciding to ad lib and "use his initiative" in a totally inappropriate way happened on a Weekend in Winchester. Come the Saturday night fancy dress party (the theme that weekend was "sweets") we had guests dressed as all manner of confectionery. My particular favourite was a guest wearing a T-shirt with "Park Lane" printed on the front (Quality Street).

Ian, one of the actors, dressed himself up as a character from a TV advert from the 1980's – the Cadbury's Milk Tray Man, a sort of homage to James Bond. He wore black trousers with a black polo neck, slicked his hair back and carried a tray, a bottle of milk and a long length of rope draped around his shoulder.

Ian's was to be the last death (a vicious stabbing) and I'd arranged to come to his room to do all the necessary preparation, which in this case mainly involved creating a realistic blood-splatter around the wound and ensuring the knife was taped securely to his back. There's nothing worse than guests seeing a knife that's supposedly embedded in a victim's back wobbling like it was about to become detached – something that was especially important in this case because the plan was for Ian to stagger along a corridor from his room, then down a set of stairs whereupon he'd fall dead at the feet of a group of guests.

I left him made up in his room, with the instruction to leave it five minutes before beginning his death stagger, and promptly bumped into a group of five guests who'd followed Ian to his room without him realising it. Once they saw me going into the room they'd tiptoed to the door to try to hear what was going on. I acted very nonchalantly with them and then raced to my room to call Ian to tell him about the potential problem – he couldn't move while guests were camped outside his door because they'd clocked my character leaving his room and it would immediately put me, at least in their eyes, in the frame for the murder. I told him to wait until I rang again because I'd create a diversion that would get all the guests together in a room well away from him. I made it very clear (or at least I thought I had) that on no account was he to move until I rang again to say the coast was clear.

Clearing the coast wasn't, however, as easy as I'd hoped; it was proving difficult to dislodge the guests who'd followed Ian to his room – they were so sure he was the next to die they would not move. This wouldn't have been a massive problem in the normal run of things, if they hadn't seen me come out of his room. I rang him again to let him know we still had a problem but that we were working on it. It may take a little time but he was to stay safely in his room until he was told the coast was clear. The other actors had, by this time, started to realise that something had gone wrong and I quietly managed to get round to each of them to explain the problem.

We were on the point of bringing a major row – one that should have happened after the death – forward to try to draw the five guests downstairs when another guest dashed into the room and at the top of their voice boldly announced that "the Milk Tray Man had been stabbed". I was momentarily perplexed by how she would know this, since Ian wouldn't have been daft enough to let anyone into his room, when what she said next left me wondering whether to laugh or cry. "And he's abseiling down the side of the hotel."

Ian hadn't listened to my instructions, possibly because he seemed to have transformed himself into "Milk Tray Action Man" – someone who would obviously not think twice about tying a length of rope to the leg of his bed, throwing the other end out of the open window and then shimmying down the outside of the building. His room was, after all, only on the third floor.

I was not very happy.

Not only had Ian's improvisational escapades gone against my very clear instructions about how to handle a tricky situation, he'd also used such bad judgement. Apart from the fact that if he'd slipped he could have been seriously hurt, he left the rest of the cast with the problem of trying to explain to guests how someone with a very large kitchen knife embedded deeply in their back was strong enough to abseil down the side of a tall building but not strong enough to either pick up the telephone or open their bedroom door to call for help.

Another example of how an actor used his "initiative" to create more trouble than he thought he was preventing, occurred when a blood bag he was wearing started to leak. This can happen because the bag, which I make, is quite fragile; it has to be weak enough to burst when an actor clasps it after being shot (we can't, of course, wire people up electronically as they do in films) but also strong enough not to leak so they can move around with a reasonable amount of freedom.

On this particular occasion Simon was due to be shot just after lunch and I fitted the bag about 15 minutes earlier so he could mingle with the guests before dying. He left my room with instructions to keep reasonably still over lunch to avoid prematurely puncturing the bag, instructions he promptly forgot as he got carried away and became very animated talking to the guests. Eventually and inevitably, the blood bag started to leak in a way that was immediately apparent to the guests he was talking to.

Most people in this situation, when it was pointed out that blood seemed to be seeping through their shirt, would make up some reasonably plausible explanation – "It's a large mosquito bite that keeps weeping" or "I was shaving my chest before lunch and the razor slipped" – make their excuses and leave so it could all be sorted out. This particular actor was not "most people" and he decided to blurt out the first thing that came into his head. Unfortunately for all concerned this was the immortal – and totally nonsensical – line: "I was walking along the corridor when I was stabbed in the chest by an M16 secret agent."

This "revelation" sent the guests into a complete frenzy and created a completely new storyline for the whole plot (which had to be hurriedly rewritten to take account of and explain this novel incident). Since it was no longer possible to shoot this particular actor (and, believe me, at the time I really did feel like shooting him) we shot the actress who was originally meant to die later on Saturday night. We then killed the original actor later that night – and when I pulled the trigger and he fell down dead I felt something of a sense of accomplishment. With a few extra clues to show the character was a compulsive liar we managed, amazingly, to get away with it!

Not all "disastrous deaths" are the fault of actors winging it of course; sometimes things just go wrong because the Universe conspires to make them go wrong. Not so long ago, for example, I was due to die on the Friday night and I'd positioned myself in a little syndicate room close to where the guests would gather but far enough away so that we wouldn't be disturbed as Mal, another actress and really good friend, strapped the knife to me and applied the blood that would make my wound look fairly gruesome. The plan was for me to stagger out of the room and stumble along a short corridor until I could fall into the guests as they were playing a quiz. Mal positioned the knife and filled my mouth with the blood I would allow to dribble down my chin as I shuffled towards the guests pleading for them to help. This is always the final bit of preparation because if you leave the blood in your mouth too long it mixes with saliva and becomes quite pink and frothy and consequently very unrealistic.

Anyway, everything was set up perfectly. I'd leave the room unseen and a few seconds later, once I'd been found, Mal could slip away without being noticed. However, as Mal pulled the door handle to let me out nothing happened. We thought for a second or two the door had jammed but, after a bit of huffing and puffing (me with a mouthful of blood I was desperately trying not to dribble over the carpet) we realised to our horror that the door wasn't just stuck – the lock was broken.

No matter how hard we tried, the door refused to budge. We looked at each other and started giggling (as you do). We were trapped in a locked room with no phone and no way of raising the alarm. To make things even worse, if this were possible, we hadn't told the other actors where I was going to be 'blooded'. No one knew we were there!

Once we got over the shock of realising we were trapped Mal, practical as ever, set about finding a way of extricating us from the mess in which we found ourselves. She noticed a large sash window at the back of the room, opened it as wide as it would go, leaned out with her little legs dangling in mid air (on a good day she's only 5' tall, even though she swears she's 5'1") and, still giggling, swung back into the room to inform me it was "only a seven-foot drop" to the ground.

I wasn't totally convinced but since we didn't have any other option we decided to go for it. Mal went first, hitching her skirt up around her armpits and disappearing through the window. I looked out to see her land, in a most unladylike heap, on the grass. Trying to manoeuvre myself through the window with a 6" knife in my stomach wasn't easy but I went for it and, still giggling like a little child, eventually managed to struggle through. We both sat on the grass, almost helpless with laughter, and it didn't help that we could see into the hotel where the other actors were wandering up and down the corridor like little lost sheep, with not the foggiest idea where we'd got to.

We composed ourselves the best we could and Mal pointed to the room where the guests were assembling and motioned for me to follow her. We proceeded to tip-toe through the damp grass, in the pitch black, like two skulking thieves in a cartoon. Suddenly, Mal heard a noise and stopped dead in her tracks, at which point I walked straight into her, stabbing her in the back with the handle of the knife that was sticking out of my tummy. This was all too much and we exploded with laughter. As our loud guffaws echoed in the stillof the night I was convinced that not only would all the guests hear the commotion but everyone in the surrounding village would too!

The blood I had just about managed to keep in my mouth (despite vaulting out of the window) spluttered over my clothes and, more importantly, splashed all over Mal's hair! Now we really were in trouble – how was a major suspect going to convincingly explain the fact "my blood" was splattered all over the back of her head?

Mal, always a cool head in a crisis, said she'd cross that bridge when she came to it. The most important thing now was to get me to the guests. She suggested I stagger up to the room they were in and bang on the French windows from the outside with my fist. If I pressed my face to the glass and dribbled blood from my mouth she thought the effect would be both dramatic and frightening. I agreed this would be the best way to salvage the situation. But there was just one tiny problem – the blood she had put in my mouth was no longer in my mouth.

We looked at each other for a second or two and realised we'd left the bottle of blood in the room from which we'd just escaped. In the normal run of things this would have been an insurmountable problem; Mal, however, simply hitched her skirt up once more and told me to give her a leg-up to the window.

She scrambled through and re-emerged triumphant with the blood bottle a few moments later. And so it was that, after giving myself a couple of minutes to stop laughing and Mal time to make good her escape (and, it turned out, time to wash the blood out of her hair), I slumped bloodily against the French windows – as much to the shock of the guests as to the actors who, they told me later, had long given up any expectation of me dying that night.

Although open windows have often proved a handy means of escape from a tricky situation, they've also been our downfall at times – quite literally in John Pendleton's case. On that particular Weekend I was the victim and the idea was I would be found dead by the guests in my room. A large knife would be embedded in my back and for this I needed help with the make-up – a task John was to carry out under my guidance. The guests would be drawn to my room because of a piece of evidence going up in the incident room and, for one reason or another, we found ourselves with only around ten minutes in which to apply the knife and make-up before the guests were likely to arrive.

The type of knife we use is one I've had specially made; it consists of a handle and half a blade that ends in a flat piece of metal that can be taped, with strong sticking plaster, to the skin under the victim's clothes. Once in place it looks very realistic, as if a knife has been pushed into a body leaving just a part of the blade and the handle in plain view. Although the taping only takes a few seconds we then have to create the illusion of a wound; "congealed blood" has to be put in place around the blade and then the more dramatic "runny blood" applied.

I was lying face-down on the bed and unable to move because of the knife taped firmly to my back, so I had to give John instructions about how to apply the make-up and, since he'd never done this before, I had to talk him through it, which meant the process took a lot longer than usual.

We'd just about finished when we heard a loud commotion that told us the guests had found the clue and were on the point of charging to my room before John had time to leave in the orderly way we'd planned. We'd had to leave the door on the latch so the guests could get into the room and, knowing they'd burst in at any moment, I quickly shouted to John to collect everything up – the make-up, fake blood and camera we use to take the in situ body shots – and "get out before they come along the corridor and see you!". He also picked up the real kitchen knife I'd been undecided about using (the idea would have been to create a gaping wound in my back with the make-up and then leave the kitchen knife next to my body so guests could see the "murder weapon"). However, I'd decided at the last minute that, because it was very sharp, we couldn't risk a guest picking it up and cutting themselves – so that had to go with John too. Whether John misunderstood my "get out" instruction or whether he just panicked when he thought he heard guests running along the corridor I'm not altogether sure – from my vantage point flat on my stomach, not daring to move in case I dislodged the knife, all I could hear was John frantically charging around the room collecting all the "evidence" – and then there was silence, followed by a loud "thud" and then a heartfelt "Fuck!".

Since I hadn't heard him open the door I knew immediately that he must have left by the window – given we were on the ground floor he probably thought it would be the surest way of escaping the guests. What I knew and he didn't was that there was a six-foot drop to the ground – as he leapt through the window he soon, of course, discovered his mistake.

As I lay there helpless I started to worry because, after the curse, I'd heard nothing; no groaning, no sound of him running away. Nothing. At that point I honestly thought he'd fallen on the kitchen knife as he stumbled through the window and fell to the ground. As the guests arrived I was forced to stay motionless for what seemed like ages as frantic thoughts raced through my head. My worst nightmare was a guest looking out of the window and seeing "another body" lying on the ground. Luckily, I needn't have worried. As he leapt through the window John realised his error and managed to adjust his body to land on his feet – the curse was one of surprise and relief rather than pain – and he then just crawled away to hide in the bushes until he could safely emerge once all the guests had been ushered away.

If this particular "disappearing act" was one that had left me momentarily with my heart in my mouth another had an altogether funnier conclusion.

"Follow me," I said to Steve Gow a few minutes after he'd been found in the hotel garden, horribly strangled. The guests had all been moved safely back to the main part of the hotel, I'd taken a couple of in situ shots of the body and now I was about to get him back to his room by the quickest possible route.

As I called out I started to run through the car park and past the rows of parked cars at great speed. Steve, however, decided that following the person who knew the way wasn't the best idea he'd ever heard and – even though he didn't know the exact route to get him to the fire escape we'd kept open at the side of the building (from where he could easily reach his room undetected) – decided he'd take a short-cut between two cars parked in front of a small wall.

What Steve didn't know at the time he was sprinting across the car park like an England fly-half about to score a winning try was that the wall was there for a reason, as I'd discovered when I'd checked out our possible escape route earlier. Steve, however, soon found out why the wall was there as he hurdled it magnificently and disappeared completely from sight. The only indication of his presence was the loud "thud!" as he hit the ground eight feet below the wall. It was just like something out of You've been Framed – if only I'd had a video camera. After the initial shock of seeing Steve just disappear I raced over to the wall and I must admit that, as I got closer, I started to get a little worried; there was absolutely no sound at all coming from the black hole into which he'd just catapulted himself – no moans, groans or even swearing – and I was genuinely worried that he might be lying dead behind the wall. As I peered anxiously into the pit all I could see was Steve looking up at me with a big grin on his face that told me nothing, apart from his pride, was broken. We both started to laugh loudly at the idiocy of his behaviour – aided by me asking "Which part of 'follow me' didn't you understand?" and him replying that he'd understood the "follow" bit but after that he'd obviously become a little confused.

While it's one thing to mess up when I'm the one dying (at least I know what's happening and can use my own best judgement to salvage the situation) it's quite another when you're responsible for someone else's disastrous death.

My crowning achievement in this respect was leaving my good friend Trudy to fend for herself in what I came to affectionately think of as "The case of the hopping mad corpse".

Trudy was playing a kidnap victim who'd been bound, gagged and stabbed in the back. The idea was to make people think she'd managed to escape from the room where she'd been left for dead and crawled to where the guests were milling around before finally expiring at their feet. I was the organiser that weekend and Trudy duly came to my room to be blooded. I fixed the knife to her back, smeared blood generously around the wound and, just before she was due to go, bound her hands firmly behind her back with thick carpet tape. I then taped her legs together and, for good measure, covered her mouth with a strip of tape so she couldn't call for help.

Normally we aim to get the final death done and dusted before 11pm on the Saturday night, mainly to give guests a couple of hours to put the final pieces of the puzzle together before they go to bed. On this occasion things had generally been running a little late and it wasn't until after 11pm that I opened my bedroom door and sent Trudy on her merry way. The idea was that she would hop along the corridor from my room until she slumped amongst the guests.

To reach her final destination however, Trudy had to shuffle down a fairly long corridor, passing through five doorways on the way and what I'd forgotten as I closed the bedroom door after seeing her safely into the corridor was that after 11pm all the doors in the corridor were automatically closed as a fire precaution.

This in itself wouldn't have presented Trudy with too much of a problem if she could have moved towards each door and leant on it gently to push through. Unfortunately, to pass through the doorway from Trudy's direction meant having to pull the door open – something she realised a few yards down the corridor from my room.

The tape covering her mouth meant she couldn't call for help and she couldn't remove it because her hands were taped firmly behind her back. Even if she could have loosened the tape to scream loud enough to be heard by guests it would have meant her falling dead in a narrow corridor – the worst possible place to fall given that 80 or so guests would all be trying to crowd into a very limited space in order to see the body properly. There was also no point in returning to my room because I had died on the previous night and wouldn't have been able to risk leading her down the corridor in case a stray guest happened along – the ultimate Murder Weekend nightmare scenario; a dying victim being helped by someone who, as far as the guests were concerned, was lying dead in the morgue...

There was, in consequence, nothing for her to do but open the fire door. She hopped up to it and, as she got close, turned her back and grasped the handle as best she could. Once she had a firm grip she then had to hop forward, pulling the door as firmly as she could manage. She then had to do a quick about turn to hop forwards through the open doorway before it slammed shut. After a couple of attempts she managed to get through and applied the same arduous logic to the second door. So far, so good. At the third door, however, disaster struck.

Although she managed to swing the door open, as she hopped through it suddenly closed violently on her. She must have finally realised that the gods weren't with her that night as the door crashed into her back, snapping the knife in two. Not only was she standing in a corridor bound and gagged but the knife in her back was now just a metal stump. The blade was lying on the carpet at her feet for all to see!

She knew she couldn't chance a guest coming along the corridor and finding half a knife, so, with great presence of mind, she dropped to her knees and, contorting her body like a limbo dancer, gradually lowered herself to the ground backwards. After feeling around for a moment or two she managed to retrieve the blade and get to her feet. She immediately realised there was now no point in continuing her journey to the guests since not only did she not have the knife in her back anymore but there was no way for the police to explain how she could be holding the blade in her hand. There was nothing for it but to turn tail and hop back the way she'd just so painfully come until she got to my room. As I pointed out later, at least this time all she had to do was lean on the fire doors to open them (but I'm not sure she fully appreciated the logic of my observation).

A few minutes later I heard what sounded like someone tapping on my bedroom door with their forehead which, oddly enough, is exactly what Trudy had been forced to do. I carefully opened the door and, with a look of puzzlement on my face said "I thought you were supposed to be with the guests" (she told me later that if it had been a real knife in her hand she would certainly have embedded it in my back – if, of course, she could have shuffled round behind me and struck the fatal blow by performing a flying backward hop!). It was fortunate her mouth was tightly covered to prevent her hurling some choice words in my direction – she was, at this stage, fuming, especially as I started to laugh out loud as she mumbled through the gag about what she'd just been through. I was going to say she must be hopping mad, but thought better of it when I saw the look in her eyes.

After I'd untied her and she'd calmed down she thankfully saw the funny side of the situation too – and when I sent her back down to the guests half and hour later I made sure that, this time, all the fire doors had been lodged open to allow her to pass painlessly through.

Although the various things that go wrong on a Murder Weekend could sometimes have been prevented with just a little forethought, this isn't always true – sometimes you just don't foresee the inevitable accident even though, with hindsight, it was obviously just waiting to happen. A case in point was that of Sarah, a new actress who was due to die on the dance floor – always a popular death with regular guests. At the appointed time and with the disco in full swing she suddenly gasped, clutched at her throat, choked violently and then fell to the floor so hard and so convincingly we all thought for a moment she really had died. Normally with this type of poisoning death the actor concerned will stumble and grab the nearest person to break their fall (dance floors, in particular, can be quite painful if you fall on them too violently and from too great a height). On this occasion however, Sarah dropped like the proverbial stone.

As part of her fancy dress she was wearing a "boob tube" (which, for those of you who've never come across them, is a small tube of elasticated fabric, worn across the chest and without a bra, that holds your assets in check by virtue of being stretched tightly around the upper body). As she hit the floor she experienced what can be politely described as a "wardrobe malfunction". In other words, her rather ample chest suddenly burst free of its flimsy covering and she lay on her back with her boobs exposed to the world.

I have to say she was a consummate professional and didn't move a muscle, a bit like the horrified guests and male actors. I like to think they were all too embarrassed to know what to do – except, of course, stare (and, in the case of some guests, take photos). I, on the other hand, immediately leapt like a gazelle across the dance floor and unable to think of anything better or more stylish to do simply flopped down on top of her. I then proceeded to weep and wail like a distressed relative obviously would, all the while trying to surreptitiously tug her top back up into position to cover her modesty before the St John's ambulance arrived to take her away.

Talking of photographs, these have been an important part of Murder Weekends from the very beginning. We use them as clues and we also photograph the bodies so that if someone didn't get to see the corpse in situ they can still get some idea of the wounds and how the individual was murdered when a photograph is posted in the police incident room. Guests take lots of pictures throughout a Weekend; they photograph arguments and dead bodies almost as a matter of course and this is something I don't discourage, I just see it as a harmless extension of the Weekend and a way of capturing interesting mementoes of exciting moments.

Nowadays guests come equipped with digital cameras for instant viewing and, increasingly, camera phones they use to send pictures of the Weekend to friends and family – sometimes just seconds after an incident or body has been captured "on film" .

Over the past couple of years Murder Weekends have embraced all kinds of digital technology – when I leave home to do a Weekend now I take not only my mobile phone but also my laptop, digital camera and printer – but not so long ago the "technology" consisted of a Polaroid camera to take photos of the dead bodies to use as clues and, if we needed shots of people injured or murdered prior to the Weekend, my trusty SLR camera and a few rolls of film. On more than one occasion photos of dastardly deeds have landed us in no small amount of trouble.

I remember one particular incident from the early days – it was around the time of my little bit of excitement with the Anti-Terrorist Squad – when the police paid an official visit to my home. As I answered the door I saw two police officers, one in uniform and one in plain clothes, on the doorstep. My brain immediately started racing and I was dreading that they'd come to inform me of a family fatality. I was almost relieved when the plain-clothed officer introduced himself as "Detective Sergeant Jones" from the Serious Crime Squad who "would like to ask me some questions about a matter that had been brought to their attention". I invited them into the living room, silently wondering what on earth I, or someone I possibly knew, had done to warrant this kind of attention. My confusion increased as DS Jones proceeded to ask what I thought were some fairly bizarre questions:

"Was I married?"

"No."

"Was I living with a partner?"

"No."

"Was I living with someone until recently?"

"No!"

"Well then Madam, could you explain this?"

As he said the words he put his hand into an inside pocket and pulled out a photo of a young man lying, half-naked, on a bed. He had been shot and there was blood on the bed, on the carpet and halfway up the wall. I looked at the picture and, despite the obvious seriousness of the situation, suddenly started to laugh. By the look on the detective's face this wasn't quite the reaction he'd been expecting. He must have thought he was about to crack the case of a twisted Black Widow who enjoyed taking and exhibiting photos of her prey – an illusion I was quickly able to dispel.

The photo was simply one of many I'd taken for a plot – an "off-Weekend murder" as I've described it – and had taken to my local branch of Boots to be developed. I quickly dug out a load of Murder Weekend literature (fast becoming my trusty standby in times of misunderstandings with the police) to show them while explaining exactly what I did. They both seemed genuinely relieved that the chatty, friendly, woman they were sitting opposite wasn't a mass murderer – but I also like to think they were maybe just a little bit disappointed that they hadn't solved the 'crime of the century'!

Over a pot of tea they told me how, when I'd taken the film to be developed, one of the shop assistants (who obviously knew nothing about me and my job) had completely flipped and panicked when she saw the developed photos and had immediately called the police. Since she'd never heard of Murder Weekends the only thought she had, as she held pictures of a very realistic, very bloody and very dead body, was that some sick individual in her community was a murderer. The two officers left on very friendly terms, each carrying the brochures I'd offered them and both promising to come on a Weekend. For my part I was rather proud that, yet again, my handy work had been so realistic it had fooled both a member of the public and two police officers; I was also pretty happy to have gained two future customers!

Luckily that was a fairly contained situation (with only the shop assistant, the two police officers and me knowing what had happened) the same couldn't be said about a similar incident in 2004 when a lot more people were witness to the mayhem I involuntarily caused in my local Tesco. I'd been sorting through a cupboard one day and came across a couple of long-forgotten undeveloped films. I had no idea what they contained but, thinking they were maybe snaps I'd taken at a wedding or while I was on holiday, I decided I might as well have them developed.

The following day I went into Tesco to do my weekly shop and dropped the films off at the photo section, thinking they would be developed by the time I'd finished my shopping. Over the years the photo counter assistants had got to know me quite well and, as I'd often chat to them about my job, they quickly came to realise that the pictures of "dead bodies" I'd occasionally have developed were all part of what I do for a living. If I knew there were violent pictures on the film that were going to be used on a forthcoming plot I'd warn them, just so they'd be aware of it. On this particular occasion I dropped the films off with the lady who normally took my order and, not thinking they contained anything she needed to be warned about, set off to do my shopping. As I got to what must have been the farthest part of the store from the photo counter I heard an almighty, ear-piercing, scream.

"Oh dear. That will be me then" was the first thought that entered my head. I raced back to the photo counter, arriving just in time to see an elderly female assistant being gently helped onto a chair by the assistant to whom I'd given the films. The scream I (and everyone else within a couple of miles I would guess) had heard had come from the shaken shop assistant. About five seconds before she fell to the floor in a dead faint.

As I arrived on the scene, I immediately knew what must have happened and began to apologise profusely; the assistant to whom I'd given the films simply burst out laughing when she saw me and this, of course, set me off laughing as well (much to the bemusement of her colleague). Once we'd both caught our breath the assistant confirmed what I already suspected. Because I hadn't warned her about the content of the films (as I've said, I thought they were just holiday snaps) she had given them to the elderly lady she was helping to train and left her alone to develop them as she went for her tea break. What she saw on the prints once she'd developed them sent the trainee into hysterics. Once we'd both explained to her what the photos were actually all about she began to calm down. She smiled and said it was okay and that she understood, but I could see she really wasn't a happy bunny and as I returned to my shopping I distinctly heard her mutter: "It shouldn't be allowed. Not with my heart!"

Guests, as I've said, also love to take photos on Weekends and consequently they too are not immune from the conscientious attentions of shop assistants, as one regular guest found to her cost. Lauren Coffey had amassed an extensive collection of photos involving both fights and dead bodies as souvenirs of her many Weekends and one day, while she was at work, there was a knock at the front door and Lauren's 16-year-old son Dan opened it to be faced by two men in ordinary clothes who, showing him their warrant cards, informed him they were policemen who would like to speak to his mother. Dan told them she wasn't home, but that she was normally back around 6pm. On hearing this they then asked to speak to Dan's father and he had to explain that his mum and dad had split up a couple of weeks ago; his father had left home and wouldn't be returning.

The two officers looked at each other and said they'd come back later and when Dan asked them why they needed to see his mother he was told it was "just some routine enquiries" and nothing to worry about.

Bang on 6pm the two officers duly returned and, when told Lauren wasn't home from work yet, asked if they could come in and wait for her. Dan said he didn't see why not and invited them in. Lauren arrived home around 7pm and shouted to Dan as she ran upstairs to get changed that she was sorry she was so late but she'd been to the pub for a drink with some work colleagues. Dan immediately followed her upstairs to say there were two detectives in the living room that wanted to talk to her.

When she was telling me this story Lauren said she can't imagine what was going on in her head at the time but, having a few days previously been on a Murder Weekend, the first thought that came in to her was "They must be actors"; since she'd told me she was keen to act on Weekends she thought I'd sent a couple of actors round to test her, to see if she was good enough to join the Murder Weekend company. With these thoughts fresh in her head Lauren then decided she'd show "the actors" how well she could role-play. She told her son to ask "the detectives" to step into the hall and, after he'd gone downstairs to relay her message, she got undressed and put on a very sexy negligee. She then went to the top of the stairs, looked down to where the two "policemen" were now standing and said invitingly: "Why don't you come up and see me, Big Boys?".

Lauren, a very attractive woman, was a little taken aback when the two officers declined her kind invitation and one of them, in a very serious tone snapped: "Madam. Would you please put some clothes on and come downstairs?"

Most people at this point would probably have thought "Err…this is for real and I've just made the most embarrassing mistake ever." Lauren, on the other hand, simply decided "the actors" were doing a fantastic job. Not only had I gone to all the trouble of sending them out to her home, but they wouldn't come out of character until they'd done what they were there to do!

She quickly got dressed and joined the policemen in the lounge, where she noticed one of the officers standing at the window that looked out over her garden. He turned to her and nonchalantly said, "Nice patio Madam!", to which Lauren quite innocently replied: "Thank you. It's new. We only had it laid last week. We haven't had much sun these past couple of days, so I haven't been able to use it yet," she continued, conversationally, still thinking she was being tested, "I've bought a new sun lounger and can't wait 'til the weather improves so…"

The detective cut her short: "Your son told us earlier that you and your husband have split up. Could you tell us where he is please?"

"I'm not sure. Glasgow I think. We'd been having trouble for ages and decided we'd both had enough because it just wasn't working. He's moved on."

Even at this stage the penny hadn't dropped. Lauren had convinced herself it was still part of some bizarre test. The policemen, however were almost salivating – because this was happening at exactly the same time as the "body under the patio" storyline running in Brookside, the two detectives seemed to think they had a copycat killer on their hands and were determined to get their man – or, in this case, woman. Lauren said the conversation went on for ages and the officers asked her increasingly personal questions and she couldn't for the life of her work out why they were so interested in her husband and his whereabouts. It was only when one of the officers eventually decided to produce the incriminating evidence that Lauren finally twigged. As she looked at pictures of a naked man lying dead in a bath, the top of his head bashed and blood splattered all around the walls, she realised that the roll of film from her recent Murder Weekend she'd taken into Boots to be developed had been picked up by a conscientious shop assistant and reported to the police as evidence of a heinous crime. It was only when she produced pictures of her husband and her together that the two policemen realised they were looking at different people. After accepting Lauren's explanation for the pictures in their possession they decided that it wouldn't be necessary to dig up Lauren's nice new patio after all.

If pictures of dead bodies sometimes come back to haunt us, the same is occasionally true of the real-life recently deceased. Disposing of the body, as I've previously outlined, is the responsibility of the actors assigned to "top and tail" the corpse and, in the majority of cases, everything goes to plan once the guests have been safely placed in the custody of the interrogating copper. There are times, however, when the removal of a body hasn't gone as smoothly as we might have liked.

Dana, for example, was eight months pregnant and had begun to resemble a Michelin man when we killed her off one Weekend. Once the guests had viewed the body and had been successfully moved away from the crime scene we were ready to "top and tail" her back to her room. The actor taking the lead indicated to me that the coast was clear and Dana was meant to leap up and follow him down the corridor to her room, closely followed by me acting as the "tail". Dana, who had died on her back because of the huge bump in her stomach, then tried to stand up and found that she couldn't; she just lay on the floor, with all limbs flailing, like an upturned turtle.

As so often happens when Dana and I get together, I started to laugh uncontrollably at her flailing efforts which, in turn, set her off; the two of us just totally lost it – the more she struggled to get to her feet, the funnier I found it and the more I laughed, the more she laughed. This must have carried on for a good ten minutes and was seriously upsetting our timings (there's only so long the detective can hold the attention of the guests and they were waiting for me to return as the signal that the body had been safely removed). Finally managing to pull myself together, the other actor and I decided we'd have to drag Dana to her feet; we each took an arm and pulled and pulled and pulled to no avail (it didn't help that we'd all, by this time, collapsed with a fit of giggles at our failed efforts).

At this point the copper returned to the scene, to check that Dana had been safely removed (he thought I'd just forgotten to return to let him know everything was okay). Quickly appraising the problem with his sharp detective's brain he realised the only thing for it, if we were ever to remove the body, was to lend a helping hand (or two). As we pulled on her arms Dave got behind her, held her under her arms and gradually lifted her from the floor.

In this way, after much huffing and puffing, the three of us were finally able to winch Dana and her unborn son to an upright position. The copper then dashed back to the guests "with some important information" while the other actor and I got her back to the safety of her room, him running along the corridor in front, Dana waddling as best she could behind and me staggering behind her crying with laughter.

Chapter 3

The corpse corpsed!

A ll actors, even the very best, corpse at some point in their career (as you'll appreciate if you've ever watched Denis Norden's It'll Be Alright on the Night). Peter Sellers, for example, was notorious for corpsing and sometimes had to shoot and re-shoot a scene many times if he got a fit of the giggles.

Without the luxury of being able to re-shoot an argument it's important that Murder Weekend actors "get it right" first time – which isn't to say we invariably do but when an actor on a Weekend corpses it's usually possible to retrieve the situation – the desperate urge to giggle or, in some cases, let rip a huge belly laugh, can be turned around so that it doesn't detract from whatever's happening at the time. Because actors usually corpse when they're in the middle of a furious argument, it's often not too difficult to turn laughter into a gushing howl of pain and tears.

A dead body, however, doesn't have the opportunity to turn things around and if a corpse corpses (so to speak) you know things really have gone pear-shaped. Having lived and died on Murder Weekends for 25 years it's probably not too surprising to learn there have been many times I've been guilty of corpsing, but not without a great deal of provocation from both guests and fellow actors.

There are a few examples of guests making me corpse that spring immediately to mind. On one memorable occasion at a hotel in Ascot, I was a character who'd been horribly stabbed (and like many of the characters I write, was so evil that I think it's fair to say my hideous demise was completely justified). I'd managed to stagger onto a terrace, a large knife protruding from my stomach and blood everywhere, before I collapsed dead on the cold tiles. The guests and actors followed me as I staggered so I was aware of being surrounded by a large group of people. Trudy, the actress playing my sister, stood over me and started screaming for someone to get a doctor and, when one wasn't immediately forthcoming (obviously) she then had a brainwave. She'd been talking earlier to one of the guests over dinner and discovered she was a nurse. Her character, a simple soul, then started to wail "Get the nurse. Get Kerry! Where's Kerry?"

When Kerry didn't appear various guests took up the plea on her behalf and from my prone position I could hear different voices shouting "Get Kerry!" and "Where's Kerry?". Finally I heard a voice say: "Here she is. We've found her. Here's Kerry." I then heard my sister shout at the aforesaid Kerry: "Do something. You're a nurse, help my sister. Please, she's going to die." I braced myself for the inevitable inspection and pulse-taking, but nothing happened. "Do something," implored my sister, to which a clearly confused Kerry responded, quite calmly and almost apologetically. "I'm awfully sorry but I really didn't make myself clear earlier. I'm a sexual health nurse". Nonplussed by this unfortunate turn (and the barely suppressed giggles of some of the guests), Trudy played her simple character to the full; as if unable to fully comprehend she said: "But you're still a nurse, you told me you were. Help her. Please." At this point I felt someone kneel beside me and I assumed it was Kerry who would to pretend to try to staunch the blood or feel for a pulse and then pronounce me dead. Instead she leant over me and said, very calmly and very loudly: "How's your vagina?"

The guests and actors collapsed in gales of laughter and it took every bit of self control I could muster to stop myself laughing with them – the best I could do was to suddenly emit a loud choking noise that I hoped would sound like the last desperate gasp of a dying woman (instead of what it actually was – the sound of a corpse being corpsed).

One of my favourite examples of a guest causing a corpse to corpse came about when I was playing a character called Mary. For the sins of my evil past I was left for dead in a corridor just outside the room where the guests were playing a game, the idea being that once the game was over they would start to leave the room and someone would stumble across me. From where I lay I heard the game finish and waited to be discovered. Sure enough, the door opened and I heard excited chatter and braced myself to be found – but what I didn't expect was that the first guest to find me would be an Irish lady who loudly shrieked, "Oh Jesus. It's Mary!". The corpse just couldn't help smiling at that one.

If guests can, wittingly or unwittingly, make actors corpse the same is also true of our fellow actors. Two particular examples have stuck indelibly in my mind, mainly because, on both occasions, I was again the unwitting victim. In the first example I was to die in the hotel car park at around ten o'clock at night and we'd arranged that my character's sister (played by Maria Allen) would find me – mainly because Maria has proven, over the years, to be a great "screamer"; we needed someone who could attract the guests' attention even though they would be some distance away, inside the hotel, from where I was to be found. I got into position and draped myself beautifully next to Maria's car whereupon, a couple of minutes later, she would find me as she went to look for something, and scream at the top of her voice for all she was worth to ensure the guests would look out of the window, see her and pile into the car park to find me dead.

Maria decided that, instead of just standing beside me, she would let out an initial scream and then run screaming and panicking towards the hotel, to ensure that the guests could both see and hear her and be drawn to investigate the commotion. This was a good plan, but it was to have a rather unfortunate consequence. Maria "found" me as arranged and leaned against her car as if in shock. She then let out the most terrifying scream, which in itself would have been enough to wake the dead, and started to run towards the hotel. I then heard her say "Oh shit!" and scream again as I felt something soft land on me. I opened my eyes to see Maria's wrap-around skirt hanging from the handle of the car door and realised she was running towards the guests in her underwear. At which point I started to laugh.

She was now in two minds what to do – continue running and screaming in her knickers or try to retrieve her skirt – and as she half twisted to look back to where her skirt was hanging her mind was made up for her when her bra strap broke and one boob dramatically dropped under her shirt. Realising she was defeated, she ran back to her car and screamed in my ear "My bra's broken!" I'm not sure why she told me this or what she expected me to do about it since at that point I was lying prone in a pool of blood on the ground. The only response her panicked reaction produced in me was further laughter.

By this point we could hear guests in the distance coming to see what all the fuss was about and Maria quickly snatched her skirt from the door and wrapped it roughly around her semi-naked nether-regions and held it in place with one hand while she used the other to hold her right boob in place inside her shirt. She then decided, for good measure, she would start weeping and wailing over my body. I was, at this stage, nearly helpless with laughter and desperately, if unsuccessfully, trying to regain my morbid composure. Just as all seemed lost Sheila, who was playing my mother, arrived on the scene, closely followed by a large group of guests.

I've no idea how but, quick as a flash (so to speak) she grasped the situation and threw herself across my face and chest in a desperate and very successful attempt to mask the fact I was nearly crying with laughter. Quite what the guests made of this scrum of bodies I can only guess but this was definitely one instance when they didn't get to see very much of the body (but they did get to see more of Maria than she might have wished).

Not content with causing the worst case of a corpse corpsing we've ever had on a Weekend, Maria was at the centre of another memorable (for all the wrong reasons) example of a corpse (me again) failing to display a level of mortality appropriate to the situation. Maria was playing a character who was something of a religious fanatic; she'd been driving everyone mad all weekend as she took every opportunity to preach to guests while trying to convert them to her way of thinking. The plan for my death was that I would be found by the guests in the room my character was using as "her office" on the Weekend (in reality it was a small syndicate room situated a short way down a corridor from the function room in which the guests were having afternoon tea). We'd also decided that Maria's character would find me first and as the guests entered the room they would see her, kneeling beside my corpse, praying frantically.

For the guests to find us an actor needed an excuse to come to look for me and we decided that Paula (the actress playing my sister) would become increasingly worried that she hadn't seen me for some time and create a little scene with the guests that would end with her deciding to "find Helena" (the character I was playing). As normally happens the guests would pick up on Paula's hint that something interesting was about to kick off and follow her to my office, whereupon they would hear the loud praying coming from inside and burst in to find my body. Maria and I got ourselves in position a few minutes before the time we'd agreed Paula would start looking for me and waited. At the appointed moment Paula, who had sat herself in the dining room with guests she knew would take the hint and follow her, pretended to be worried about me, asking the guests "Has anyone seen Helena?" and, when no one said they had, suddenly became very worried and said she had "a nasty feeling" that something may have happened to her. She then loudly announced she was "going to find Helena to make sure she was alright" and promptly marched out of the room with guests in tow.

As she set off the realisation struck her that she hadn't actually got the foggiest idea in which room I was going to be found dead, mainly because she hadn't been paying sufficient attention in the actors' meeting a couple of hours earlier when we planned everything out. Undeterred by this minor consideration she reasoned she would know which room I was in because she would hear Maria loudly praying. This was, up to a point, a reasonable assumption and a good example of an actor thinking on their feet when something goes slightly wrong.

What Paula didn't know, however, was that just as Maria was due to start praying she suddenly looked at me and confessed, in a loud whisper, that she wasn't in the least bit religious and didn't know enough prayers to keep things going for any great length of time. Consequently, she suggested she would only start praying just as everyone was outside the door and about to enter the room. Since there was nothing I could do at this late stage about Maria's sudden lack of religious knowledge I agreed that this was what she should do (little knowing that when Maria said she didn't know "enough prayers" what she really meant was that she didn't know any prayers).

As I lay on the floor with Maria beside me we heard Paula's voice in the distance and the satisfying sound of a lot of guests with her. I started to shallow breathe and Maria prepared herself for prayer. The gaggle of guests approached "my room" but instead of stopping they walked straight past it. We heard them clump off into the distance and then there was silence – until about five minutes later when we heard Paula's voice loudly announcing: "She's not in her room and I haven't a clue where she is! I'm getting seriously worried about her now."

We heard approaching footsteps but then they promptly veered off in a completely different direction to our room. All Maria and I could hear at this point was the muffled sound of the guests tromping backwards and forwards around the hotel, with the occasional sound of Paula's voice "encouraging the troops". The fact that we both knew Paula was completely lost and hadn't got a clue about where to look for us set us both off with a fit of the giggles.

After a few more minutes we heard someone outside the door and that snapped us back to the business at hand. We both immediately regained our composure and as I lay on the floor, as stiff as a board, Maria readied herself to start praying. Luckily for all of us (or else we could have been there all night), a guest had decided that instead of just marching aimlessly around the hotel they would try every door they passed on the premise that since they suspected I was dead and waiting to be found I'd probably be behind one that wasn't locked. As Maria saw the door open and the guest pop their head into the room she clasped her hands tightly together over my body and began to chant the only "prayer" she could think of:

"All things bright and beautiful, All creatures great and small," she solemnly intoned, at which point I was a goner and couldn't stop myself from convulsing uncontrollably with laughter. Realising what she was saying was ridiculous, Maria also started to laugh and it was fortunate for both of us that the guest who'd found us had immediately dashed off to find their companions to tell them the "good news". When Paula and the others discovered us a few seconds later Maria had managed to throw herself across my prostrate body and was masking her laughter (and my guffawing) with an Oscar-winning performance of weeping and wailing…

When we have a large number of guests on a Weekend (usually around 80+) we include an "extra character" (a police sergeant) who's main role is to help his superior officer (the detective inspector) with everything that needs to be done on a Weekend; this involves things like helping to control the guests after a death and making sure that everyone has all the relevant information about the deaths that has come to light during the Weekend.

Marc Steatham, who is incredibly sharp and quick-witted, decided to make the role his own and created what we've since come to affectionately call the "comedy sergeant" – a very dim-witted character who's always several steps behind in the investigation, much to the guests' amusement and the inspector's exasperation.

At the actors' meeting we'd decided Marc should find my body in the hotel garden after lunch on the Saturday afternoon. My character was an evil woman who was to be killed horribly in a mock crucifixion and the make-up I'd used was, I like to think, one of my best efforts – it looked as though nails had been hammered through my hands and my feet and, to make the image complete, I was to be found in the crucifix position, my legs bound together and my arms spread wide at right angles to my body. It wasn't, however, the most comfortable position in which to lie.

To make matters worse, lunch took more time to serve than we'd initially calculated and, taking into account the need to be "in position" well in advance of being found, I ended up lying on cold concrete for around 45 minutes – by which time every part of my body was aching and my arms and legs had gone to sleep (when you're expecting to be found at any moment you can't keep shifting your position, just in case anyone's watching). You can imagine my relief, therefore, when Marc eventually came up to me and said he was about to let the guests know he'd found me. At our meeting the plan we'd mapped out was that Marc would find me and then run through the hotel gardens until he came to the French windows that led from the restaurant, where the guests were having lunch, to the gardens. These would be closed and he would then bang on the glass to alert both the guests and the inspector to the body he'd found.

Although I was some way distant from the restaurant and didn't personally witness what happened next, one of the actors told me that one minute they were sat at a table chatting away to a guest and the next they heard what sounded like a gunshot. Marc, it seems, had rushed up to the French windows and instead of tapping lightly on the glass to attract people's attention had, in his excitement, hit it so hard that his fist went straight through, shards of glass were sent cascading into the room and everyone rushed to see what all the fuss was about.

As Marc, on one side of the window, tried to breathlessly explain to the guests on the other side that he'd found a body, the detective inspector, after rebuking his hapless sergeant, instantly worried about guests cutting themselves on the broken slivers of glass, began to usher people away from him. Denied the opportunity to question Marc, the guests then had to make their way out of the restaurant and around the side of the hotel to where he was standing; by this time I had been lying on the ground for around an hour and was cold, stiff and very, very, fed up.

When Marc finally managed to get the guests to where I was lying they were suitably impressed by the efforts I'd made with the make-up. I was, judging by the reactions, a pretty horrific sight, with lots of blood and nasty wounds created by the nails in my flesh (which were, in fact, made of wax). Despite his earlier, albeit inadvertent, efforts at sabotaging my death, Marc wasn't quite finished. He managed to corpse me by standing over my body and exclaiming in his very broad Birmingham accent: "Oh my God, I don't believe it. I'm bleeeee-ding." He then, by all accounts, proceeded to wave his hand in the general direction of any guest who wanted to bear witness to the fact that, yes indeed, there was a miniscule drip of blood coming from a very tiny wound caused when he stupidly broke the pane of glass.

I had to smile at the thought that there I was lying dead in a pool of blood with multiple stab wounds in my body and all the majority of the guests were concerned about was making sympathetic noises about Marc and his "wound". Mind you, it took all the effort I could muster not to burst out laughing when one witty guest sidled up to the inspector and loudly said: "I know you're supposed to 'Break the glass in case of an emergency' inspector, but don't you think your sergeant's taken things a bit too literally?"

At the start of Chapter One I talked a bit about how a Murder Weekend is all about role-playing and the fact that, in order to allow the actors scope to develop a role, I only provide them with rough sketches of their character. This allows each actor to create the most wonderfully rounded personalities and, I think, adds to the overall realism of the plot as the characters, within reason, behave in a believable way towards each other and the guests.

This freedom, as some of the stories in the previous chapters have shown, occasionally creates problems – something brilliantly illustrated by the behaviour of Becky (one of my actresses who is particularly good at creating very humorous and ingenious characters) in my final "corpsing corpse" story.

For one particular plot she was playing a character called Geraldine – a decidedly dodgy but essentially harmless individual who was stalking one of the other characters over the course of the Weekend. Geraldine, as I envisaged her, was a rather sad individual with just a few too many screws loose – something Becky took to heart.

When we'd done this plot on previous occasions we'd decided that the guests would initially discover Geraldine in her role as a stalker, hiding behind some bushes in the hotel garden as she tried to sneak a closer look at the object of her affection, a very well-known and very pompous actor called Maxwell Hart. We first met Becky's interpretation of Geraldine at the Friday evening actors' meeting when she knocked the wind out of everyone's sails by arriving dressed in combat fatigues, complete with binoculars, night goggles and a survival pack slung around her neck. No one at the meeting thought to ask if these were things she'd acquired especially for her character or whether, worryingly, they were all part of her general wardrobe – mainly because she'd brought with her a book called How To Survive Anything that proved to be an endless source of fascinating tips about what to do in the event of a crisis.

As Geraldine, Becky took every opportunity to tell guests what they should do "if a bear attacked them" or "they were caught in a sudden earthquake", neither of which were likely to occur in suburban Surrey!

The guests loved this behaviour and took every opportunity to question Geraldine about what they should do in the most ridiculous of circumstances – and if no one was interested in asking her anything, Geraldine was not backward in volunteering sound advice.

One piece of information she discovered while rifling aimlessly through her book was what to do if someone was stabbed and bleeding to death: "You must throw sugar on the wound," she proudly announced to anyone who would listen, "and lots of it!", she added for effect. "That sterilises the wound and bungs it up!" she concluded triumphantly, just in case anyone doubted the wisdom of her words – yet another piece of useless information until, of course, I found myself lying motionless on the incident room floor on Saturday night, bleeding profusely from multiple stab wounds...

When playing the corpse you get used to not reacting to loud screams and gasps fom the guests when they first stumble across the body. On this occasion I had been lying on the floor for a couple of minutes after I had been discovered when I started to hear a few loud gasps from the guests. I had no idea what was happening as I lay prone with my eyes tightly closed and was a little confused to hear someone shout: "Oh no!" This was quickly followed by another guest saying "You can't!" and finally someone screeching "You mustn't!"

It was at this point that I heard Geraldine shriek: "Don't worry, I'll save her. I know exactly what to do. Stand back!". I was expecting the worst and I wasn't disappointed. I felt the floor rumble as Geraldine thundered across the room and the next thing I knew I was being showered with sugar! Although I could just about stomach a bag of granulated sugar tipped over me, the fact that she followed this by pelting me with sugar cubes really took the biscuit. "It was, after all", she announced disarmingly, "such a very large wound". This produced much laughter from the guests and it took levels of self control I never knew I possessed to stop me from joining in the laughter – I had to bite my cheek so hard it was sore for several days!

Once safely back in my room, Becky eventually dared to show her face to check that everything was alright and the first thing I did was warn her that one day I would get her back. As yet it hasn't happened but one day Becky, one day!

Chapter 4

A bedroom farce

From the very beginning of Murder Weekends one of the most frequent plot devices I've used is that of an affair between two or more of the characters. Not only does this suggest a possible reason for murder (at least in the mind of some guests) but more importantly the discovery by a guest of evidence pointing to the affair draws them into the action by giving them the opportunity to initiate confrontations between the characters; this sets up the possibility of some really cracking rows, especially when the characters are caught in the act, so to speak, by guests and suitably outraged partners.

Although we've performed, if that's the right word, numerous bedroom scenes over the years, one that created the most consistent trouble for the actors was our first ever gay affair a couple of years back. The storyline involved two male actors being discovered naked in a bedroom when the wife of one of the characters, prompted by a piece of evidence brought to her attention by guests, became convinced her husband was having an affair with another woman. To make matters worse the evidence suggested they were, at that very moment, in bed together in "the other woman's" room. The wife, followed by the guests, would then go to the room and demand to be let in – at which point her husband would "panic" and hide in the wardrobe (with only a small cushion to hide his modesty). His erstwhile partner, meanwhile, opened the door wrapped in a towel as if he was just about to take a bath. The wife was then suitably embarrassed and apologetic until she saw her husband's watch on the bedside cabinet, whereupon she would force her way into the room followed by inquisitive guests who would, of course, search the room for the missing husband and, eventually, find him cowering in "the closet".

Things, however, started to go wrong from just about the first time we performed the plot. When the cowering husband emerged contritely from the wardrobe to face his furious wife, she picked up the first thing that came to hand to throw at him, which just happened to be a full glass of beer. Fortunately for him the husband saw it coming and ducked, which meant the alcohol missed its intended target. Unfortunately, given he had been standing in front of a wardrobe filled with his clothes, for the rest of the weekend everyone knew when he was about to enter a room because the stench of alcohol alerted everyone to his imminent arrival.

Although we'd tried to avoid the obvious problem of two naked men standing in a room displaying their wares to the world through the clever use of strategically placed towels and cushions, things went from bad to worse when a couple of weeks later we made the cardinal error of casting a real-life husband and wife to play the fictitious husband and wife.

As a guest found her husband, Chris, hiding in the wardrobe Julia Livesey duly went berserk. She dragged him into the room and began to slap him around the midriff, but since he had the cushion safely covering this part of his body it didn't have the desired effect. In her frustration and blind fury she did what came naturally (a little too naturally it seemed to me); she started to slap him around the head. Chris, not being coordinated enough to keep one hand on the cushion while using the other to ward off the blows, raised his hands and, of course, the cushion that was supposed to protect his (and the guests') modesty. I don't think I'm alone in saying it wasn't a pretty sight.

Chris later said the worst part of it wasn't being hit (as actors we're usually pretty good at faking slaps and punches in ways that make them look quite real), nor was it the fact that as he lifted his hands something other than Julia hit him – the realisation he was effectively standing naked in a room full of almost total strangers. What really got him was that as he peeked past the cushion he was desperately using to ward off his wife's attack he saw three guests (all sisters we later discovered) standing about six feet away from him in a neat line, each with a camera and each clicking away like there was no tomorrow.

Chris was involved in yet another unscripted moment the following week, although in this instance it wasn't (he claims) his fault. This time he was playing the gay lover while Tim, who is a really lovely bloke, was playing the husband. At our meeting a couple of hours before the scene Tim said he was a bit nervous about the possibility of guests seeing "his bits", so we decided his wife wouldn't pull him into the middle of the room once he'd been found – she'd just keep him backed into a corner of the wardrobe so guests could see she was hitting him but couldn't really see much of his naked body. The fact he is 6'4" tall (and also one of the clumsiest men I have ever met – but more about that later) did make this seem a little unlikely but Tim seemed happy enough with this plan.

We also decided that since Chris was going to be found dead in the same room about half an hour after the bedroom scene we'd need to hide some of the blood and equipment in the bathroom beforehand, while the guests were occupied elsewhere. Chris would then have to ensure that once he'd got Tim safely into the wardrobe and let the guests into the room, he stood in the bathroom doorway to stop guests going in. We couldn't just shut the bathroom door because this would simply have invited guests to search for Tim in the bathroom.

A few minutes before the "irate wife" was about to find them Chris got Tim safely into the wardrobe (complete with two modesty cushions, one for the front and one for the rear). When Tim's "wife" arrived and forced her way into the room (closely followed by a posse of guests) Chris moved casually towards the bathroom to block the doorway and was surprised, to say the least, to see the wardrobe doors suddenly burst open and Tim, his adrenalin obviously pumping, leap into the room.

Ali, the startled wife, didn't stay that way for long; she began to shout and scream at Tim while trying to hit him across his back and shoulders. Tim, like all the actors playing this particular part, had been told he had to grin and bear it (in a manner of speaking) but, as is often the case with Tim, things took a different direction once "the lights were on" and the action had started – he decided to fight back by hitting his wife with the cushions he was holding. She, in turn, managed to pull one of the cushions from his grasp and began hitting him with it. One of the things I try to impress on actors when they're involved in an argument is to "move around the room" – with a big group of guests in large rooms it's important that the actors move around (as naturally as possible I should add) so that everyone gets a chance to see and hear what's going on. Tim obviously took this instruction to heart because he then decided to move – and in a tiny bedroom that hardly had enough space to contain the twin beds he and Chris had pushed together to make it look as though they'd been together in a double bed – there was only one place to go. He jumped onto one of the beds.

Ali, at this point, leaned across one of the beds and tried to hit Tim with the cushion she was holding. Tim, of course, tried to get as far away from her as possible which forced Ali to chase him around the room in an increasingly unsuccessful effort to give him the beating he so richly deserved. Tim, by this time, was squealing and jumping from bed to bed (while inadvertently showing his considerable talents to the assembled guests) until, under the strain of one final leap too many, one of the beds broke (not the first thing he's managed to break in the 15 or so years I've known him) and he fell into a heap on the floor as the beds were pushed apart.

If any of the guests hadn't seen enough of Tim by this time they certainly got an eyeful as he lay, half on his back with his legs akimbo showing everything he had to the world. The male guests were impressed, the female guests were screeching with excitement and Tim's wife was beyond help; having given up chasing him round the room she dissolved into tears on the floor (she was actually laughing so hard she thought she'd pretend to cry to salvage what little dignity she could from the scene they'd just played out). At this point the copper decided it might be a good idea to intervene and, covering Tim's assets with a bedspread, led him out of the room and away from the trail of devastation he had left in his considerable wake.

The final bit of trouble we suffered with this particular scene was, in many ways, the most embarrassing for all involved – even though there wasn't a guest (or irate wife) in sight. The two male actors were, as usual, in the bedroom getting ready for their big scene. Both had stripped down to, well, nothing and one of the actors was just about to get into the wardrobe when, much to their consternation they heard a key turn in the locked door. Before they could say or do anything the door opened and in walked a chambermaid.

"Oh," she said, clearly a little shocked and embarrassed by the sight of so much pale white male flesh. "It's…err…not what it looks like," replied one of the actors hopefully. "Okay," she shrugged, as if the sight of two naked men in a wardrobe in a hotel bedroom at 2.30 in the afternoon was something she encountered everyday. "I'll come back later – when you have finished."

Although our all-male bedroom scene probably caused more than the usual number of problems, male-female bedroom encounters have also, over the years, given both actors and guests their fair share of amusement, with the women involved in these scenes each taking to them in their own inimitable manner.

Linda White, for example, an actress who's been with Murder Weekends for many years, is very confident in her voluptuous body and has surprised more than one male actor by simply whipping off all her clothes and leaping into bed before you could say "Jack Robinson". Others, like Maria and Mal, tend to be a little more demure, taking great care to wear their best undies and slip quietly under the covers while the male actor turns his back. I, on the other hand, was always filled with embarrassment whenever I had to play a bedroom scene – mainly, I think, because I hate my body. Over the years the actors have come to joke that I was the only person they knew who put on more clothes to get into bed – and on one occasion this nearly got me into terrible trouble!

Chris and I were doing a bedroom scene, one he'd already done a couple of times with different actresses so he was quite blasé about taking his clothes off and getting into bed ready for the arrival of the guests. As he got between the sheets, naked except for his underpants, I climbed in next to him – fully clothed – and pulled the sheets and blankets tightly around my neck. He looked at me and laughed. "What if the guests pull the sheets off the bed?" I told him in no uncertain terms that there was no way on God's earth that the sheets were coming off that bed while I was in it. However, as a small concession to his sensibilities I pulled my shirt and bra down to reveal bare shoulders and held the sheets across the top of my chest. I thought that to all intents and purposes I would look naked too (although by this time Chris had decided to remove his underpants "just in case").

When the guests burst into the room to find us in bed together Chris started shouting and screaming at them to get out and, as if to make his point more forcefully, he picked up a small cushion to cover himself, pulled back the sheets and got out of bed. There was a sharp intake of breath from the guests because, as he'd obviously planned, they could see his bare bum reflected in the mirror on the wall beside the bed. I thought this diversion might satisfy the crowd but unfortunately I overlooked a group of seven overzealous guests who decided that since Chris was standing in the middle of the room naked except for a small cushion, I should be forced to face the music too; as they grabbed the bottom of the bedding and started to pull. I knew I couldn't let them remove the sheets – it would just have been too ridiculous. Not only had I got all my clothes on, I hadn't even taken my trainers off! I can honestly say it took a truly superhuman effort on my part to hang on to the bedclothes as the guests pulled at them. At that particular moment it seemed like I had the strength of ten men and there was no way in the world those sheets were going to be removed – although I have to say I was genuinely thankful for the timely intervention of the detective who stepped in to stop the guests exposing me (or not, I suppose).

Although I can't be certain, I think my fear of being 'overexposed' stems from an incident many, many years ago – one again witnessed by a large crowd of guests and, I suspect, recorded on several cameras and videos for posterity! I was playing a character who was both madly in love with her husband and pregnant with their first child. Over the course of the weekend, however, I came to learn that not only was my lovely husband a serial adulterer, he was also responsible for the death of a close associate. As more and more was revealed my character took to the bottle and by Saturday night was very drunk – so drunk, in fact, that she decided she was going to bring on a miscarriage using a very hot bath and a bottle of gin – the Old Wives' Tale may have been just that, but it definitely made for a good storyline.

Each week on the plot I filled the bath with lots of hot water and masses of bubbles, stripped off and sank into the relaxing foam. I folded my arms across my bare boobs and held an empty gin bottle in one hand for drunken effect. This worked splendidly for a number of Weekends – each time I was found within a few minutes of getting into the bath, my naked body well-covered by the copious bubbles. One fateful Weekend, however, the guests missed the clue that normally led them en masse to my room. I lay in the warm water for 10 minutes or so with no sign of the guests. 20 minutes passed and I was starting to wonder what was happening. After 30 minutes I was beginning to worry, thinking that something had gone wrong and I'd been forgotten. The water had, of course, been getting cooler and cooler until, by this stage it was really quite cold; more importantly, as far as my modesty was concerned, the magnificent mass of foaming bubbles that had covered me half and hour earlier had, by now, dissipated to almost nothing.

I tried stirring the water as best I could, to no great effect and I couldn't get out of the bath and re-run the water to create more bubbles because I was expecting the guests to burst into the room at any moment. After 45 minutes I finally heard the guests at the bedroom door and then Laura, the actress playing my sister, ran into the bathroom to find me lying in a bath of tepid water with hardly a bubble worth the name to be seen.

She looked at me and instantly knew I was in trouble. There was only one thing for it. She ran over to where I was lying and, as I began to loudly cry, threw herself over my soaking wet body. As she did this she started to thrash around with her hands in the water as if she was struggling to get me out of the bath; in reality she was madly – if semi-successfully – trying to regenerate the bubbles to hide my naked body. As the other actors arrived on the scene to be met by the sound of frantic splashing coming from the bathroom they realised what must have happened, but since they were all playing characters that hated me they couldn't be seen by the guests to help me in any way – the best they could do was ignore me in the hope the guests would conclude nothing very interesting was going on. Judging by the multitude of video cameras suddenly pointed in my direction there was no chance of that happening; it makes me shudder to think about the footage the guests shot, the number of different people who've seen it and, even more embarrassingly, what they thought about it!

If bedroom scenes and the possibility of being found naked generally make me nervous and embarrassed, one thing I've learnt to come to terms with is the ravages of age. Whereas once, when I was but a mere slip of a girl, I could laugh like a drain on Weekends, now I've become a "lady of a certain age" hysterical and uncontrolled laughter can have dire consequences! On one particularly memorable (for all the wrong reasons) occasion I was lying dead on the ground in a rotunda that had a balcony all the way round from which guests could enter each of the different corridors to the bedrooms. I was supposed to be found by my "mother", played by Shirley, a very witty older actress, who's loud crying would then alert the other actors and, of course, the guests.

After what seemed an age lying by myself I was eventually "stumbled across" by Dana (the aforementioned upturned turtle and one of the funniest actresses I have ever met – she often reminds people of Julie Walters in terms of both her range of facial expressions and dry sense of humour) and another great pal of mine, Mal; they had both come to check I was okay because Shirley, although she had been "missing" for some time before my demise, was nowhere to be seen. This was not, it has to be admitted, a wholly unforeseen possibility because Shirley was legendary for her ability to get hopelessly lost on even the simplest of journeys.

As we waited Dana and Mal started to make me giggle by relating Shirley's master plan. We were in a new and particularly sprawling hotel and Shirley had decided that to avoid getting lost – and suffering our consequent micky-taking – she would adopt a foolproof plan that involved the clever and discreet use of marbles. Having earlier worked out the route from her room to the rotunda, she had put a marble in the corner of each corridor. In this way she would, come the time to discover my dead body, be able to retrace the route using her marbles as a guide. This cunning plan had only one tiny fault, which she quickly discovered when she realised that, although the marbles indicated where she'd been, they didn't tell her in which direction she should be travelling. Needless to say, she became hopelessly lost in the maze of hotel corridors when the time came for her to find my body.

Dana and Mal were just debating about whether they should go and look for "their mother" (the three of us were playing her daughters on the Weekend) when Shirley suddenly appeared on the balcony quite a way above us.

Just in case any guests were within earshot, Mal and Dana went into acting mode and gave Shirley hurried instructions about how to get down to us while I went back to being dead since I was expecting to be found at any moment. A few minutes passed, however, with no sign of Shirley. The next thing we heard was a door opening on the balcony immediately above us and then Mal saw Shirley's face peering down to where I was lying; I knew she was above us because I heard a muttered, if heartfelt, "Oh dear" and this, of course, set each of us off laughing once again. With Dana cradling me in her arms, Mal then explained in painful detail to Shirley how she could get down to the ground floor and her daughter's body.

A few more minutes passed and then, once more we heard a door open above us and Shirley appeared on the balcony for the third time. She seemed genuinely shocked to be looking down on us since, as she said later, she had been certain Mal's final directions had definitely put her on the right track. We all looked at each other for a split second and then the four of us started laughing – the sort where you laugh so hard the only sound that comes out is one that resembles the hissing of a steam engine. Dana and I laughed so hard we both experienced what we now call our "Tena Lady" moments and it was left to Mal to retrieve Shirley from the balcony since, as she perceptively pointed out, "I'll have to go because I'm the only one with dry knickers."

Embarrassing as this episode was, at least with Dana I was in good company. By far my most spectacular "knicker incident" however occurred in January 2006 in front of a film crew from the BBC Holiday Programme. The Weekend was going brilliantly, the guests were having a ball and the presenter and crew were thoroughly enjoying themselves and extremely pleased with the marvellous footage they were getting. I'd arranged with the director that, on the Saturday afternoon, I would find a body in a function room at the opposite end of the hotel to where everyone was having afternoon tea in the restaurant. The room could just be seen from the restaurant and guests could get to it quickly and easily across a beautifully tended lawn that ran through the lovely garden.

My plan, which at the time of our midday meeting I thought was a good one, was that I would discover the body, leave the function room through the French windows and run across the lawn towards the restaurant screaming as loudly as I could. Once there I would bang as hard as I could on the window as if I was in a blind panic. The TV crew were primed to be near the window so that, as they heard me start to scream, the camera could be quickly turned in my direction in order to film my mad dash through the garden. This would have been perfect for everyone – guests and crew alike – but for a couple of minor details. Firstly, at around 1pm there was a very heavy and sustained downpour that completely soaked the garden and lawn and, secondly, I was on a strict diet that involved drinking four litres of water a day. Although I didn't appreciate it at the time, these two unrelated facts combined to create a recipe for disaster.

At dead on 4pm I "found" the body, pushed open the French windows, screamed very loudly and started to run across the muddy lawn. This would not, at the best of times, have been a great idea. Trying to do it while wearing high heeled boots and a long flowing skirt was just asking for trouble – and sure enough I got it.

After a few strides my heels stuck in the grass and as I tried to drag my feet I slipped and did the splits – at which point what felt like the three litres of water I'd already consumed that day came gushing out like Niagara Falls. On any other Weekend I would have cut my losses, stayed where I was and screamed blue murder until someone came to find me. On this Weekend, of course, I couldn't do that because the crew were waiting to film my exciting dash and breathless entrance; it wouldn't be possible to do a second take so, being a real trooper, I picked myself up carried on running until I got to the restaurant – at which point, having alerted everyone to the body with my ear-piercing screaming, I hid behind a bush and refused point blank to come out.

The actors were rather confused by this odd turn of events and, thinking I'd decided to change things around in the heat of the moment, tried in vain to coax me into the open.

They found it difficult to understand why I was partly hidden behind a bush while simultaneously gesticulating madly in the direction of the function room. The penny didn't drop until about ten minutes later when the guests were safely out of the way being interrogated by the copper; I finally emerged from my hiding place to explain my "accident" and to add insult to embarrassment, the BBC crew went away with so much good footage of the Weekend that they didn't use a second of my muddy dash across a swampy lawn!

Chapter 5

A policeman's lot is not a happy one

The role of the police inspector on a Weekend is an important and highly specialised one and not every actor is up to the challenge of playing the part. Those who play it regularly however generally find it interesting and different to the usual types of role they're asked to play – and nowhere is the difference and challenge more in evidence than on the Friday night when the inspector normally makes his or her first appearance.

Unlike when you're playing a normal role and can ease yourself into the part by getting to know the guests at the reception and over dinner, the detective comes "cold" to the scene and the first thing they're required to do is control the excited and boisterous crowd gathered around the body. Once they've successfully moved everyone away so the body can escape they then have to perform what most of my regular coppers say is the hardest part of any Weekend – the first interrogation of an invariably lively (and sometimes slightly tipsy) group of strangers. At this stage the actor playing the copper has to be prepared to be heckled, booed and insulted by uncooperative suspects and interrogated by guests who want to know everything about them (name, rank, force, inside leg measurement…), while remaining cool, calm and collected as they establish a rapport with the guests. Those actors with an aptitude for playing the copper quickly learn how to earn the respect of their audience.

A lot of what the copper does on a Weekend goes on "behind the scenes", away from the eyes of guests. Some of this is just general administration (ensuring every guest gets a clue sheet at the appropriate time and collecting completed questionnaires on the Sunday morning, for example) but the detective also plays a significant role in ensuring the Weekend runs smoothly and to plan – evidence, for example, has to go up in the incident room at the right time and in the right order. The timing of evidence being made available to guests is often vital because a particular clue may be used to spark off a row and the actors involved need to be able to count on the copper. When a clue fails to appear at the right time it can throw the actors, characters and rows completely. Having said that, the nightmare scenario, as far as the copper is concerned, is putting clues up in the wrong order; if a clue is supposed to appear after a character is dead and it appears while they are still very much alive it not only makes it very difficult for that character to explain, it very, very occasionally makes it crystal clear to the more alert guests that the character is the next to die. As an actor there are few things more disconcerting than guests confidently telling you to your face that "You are next" when you know they're right.

The copper also plays an important role with the guests; they can, for example, be a good sounding board for different theories when the guests are wrestling with all the clues late on Saturday night – the copper not only has to be absolutely clear about the whole of the plot, they also have to walk a fine line between being "distant but approachable". By this I mean guests have to feel comfortable about being able to talk to the policeman while testing their ideas but, at the same time, they can't expect the copper to solve the case for them (since this would defeat the object of the Weekend). In this respect one of the most important jobs the inspector does is very much in the public eye – presenting a succinct, clear and witty interpretation of my denouement on a Sunday morning.

A well-delivered denouement that explains the complex plot clearly and concisely invariably means the guests go home happy, having understood how all the evidence fits together and, usually, kicking themselves that they've missed the vital clues that clinched the case.

Given that the detective always has a great deal of vital work to do on a Weekend (both with the guests and behind the scenes) it probably won't be too surprising to learn that the detective's lot is not always a happy one; more often than not our coppers are fantastic and do a wonderful job, but sometimes things do go wrong. Trudy Lowe, for example, plays a very authoritative and funny copper with a dry sense of humour. She's rarely lost for words or a witty response to even the most persistent and truculent of guests – but she's not always as observant as a good police officer should be.

One Weekend Trudy was loitering quietly in a room a little way from where she knew a body was about to be found; sure enough she heard the guests cry out: "Inspector! Someone find the inspector quickly!" which was her cue to dash across a small courtyard and along a length of path to the room where everyone was congregating. She crossed the courtyard and sprinted up the path to enter the room through what she thought was an open door. It wasn't. Instead of a dramatic and breathless entrance to the scene of the crime Trudy dramatically ran straight into a sliding glass door. The guests were a little taken aback to see her suddenly ricochet backwards off the window but, professional to the core, she carried on as if it was the most normal thing in the world to do. She staggered into the room, clearly stunned and with tears running down her cheeks from the pain of what she thought was a broken nose. Understandably, her inspection of the body wasn't carried out as thoroughly as she would normally have done (unless Trudy's normal inspection consists of a quick glance and a blurted "He's dead", with one hand held to her nose as if the corpse might already have been giving off a funny smell) and it took her a great deal of effort to muster up the authority to shout: "Rite. I deed ebrydoddy doo doh dack doo de functshn dwoom." As the guests looked at each other quizzically for a few seconds one eventually piped up to translate: "I could be wrong but I think she means she wants us to go back to the function room!"

Being in a hurry – and running fast without bothering too much about where you're running – is an occupational hazard for coppers on Murder Weekends, especially when they're helping to get a body away from the scene as quickly as possible without being spotted by guests. We usually manage to do this successfully, with the guests being none the wiser about the sudden disappearance of a body, but on a Weekend at Whately Hall in Banbury things didn't run (quite literally) as smoothly as we would have liked. The body had been found in the main lounge and the quickest way for the corpse to get back to his room was to run out of the main door, into the street for about 20 yards and then down a side alley and back into the hotel safely away from any stray guests.

The body was being "topped and tailed" by the actress playing his wife and the copper who, once they'd got the nod from another actor that the guests had all been moved safely away, threw the main doors open and dashed blindly into the street – straight into a large crowd queuing for the late night horror movie showing in the cinema just next to the hotel. They certainly had more horror than they were bargaining for when the victim, covered in (fake) blood tried to weave his way unsuccessfully through the crowd, causing a real commotion as he did so. The copper, however, was unfazed by this unexpected turn of events; cool as a cucumber he reached into his jacket pocket and produced his (fake) police ID.

He then held it aloft (just like they do on TV!) and pushed his way through the crowd, followed by the corpse and his wife, proclaiming "Everything's under control; let me through please, I'm a police officer. There's nothing to see here. Thank you." I shudder to think what the film fans were left thinking that night!

Whenever Tim (the shy, retiring, jumping flasher of a previous story) plays the copper he always looks the part. At our Friday evening meeting I'd given him clear instructions about the room where the body was going to be found and how to get there and Tim, as he usually does, nodded sagely as if he were taking everything in. A few hours later he got the call to let him know the body had been found and he made his way to the front of the hotel, whereupon he came flying through the doors, stopped briefly at the reception to check the location of "the incident" and, without listening too carefully, went hurtling off down a corridor until he came to the closed doors of a large function room. Tim must have looked fantastic as he made his grand entrance – the double doors flying open and his police raincoat billowing like a superhero's cape as he burst into the room, notebook and identity card in hand. "Ladies and gentlemen. My name's

Detective Inspector Rutherford. I received a call that someone has been murdered... someone attending this function, I believe..." he began promisingly before he realised his impressive entrance was wasted on the couple of hundred male Law Society members, dressed in dinner suits and black bow ties, who turned to look at him with blank astonishment. Suddenly realising he was in the wrong room he quickly mumbled an apology and then beat a hasty retreat back to reception and this time he listened properly to the directions he was given.

Although Tim wears glasses I didn't realise he was quite so short-sighted until he was the copper on a plot that involved one of the male actors playing a transsexual. The basic idea was that this particular character was committing murders disguised as a woman and in order to convince the guests this was plausible I decided it would be fun for the murderer to don his female clothing and spend a few minutes walking among the guests.

Stuart Hatcher was brave enough to volunteer for this part and after a lot of discussion I created a perfect female disguise for him, complete with a very realistic long-haired wig. I spent a lot of time making Stuart up each time and I'm happy to say none of the guests ever twigged, until all was revealed at the denouement, that the "pretty young woman" who briefly appeared and disappeared on the Saturday evening was, in fact, the same Stuart they'd been chatting to all weekend.

Although most of the actors had seen Stuart being made-up we'd decided that none of them should be around when he took his brief stroll through the hotel; the idea was to make the guests think all the actors were in their rooms getting ready for the evening fancy dress and, in this way, make them less suspicious (although since, once properly dressed and made-up, Stuart made a very presentable woman, I needn't have worried). However, just in case a guest recognised Stuart as he walked around the hotel I thought it would be a good idea if the copper was around. If something did go wrong he would then be in a position to intervene.

I told Tim that Stuart would be starting his stroll at 5.30pm and that he should be in the bar chatting to guests as Stuart walked through. I made Stuart up and at 5.25pm I sent him off to walk right around the hotel so that as many guests as possible would have the opportunity to see him.

He returned about 10 minutes later with a huge smile on his face and when I asked him why he was looking so pleased with himself he just grinned even more, said: "No reason," and when I pressed him further, just said: "I'll tell you when Tim comes back."

He then quickly changed into his normal clothes (unlike New Year when, you may recall, he sat around stark naked in his guise as "Mr. January") and was sitting comfortably in an armchair when, about ten minutes later, Tim wandered back to the room. On seeing Stuart his first words were: "When are you going to do it then? I've been waiting in the bar and the guests are starting to go back to their rooms." Stuart said nothing for a second or two, then said: "We've had a bit of a problem mate. You know that woman that walked through the bar about twenty minutes ago?" Tim looked a little confused. "You know," Stuart continued, "when you were leaning on the corner of the bar she smiled at you and you smiled back?" "Ye-ess" said Tim a little warily, still not really twigging what Stuart was getting at.. "Well mate. When you winked at me I thought my luck had changed."

I said earlier that Tim is probably the clumsiest person I know – he's always knocking things over or breaking something, but his most spectacular act of accidental destruction came early one Saturday morning when he was once again playing the detective (although at least on this occasion there was no doubt who the culprit was). He got out of bed and decided to have a stretch to wake himself up. If you're five feet nothing this is not such a bad idea; when you're as tall as Tim it's definitely a mistake. His arm smashed into the chandelier and there was a massive spark of electricity, a loud "bang" and the smell of burning flesh (Tim's arm). To make matters worse, when he went to the bathroom he discovered that he'd managed to fuse the lights – not just in his room but also in the entire bedroom block. In the middle of winter this, as you may imagine, made things difficult for those guests struggling to get ready for the day ahead in bathrooms without windows. Despite the pain from his bad burn (he still has the scar to this day), Tim bravely soldiered on at breakfast and was clearly thinking about the disconsolate guests, their rude awakening, the inconvenience of having no electricity and, in some cases, sopping wet hair they'd been unable to dry properly – although the fact that his exact words were: "Yes, it has made my investigation very difficult," probably didn't adequately convey his concern (or his guilt, come to that).

The copper's role, as I've suggested, is frequently a demanding one. One Weekend in Windermere the actors and guests had just settled down to afternoon tea and I was waiting for another character – having seen a piece of evidence go up in the incident room – to come storming up to me and accuse me of causing the death of his sister. The time for the argument came and went and nothing happened – there was no evidence to be seen. We had our tea and scones, played a couple of games and then the character with whom I should have rowed toppled over and died as we'd previously planned. The guests started calling for the inspector, who was singularly noticeable by his absence; a couple of the actors sloped off to see if they could find him, but he was nowhere to be seen. By now everyone was calling loudly for the police, at which point a young and very attractive guest walked into the room and nonchalantly said: "If you want him you'll have to shout a bit louder – he's out on the lake on my boyfriend's speedboat!". I'm surprised Wes didn't hear the thud of our collective jaws hitting the floor. Everything, at that moment, became crystal clear; no evidence had been put in the incident room because Chief Inspector Beard (aka Wes) of the Cumbrian police was playing boy racer on Lake Windermere!

Wes and I have laughed about this particular story ever since, but he's still at a loss to explain why he thought his police work was done by coffee after lunch!

Wes is not alone in having lost himself in the moment. Ron, a lovely chap who is now sadly investigating in that great police control room in the sky, used to really enjoy the themed games on a Weekend and more than once the actors discovered that the inspector had forgotten about the murders he was there to solve; he clearly had more important things to do, like removing his jacket, rolling up his sleeves and getting stuck into a miming game with the guests!

If this kind of behaviour on the part of the police is, thankfully, quite rare. I try to encourage the copper to keep a certain distance from the madness that may be going on around them but there are times when the inspector is drawn inexorably into the action.

A case in point was when I cast Dana as a police sergeant on a Weekend. This role can be a particularly difficult and thankless one for the actor concerned since the guests' focus is mainly on the other actors and the inspector – the sergeant usually stays in the background to offer help and assistance where necessary. Dana, however, had other ideas; she quickly decided she would develop her own inimitable version of "comedy sergeant", based around the idea her character was in love with her superior officer.

Dana gave a wonderfully potty performance as the sergeant and, egged-on by guests who were loving her own inimitable interpretation of romance, she invited the inspector onto the dance floor at the Saturday night disco. The inspector quite rightly initially rebuffed her frantic (some might say desperate) attempts to tempt him, but eventually the sight of her sensuous dance moves (and possibly 70-odd guests braying their encouragement) weakened his resolve. And so it was that the inspector found himself "grooving on down" with Dana – at the centre of a huge circle of guests, clapping and cheering as though they were witnessing the first dance of a newlywed bride and groom.

In the heat of the moment, with the crowd all cheering and the music setting his feet a-tapping I could, I suppose, forgive my inspector for momentarily losing some of his legendary reserve and deciding to show off his dance prowess with a quick foxtrot or tango in the interests of fostering police-community relations (although I'd hazard a guess and say these weren't the kind of relations Dana's character had in mind). I think, however, that the inspector suddenly deciding to remove his jacket and rub it sexily across the shoulders of his sergeant before swinging it and flinging it into the crowd as if he were John Travolta in full Saturday Night Fever mode was taking things a bit far.

If Dana's behaviour, in the context of the character she'd developed, caught the mood of a particular group of guests on a Weekend to create a bit of fun between sergeant and inspector, it's not always the case that the copper is allowed to share the joke. Guests (and occasionally actors) try to back the copper into a corner – usually over the absence of a full squad of police officers to cover what, in reality, would be a major crime scene. Although I try to maintain as much realism as I can (with the exception of allowing Dana or Marc to play comedy sergeant) it's clearly not possible – or even desirable – to have a murder squad of ten or so police officers, as happens in Prime Suspect or Taggart, on a Weekend.

Employing extra actors to stand around in uniform "guarding crime scenes" or sneak around investigating the rooms of the suspects would make the cost prohibitive and there is a point at which striving for a certain level of realism (such as not allowing guests near a body) would positively detract from the purpose and enjoyment of the event. Everyone, guests and actors alike, has to accept the general limitations of the Weekend and "suspend their disbelief" in order to imagine there are plain clothes officers all around the hotel and uniformed constables working flat out in a control room somewhere.

When guests jokingly try to put the copper on the spot by saying they haven't seen any other police officers around, the inspector is usually able to explain their apparent absence by reference to such officers working behind the scenes, patrolling the hotel grounds unseen and so forth.

When actors try to put the copper on the spot, however, it's often a lot harder for the inspector to respond. Paula, one of my actresses, was notorious for putting the inspector in impossible situations; as part of her character she would do things like demand to know why the police were doing such an inferior job, why her relatives were dropping down dead in the, obviously incompetent, presence of the police and, a particular favourite of hers, doubting that there were any other police officers in or around the hotel as the inspector had claimed. The coppers on the receiving end of one of Paula's tirades frequently wanted to strangle her for pushing her luck and on one plot she went a step too far. So we decided to teach her a lesson.

Paula was playing a character who had been raped in the past and when the (male) inspector and his male sergeant tried to interrogate her in front of the guests Paula's character refused point blank to say anything until they did what they were supposed to do – provide a female police officer to take her statement! No matter what they said or how hard they tried to persuade her to cooperate, she refused to budge.

Both coppers came (fuming) to my room and described what had just happened – how Paula had just sprung this on them and made them look small and foolish in front of the guests. They were both desperate to think of some way to repay the compliment. We thought about various possibilities and then Jerry (the sergeant) remembered that since we were in Ascot and Trudy lived close by it might be possible for her to drop by to help us out. I rang to see if she was busy that afternoon and when I explained the situation Trudy readily agreed it would be great fun and would certainly shut Paula up for once!

A little later we smuggled Trudy into the hotel without telling any of the other actors and over afternoon tea the inspector and his sergeant once again tried to convince Paula, in front of the guests, to cooperate with the investigation.

Paula being Paula wasn't having any of it and refused to talk to male officers about such a sensitive subject. "You know my demands," she said dismissively to the inspector "and if you had any respect at all for women you'd treat me with the respect I deserve." Since she was enjoying the situation she added, loudly for everyone to hear, that she would be lodging a complaint with the inspector's superior officer. What Paula didn't know, but the guests could clearly see, was that Trudy – the female officer Paula was so vehemently demanding – had quietly entered the room through a side door and was now standing, out of her sight, a little way behind her.

The inspector, pretending to be exasperated with Paula's lack of cooperation, looked at his sergeant and, with a sigh suddenly said, much to Paula's evident surprise and the guests great delight: "As you wish madam. Chief Inspector Lowe has been called to the hotel."

Paula, thinking he was bluffing, started to say something in response but was abruptly stopped by the copper with the words: "I know she'll be more than happy to talk to you – won't you Ma'am?"

Paula, realising something odd had happened, turned around to look in the direction of the inspector's question and, for once, was completely speechless as she was confronted by a very cross chief inspector who proceeded to inform her, in no uncertain terms, that both she and her officers had far better things to do on a serious murder investigation than play "bloody silly games" with a stroppy suspect!

Chapter 6

Hotels...

When I wrote in an earlier chapter about the logistical problems we've encountered over the years the one thing they all had in common is that they were in some way down to us. By this I mean that although it's difficult to cater for something like a gun failing to fire properly, I would always risk it for dramatic effect. The same can't, however, be said about another "unknown quantity" that has created numerous problems over the years – hotels and their staff.

Although we've frequently performed in many excellent establishments filled with friendly, helpful staff for whom nothing is too much trouble and who've bent over backwards to ensure everyone has felt welcome and valued, the reverse is also true; we've encountered hotels and their staff that make Fawlty Towers seem like a five star experience and, unfair as it my seem, it's the bad times that tend to stick longest in the mind.

At one corporate event, I had no control over the choice of venue. We sat through a very poor meal at the hotel, served by waiters who were uniformly slow, unpleasant and well past their sell-by date. The meat was very tough, barely edible and accompanied by soggy cabbage and stale bread. While the pudding was a quite passable plum crumble it was very dry because no custard or cream was offered. Although we all grumbled about the crumble to ourselves only one of our number plucked up the courage to very calmly and very politely ask "Attila the Hun" (as we had affectionately named our waitress) "if it was possible to have some cream, please?"

Attila's furious response was akin to the guest not merely asking for some cream but demanding that Attila milk the cow into the bargain; she whirled round, gave the guest the most withering look of distain I think I've ever seen and curtly said "No", adding as an afterthought as if to somehow justify her woeful behaviour "It will make you fat"!

While we were in another hotel on my list of shame a guest suddenly dashed into the room and screeched "I've found a body". This caused a certain amount of confusion and consternation among the actors since, as far as we were concerned, there was no body to be found at this particular time. Taking the guest's lead however, everyone followed them to the hotel terrace and there, slumped against a wall, was someone I didn't recognise and who was to all intents and purposes as dead as a dodo – he wasn't moving and, more worryingly, didn't look as though he was breathing. I was at the point of thinking we probably needed to call for an ambulance when the actor playing the police inspector suddenly appeared with the hotel manager in tow.

The copper immediately started to usher everyone back inside the hotel just as if there really had been a Murder Weekend "death". I realised that something was amiss, but the involvement of one of the actors also told me it wasn't something serious and once the guests had been safely cleared from the terrace the hotel manager asked if he could "have a word".

I followed him to his office where he explained that the "body on the terrace" was a member of the hotel staff who had drunk himself into unconsciousness following the unwelcome news that his girlfriend, one of the chambermaids, had just finished with him. He then pleaded with me to write another death into the plot to explain the sudden and unusual appearance (and equally rapid disappearance) of this "character". He was very concerned that the guests shouldn't know it was a member of his staff since such an unfortunate incident would reflect badly on the hotel. Since I had some sympathy with the predicament in which he found himself I did write the "dead waiter" into the plot and I think to this day the guests on that Weekend are none the wiser.

The "chicken in the basket" incident with the distraught Italian chambermaid wasn't the first and probably won't be the last instance of hotel staff getting the wrong end of the stick. We were, for example, at a hotel recently in the company of a BBC film crew who were recording for a documentary programme about Original Murder Weekends (the company I formed way back in 1981).

They were using two cameras on the Weekend, one to film all the action and the reactions of the guests and the other to follow me to capture everything that goes into a Weekend – the meetings and discussions, the preparation of bodies and the like – that is never seen by guests. On the Friday night I'd arranged with the director that, as the first body (Ros Hodges) staggered into the bar, both cameras would follow the reactions of the guests and the actors playing the grieving, shrieking relatives.

Once the police arrived and everyone – guests and actors alike – had been safely moved away to a nearby function room, the main camera crew would follow them to film the detective's interrogation while I (playing the part of the dead woman's sister) and Mark Braithwaite (her fictional husband) would stay with Ros and "top and tail" her as she got away. The smaller camera crew stayed with us and filmed me chatting to Ros, who looked very bloody and quite dead, while we waited for the "all clear" from another of the actors.

At this point a South African waiter (who the management later admitted hadn't been briefed about the Murder Weekend) came strolling into the bar from the kitchen. He stopped suddenly in his tracks and I could see he was a both a little confused and concerned by what he saw. I looked at him and said "everything's okay" and that we'd called for an ambulance – which was a bit naughty of me because I knew the crew were still filming and I wanted them to get the waiter's shocked reaction. After a few seconds he turned on his heels and shot back into the kitchen. Mark then rang for the nearby lift we were going to use to get Ros to her room and, as we got the nod that the guests were safely occupied, I whispered to Ros "Quick, go now" as the lift doors opened. The camera then filmed Mark and Ros as they escaped into the lift and although, as I've said before, I would have gone with them if this had been a "normal" Murder Weekend, I wanted to stay with the crew to check that they'd shot everything they wanted.

At the very moment the lift doors closed, however, who should suddenly reappear but the confused waiter and this time he'd brought help in the shape of the hotel manager. "There!" he exclaimed, pointing to where Ros had, just a few seconds ago been lying, "She's…" and he stopped in mid-flow as the camera crew recorded his disbelief as he pointed to an empty carpet!

Although I've never written a plot about a hotel and its staff I really think I should at some point because, in my extensive experience, there's an almost bottomless pit of rivalries and intrigues (not to mention affairs) bubbling away just beneath the surface – the most shocking of which was probably the time we nearly witnessed a real murder! We were at a hotel in the Lake District and everyone was sitting down to dinner. It was a lovely summer's evening, the sun was just going down and the restaurant gave us a spectacular view across the hotel gardens, a small wooden jetty and a lake. It had been a very hot day and since hotel kitchens are, at the best of times, sweltering places in which to work on this particular occasion it must have been hotter than normal. Dinner was very slow and the waiters were looking flustered as guests began to get restless about the lack of food. The murmurs of complaint were suddenly replaced, however, by the sound of jaws dropping as, through the restaurant window, we saw one of our waiters running through the garden as if he was being chased. As indeed he was – by the chef brandishing a very large kitchen knife!

As he reached the jetty at the end of the garden the poor waiter was clearly faced with a career (not to say life) defining moment – either to stop and try to placate the irate chef or jump into the lake. He chose the latter option. The chef, seemingly satisfied by this turn of events, then promptly turned on his heels and returned to his kitchen. Oddly enough, any complaints we had been harbouring about the food were quickly forgotten.

Chapter 7

...and guests

Although hotels and their staff failing to meet their guests' high standards are thankfully quite rare as far as Murder Weekends are concerned, there have been a couple of times when my actors have also failed to meet some guests' high expectations but only, it has to be said, when they're "in character" and playing it just a little bit too well.

A good case in point was demonstrated by my very dear friend Becky – the 'sugar babe' as I now call her. We were at The White Hart in Salisbury, a very pleasant and respectable hotel where lots of retired people come for a spot of lunch on a Saturday and Becky was very convincingly playing the part of a cheap and outrageously tarty prostitute. She was dressed in a garishly patterned blouse that was at least two sizes too small, under which she wore a Wonderbra that created a very voluptuous cleavage. Her leather miniskirt was the size of a small belt and her fishnet tights ended in a pair of white stiletto shoes with the highest heels I've ever seen – so high, in fact, Becky had great difficulty walking in them.

This ensemble had the effect of making her very long legs, accentuated by the extremely short skirt, look very odd indeed – an impression that was forcibly brought home to her during one particularly heated row with her "mother", played by Sheila (an actress who has the most wonderful way with words) .

Becky and Sheila were battling each other in the middle of the dance floor, surrounded by eighty "oohing", "aahing" and laughing guests.

As the argument heated up they both became increasingly angry – screaming and shouting at each other like a pair of fishwives – until Sheila suddenly stopped, took a step backwards, slowly looked Becky up and down and sneeringly said: "Who the hell do you think you are, standing there with your legs on the wrong way round?". This announcement immediately stopped the argument in its tracks and silence descended as eighty pairs of eyes suddenly turned their attention to Becky's legs – and yes, the way she was standing, with her feet splayed outwards, did make it appear they were almost at right angles to her legs (a legacy of years of arduous ballet training!).

At this point, everyone, including the supposedly livid Sheila, burst out laughing. Becky, however, was professional to the end and just became angrier, planting her hands firmly on her hips and giving Sheila as good as she got in return. This action, however, just had the unfortunate effect of making her legs seem even more twisted than before and it wasn't long before both she and Sheila had to give up any further pretence of argument as they both fled the room, to all intents because they were furious with each other but in reality because they couldn't stop themselves laughing at Sheila's ridiculous observation.

After lunch I came out of the restaurant and saw Peter Watt, one of my favourite managers, deep in conversation with a tweed-suited, cravat-wearing, colonel-in-chief type who was looking and sounding extremely cross. There was much sympathetic nodding of the head on Peter's part and much finger-waving on the part of the colonel. It transpires, Peter told me once the colonel and his good lady had left the hotel, that the man was complaining bitterly that his "gentle and innocent wife" was extremely upset that her lunch had been spoilt by being "exposed to the likes of this". When Peter had politely enquired "The likes of what?" the colonel pointed in Becky's direction and blustered "Openly allowing prostitutes to tout for business".

You might, at this point, be thinking that managing to convince the colonel she really was a prostitute was the height of Becky's achievement in this particular role (in reality she is a highly respectable and very well known tax lecturer!) but you would be wrong – her ultimate triumph was to come a couple of weeks later at a hotel in Surrey.

The England Rugby team were staying at the hotel on the Friday night as part of their preparation for an important International they were about to play against South Africa at Twickenham and on the Saturday morning, as they were checking out to leave for the ground I happened to be walking through reception with Becky. Even at 10 in the morning she was dressed in "her gear" and as we passed by I overheard Will Greenwood say to Jonny Wilkinson "I wouldn't touch her with yours, mate!".

Playing a prostitute is something many of the female actresses have done over the years, without necessarily attracting as much (unwanted) attention as Becky achieved – with possibly one exception. Ros Hodges, a very bubbly and fun actress, was a successful (and single) career woman who, a couple of years ago, decided the time was right to find the perfect man with whom to settle down. With her busy lifestyle it made sense to join an online dating agency and after a few introductions she found one man she was particularly keen on. They got to know something about each other through chatting online and exchanging emails and, after a few weeks decided they'd like to meet each other "in real life".

They chose a romantic location (Pizza Express) and were soon chatting easily over the garlic bread; he was as good looking, funny and intelligent as she'd hoped and everything seemed to be going perfectly. Things continued to go well between them until Ros heard a male voice loudly exclaim "Oh My God! It's the prostitute!" It wasn't until she saw the look on her date's face that she realised these words were aimed at her. As she turned her head the voice said "Hello Gemma."

By a strange quirk of fate Ros had been recognised by someone who'd just been on a Weekend on which she'd played the part of Gemma the prostitute. Ros, unfortunately, hadn't told her date about her hobby (acting on Murder Weekends rather than standing on street corners) and it took a lot of explaining to account for the fact that a good-looking stranger was calling her "Gemma" and announcing to all and sundry in a crowded restaurant that she was a prostitute. It would be nice to be able to end this story by saying that her explanation was accepted by her date and that they're now living happily together, but unfortunately the shock of hearing his date referred to in public as "a prostitute" seemed to put a dampener on their relationship and Ros never saw him again!

By an odd coincidence a similar thing happened to me in a West End theatre, of all places, where I was having a lovely time watching the wonderful musical The Producers. During the interval I was walking out to the foyer with my friend, following several hundred people going to the bar for a drink, when I felt a tap on my shoulder. As I turned around I heard a voice very loudly say: "So when did you get out of prison then?" With the eyes of a couple of hundred people suddenly on me I couldn't for the life of me place the face of my questioner. I'd twigged that he must be a Murder Weekend guest but his name simply escaped me – l laughed and knowing that everyone was listening (and for the sheer hell of it) simply replied: "Of course. They gave me an early parole when I admitted the murders." It seemed funny at the time but I really regretted saying it because during the second half I could feel several people warily watching me rather than the show...

On numerous occasions over the years we've staged Murder Weekends at hotels that are also hosting wedding receptions and although the two may at first sight seem incompatible bedfellows the two events usually pass off successfully with minimal disruption to either. This is not, however, always the case. Although I always remind the relevant hotel manager that the wedding guests need to be warned in advance that a Murder Weekend is taking place, there are inevitably some guests that either don't get the message or are unprepared for the kinds of things – such as gruesome, blood-splattered, bodies and ferocious arguments – that happen on a Weekend. Generally this only seems to cause amusement to the bride and groom; they often seem to enjoy the fact that we're sharing the hotel with them and I have, on more than one occasion, had requests for the bride to have an official photo taken with a body or warring relatives!

I try, of course, to make sure our event doesn't overshadow or disrupt the happy couple's big day and by liaising with the hotel's management, to discover things like the time of the bride's arrival, for example, it's not too difficult to ensure that anything we're planning to do doesn't create conflict because we're in the wrong place at the wrong time.

Speaking of which, on one Weekend the hotel manager managed to get his timings confused and informed me that the bride, groom and their guests would be arriving an hour later than was actually the case. This meant the blazing row we'd planned between our actors – a married couple who were, shall we say, experiencing some "personal difficulties" – should have been safely done and dusted long before the wedding reception began.

We were at a hotel that had a lovely old oak-panelled lounge and reception area with a sweeping oak staircase that led up to a first floor with a huge balcony overlooking the reception.

The plan was for Martin and Trudy, the "married couple" in question, to start their argument on the first floor (just outside their actual bedroom, as it happens) so that our guests, in the lounge below, would be able to hear something kicking off on the floor above; gradually, as the argument became fiercer, they could then either watch from below or follow the action from the staircase.

The row started quietly but quickly escalated into a massive bust-up, with Trudy's character getting more and more annoyed and agitated; the row culminated with Trudy very angrily telling Martin that "their marriage was over" and that she could no longer share a room with him. Leaving him standing by the balcony, looking very sheepish and contrite, she stormed off to their room, still shouting and screaming.

Two unrelated things then happened (which, if they had occurred five minutes apart, wouldn't really have mattered. The fact they occurred at exactly the same time was, however, a little unfortunate).

The first was the arrival of the bride and groom and the second was Trudy storming out of her bedroom carrying a huge pile of Martin's clothes, which she then proceeded, in a blind rage, to throw over the balcony, piece by piece; socks, trousers, shirts and underpants sailed over the balcony like confetti – to land at the feet of the startled happy couple. And if this wasn't enough (Trudy couldn't actually see the bride and groom from where she was standing on the balcony) she then applied the icing to the cake, as it were, by shouting "Marrying you was the worst decision of my life. You've given me twenty years of misery and now I'm free. Why anyone would want to get married is beyond me!". The guests, seeing and hearing all of this happen in front of the bride and groom, didn't know whether to laugh or keep a respectful silence – at least until the newlyweds thankfully seemed to see the funny side of it, at which point the place erupted in raucous laughter.

If this represented something of a rude introduction to married life another incident (that always makes me chuckle whenever I think of it) was an introduction of a different sort altogether – one that I hope the bride, groom and wedding guests also have a smile about whenever they flick through their wedding album. It happened just before the fancy dress party we always have on the Saturday night of a Weekend.

The party always has a theme in keeping with the plot and this particular plot was constructed around the idea of a very famous children's author (a character I'd very loosely based on JK Rowling) who had published five highly successful books featuring an Elf called Karma Miranda. The theme for the fancy dress was "My Favourite Children's Book, TV or Film".

I always try to encourage guests to make their own costumes, not only to save a bit of unnecessary cost (as costumes can be very expensive to hire) but also because I think it helps guests get into the swing of a Weekend if they take some time to think about and prepare their fancy dress. In addition a spot of "do-it-yourself" also means we get some fabulously creative costumes – the best of which are usually "simple but ingenious".

On this particular plot, for example, I remember a guest wore a plain white T-shirt on which they'd drawn two trees with a bottom appearing between the trunks. With a puff of wind drawn in the sky they became The Wind in the Willows. Another guest whose costume stuck in my mind wore a T-shirt on which they'd printed a map of the London Underground. Just above one particular station they'd pasted a very small picture of a naked body to create, you've probably guessed it, Paddington Bear.

Good as these were, the most memorable fancy dress on this particular Weekend was a guest kitted out as a perfect adult-sized replica of Enid Blyton's Noddy; from the little silver bell on his hat to the points of his bright red shoes he looked absolutely incredible. On first seeing him I was sure the costume must have been hired (it was that good) and I felt doubly sure when his wife, dressed – just as perfectly as her partner – as Big Ears appeared. I was pleasantly surprised to be proven wrong, however; "Big Ears" told me she worked as a seamstress and that she'd made both costumes in the weeks running up to the Weekend.

The fancy dress party normally starts at around 8pm and Noddy had come down from his room and was mingling with the other guests. He then noticed that a large group of wedding guests were assembling in the lounge, prior to making their way to the room where the wedding breakfast was being held.

As they filed into the function room the guests were met by the receiving line where they were welcomed, in turn, by the bride's mother and father, the groom's mother and father, the bride and groom, the best man…and Noddy. Feeling a little mischievous he'd crept into the breakfast room through a side door and silently joined the receiving line. The groom's family thought it was a joke on the part of the bride's family and her family thought the same; Noddy dutifully introduced himself ("Hello, I'm Noddy. So glad you could come") and shook hands with each of the wedding guests in turn. And no one from either family said a word; it was if it was the most normal thing in the world to be welcomed to a wedding breakfast by Noddy. What a hoot – and the pictures for the wedding album must, I think, have been something to treasure!

The fancy dress party is always one of the highlights of any Weekend, for both actors and guests; it's a chance, after all the dastardly deeds, rows and sleuthing for everyone to relax and, for most, to let their hair down on the dance floor.

I've been amazed at how creative our guests have been with their costumes and I only wish I'd taken photos of some of the best for posterity. Having said that, some actors can be very creative too; Shirley (she of the marbles and appalling memory), for example, always spent a lot of time and effort on her fancy dress and she invariably came up with the most wonderful costumes – a particular favourite of mine was the time she dressed as Mrs Overall from Acorn Antiques and spent the whole of Saturday night tottering about with her tray causing havoc amongst the guests.

On another Weekend, in Manchester and very near to Granada Studios, we happened to be sharing a hotel with the cast of Coronation Street who were holding a farewell party for Liz Macdonald. The fancy dress theme for the Weekend was the jobs people might perform in a zoo and Shirley decided to come as an elephant keeper. She plastered her hair to her scalp, applied grey make-up so her face looked very sallow and stuck a big bushy moustache to her upper lip.

She wore a big baggy jumper, baggy pants with braces, huge socks and enormous Wellington boots, topped off with a brown, heavily stained, overall. Her final accessory was a massive tin bucket filled with balls of "elephant dung" (she'd actually bought some bread rolls, painted them dark brown and put something on them (some sort of stink bomb!) that stunk to high heaven. Shirley, as always, looked amazing.

On her way down from her bedroom on the top floor to the fancy dress party on the ground floor, the lift stopped at the third floor and Paul O'Grady – dressed from head-to-toe as his marvellous creation Lily Savage and obviously on his way to the Coronation Street party – stepped in.

As the lift moved off he could, in the very confined space, clearly smell Shirley's elephant dung and he looked her up and down in disgust. As they reached the ground floor he turned sideways to look at her and said, in a broad Liverpudlian accent: "I used to work in social services, luv. Before I was in show business of course". Before Shirley could reply he added, just before the doors opened "and all I can say is I 'ope t'god they're waiting when these doors open 'cos no one in this hotel's safe if you've bin let out on yer own." For once Shirley was left speechless.

This brush with fame wasn't, of course, our first on Murder Weekends. Over 25 years we've welcomed a wide range of celebrities as guests, something that has invariably created great excitement – and occasional confusion – amongst the other guests on the Weekend.

A few times the regular guests have thought the celebrity is actually there to act on the Weekend and have tried to interrogate them to discover their dastardly life history. Sometimes the celebrity has made life difficult for themselves by playing along and then becoming hopelessly embroiled in the plot.

In the main, however, most make it clear that they are there to play "the Murder Weekend game" like everyone else. Having said this, it hasn't always been possible for the celebrity to blend into the background. One Weekend in Bournemouth I remember well was attended by the members of Spandau Ballet (a very good-looking 80's pop group that included the Kemp brothers and Tony Hadley). At meal times it was as though the other 80-odd guests and actors didn't exist; all the waitresses were buzzing around the "celebrity table" like bees around a honey pot!

I think, however, the "celebrity Weekend" that really stands out most in my mind was an event we did in 1987 after I received an unusual request. A hugely successful London theatrical agent wanted to celebrate his 40th birthday by inviting all his clients to a private Murder Weekend at a spa hotel in the Lake District.

The guest list, when I received a copy, read like a "Who's Who" of British drama and comedy; it included Beryl Reid, the actress known for her fantastic sense of humour, Barbara Windsor of Carry On and EastEnders fame, half the cast of Coronation Street, (including the late Lynne Perrie who played Ivy Tilsley), Gordon Kaye of 'Allo 'Allo! fame and many, many more – the guests were virtually all famous actors and we knew we would have our work cut out to perform our roles to the best of our ability; we all felt our every move and gesture would be critically analysed.

We needn't have worried too much, however, because the guests really enjoyed the Weekend, especially the deaths and the rows – although the amount of alcohol consumed each night certainly took its toll on their sleuthing skills.

The most striking thing about the whole Weekend, however, was that although we were all prepared, as actors, to be upstaged by our famous (and sometimes hugely witty) guests we weren't really prepared for the fact that, due to the underlying rivalries and hostilities between some of the guests, we would be upstaged on the Saturday night by drunken rows that certainly weren't in my script!

Thankfully, by Sunday morning all was forgiven and forgotten and the Weekend was deemed a great success by guests and actors alike – even if our nerves were left a little jangled.

Chapter 8

...and ghostly encounters

Sheila and Grant, my great friends and co-conspirators in the "Hurricane Hancocks" story, are mother and son in real life and were acting together on a Weekend – but, stupidly as it turned out, I had cast them against life and Grant became the son of another actress (Shirley).

Sheila died and was safely tucked up in her room enjoying her evening meal and watching her favourite TV programme at the time Shirley was found horribly stabbed in her room that was just a short distance along the corridor from Sheila's. When Grant was told his mother had been murdered he immediately charged along the corridor towards Shirley's room and, as he approached the room, followed by 70-odd guests, he started to loudly scream for his mother. Sheila, nicely relaxed in her room, suddenly heard her son's voice crying "Mum, mum!" and, without thinking, rushed to the door. As she opened it she came face-to-face with Grant and it's questionable who was the most surprised – Sheila, who suddenly realised her terrible mistake; Grant who wasn't expecting to see his real mother or the guests who'd seen her die several hours before her "miraculous resurrection".

Although there was no earthly way to explain Sheila's dramatic reappearance, word soon got around (encouraged, it has to be said, by a few choice comments planted by different actors) that the hotel was haunted which, judging from a few of the experiences we've had at different hotels, it might well have been (although thankfully Sheila is,

I'm happy to report, still very much in the land of the living).

The majority of the hotels where we perform are old and very atmospheric – a deliberate choice on my part because I think Murder Weekends are at their most effective when the location is well-suited to their general theme. They often have lots of oak panelling everywhere and, more often than not, very creaky floorboards. I've lost count of the times, particularly when going back to their rooms very late at night when there's no one around, actors have been spooked by noises, feelings and "unusually cold" areas in corridors. There have also been a couple of times when I've had very strange and, looking back, actually quite scary "ghostly encounters".

One was at The Talbot in Oundle, a hotel built around a central staircase that originally came from Fotheringay Castle, the prison where Mary Queen of Scots was executed. The local talk was that Mary walked up and down the stairs, particularly near the day (February 8th) she was executed in 1587.

Night managers and other hotel staff had often told me how, especially late at night, they had seen, heard and felt strange things. Simon, one of my actors, wasn't someone easily scared and he was always very sceptical of these stories until very late one night he offered to deliver cluesheets to the guests. As he was making his way up the staircase he felt a sudden and extreme change in temperature, like a very cold gust of wind settling around him, and he was immediately aware of some kind of presence standing on the stairs directly behind him – he didn't wait to find out what it was; this big, burly, rugby-playing toughie was reduced to rubble – and never offered to deliver cluesheets in the middle of the night again.

Sheila, Grant and I were always interested in ghosts and, being both intrigued and adventurous, we decided to book into The Talbot on the anniversary of Mary's execution; the plan was for an all-night vigil in the room that now occupied the same position at the top of the stairs as her original room at the castle. We arrived with supplies of food and (non-alcoholic) drink and settled down together for what we'd hoped would be a night of ghost watching – Sheila and Grant in the double bed and me in an armchair facing them.

To pass the time we chatted away about the important things in life

– like fashion, food and fun – until we all became a little tired around three in the morning. It was then I realised the room had become strangely cold and, as I was nattering away to Sheila and Grant, I realised they weren't looking at me and had both gone very quiet. Both seemed to be staring at a point about a foot above my head. I said "What is it?" and they both whispered they could see a smoky, balloon-shaped mass just behind me, about five feet off the ground. This smoky shape moved around the room, but kept coming back to settle just behind my left shoulder. This went on for about half an hour and it was seriously scary stuff. Having spooked ourselves silly, we decided enough was enough – as soon as it was light we decided it was time to head off (sorry!) home for a good day's sleep!

The second happened at the Hotel de la Bere in Cheltenham, part of which dates from the 16th century; the turret at the top, where I used to stay (note the past tense!), is the oldest part of the building – a huge room with a very old fireplace. The room was perfect for our meetings because of its size.

As I lay in bed each night I often imagined all the people in their fine costumes who must have gathered in what I was sure was the living room of the original building. Although I had been going there for years, I never slept in that room again after one particular night. I had just switched off the light and was snuggling under the bedclothes when I smelt the most horribly bad breath and then a very deep, very loud and very malevolent male voice shouted in my ear: "Get the fuck out of here!" I was, as you can imagine, in a place somewhere beyond scared; my heart was jumping out of my chest and I knew I had to get away, so I just ran to the nearest actor's room, banged frantically on the door and sat in a chair jibbering as I tried to explain about "the presence" in my room.

Keith, the actor in question, must have been pretty convinced because he refused to swap rooms with me (what a gentleman!) and since there was no way I was going back to my own room he generously let me sleep in the other twin bed in his room. Not that I did much sleeping that night – I couldn't get that terrible voice out of my head and it still makes me shudder whenever I recall it.

Although each of these "ghostly encounters" was quite strange and spooky in different ways, my most memorable encounter with the "spirit world" is one that happened a lot closer to home, involving my deceased father, Norman.

Towards the end of Mum's life she seemed convinced that the spirit of my Dad was around in our house. She occasionally smelled pipe smoke in the room (as I did on a few occasions) and a couple of years before Mum died a clairvoyant told me that Dad was with my uncle Tommy and that they often went to the cottage in Wales where we had spent many happy holidays together as a family. Dad told the clairvoyant that he was often with Mum and that though he wouldn't be with her "in spirit" for a while, when it was "her time" he would be there ready for her. Although it seemed to comfort Mum, I took all of this with a healthy pinch of salt. I was pretty sceptical about ghosts and clairvoyants... until the Murder Weekend when I met Norman!

Every April 27th (the anniversary of Dad's death) Anthony Hill – an old family friend whose birthday happened to be on the same date – invariably sent Mum a beautiful bouquet of flowers. Anthony was originally a friend of my brother's. He'd lost his own father and was someone to whom Dad had almost been a surrogate father. Caught up with business, I would always forget the anniversary and would ring Mum from wherever I happened to be working and she would invaribly say: "Anthony has sent some lovely flowers..." and – clang! – I knew I'd forgotten again...

One year I was hosting Weekend at the Bear Hotel in Rodborough, near Stroud, and like so many times before I rang Mum that evening to be told she'd received a lovely bouquet from Anthony. As usual, I was guilt-ridden that the pressure of work had once again let the anniversary slip from my mind. That night the disco played a record from 1970, one that I'd seldom heard – "Spirit In The Sky" by Norman Greenbaum. This was the very same record I had bought the day Dad had died (it was number one in the charts that week). Hearing it once again made me think "Heck. Now Dad's telling me off for my forgetfulness" and I silently vowed to buy something special for Mum, both to comfort her and to make up for all the times I had been so tardy.

I was thinking about this as I walked downstairs to the hotel reception where I ended up staring at a large glass case that must have held at least 50 teddy bears, each of which was hand-made, gorgeous and beautifully dressed. A very small bear at the back of the case caught my eye. He was a bit different to the rest beacuse he didn't have any clothes, just a lovely rounded tummy and the cutest little face. He just stood out and I found myself thinking that, knowing my luck, he will probably be the most expensive of all the bears on show as he's so beautifully made.

I spoke to the recptionist and she unlocked the case and took out the lovely bear. He had a little silk rope around his arm and attached to it was a message that read: "Hello, my name is Norman. I am all alone and need a loving home".

Well, if that wasn't Dad telling Mum that he was around and with her, I don't know what was. I just knew I had to buy the beautiful bear then and there and Mum had 'Norman' with her until the day she died. I lovingly put him in her coffin, hoping that very soon she would be with the real Norman forever.

Although I'm sometimes accused, by actors, of having an overactive imagination as far as all things spectral are concerned, it's not just me who's been scared stiff by ghostly goings on. One of my regular guests, Emma Conway, had an encounter in her room at Whately Hall in Banbury where, local rumour has it, there are a few ghosts that supposedly haunt the hotel.

Emma never imagined, however, that she would wake up in the middle of the night to find one sitting on the end of her bed – an elderly, grey-haired woman dressed in a Victorian nightgown. Emma came down to breakfast the next morning looking very grey herself, having been too scared to sleep a wink following her unwanted encounter. You could tell how badly it affected her because although she's a keen sleuth who always gets the correct solution, she didn't on this particular Weekend; as she said to me afterwards: "I just couldn't think straight after what happened that night."

Chapter 9

Guess who's coming to dinner?

Murder Weekends wouldn't exist without guests and the vast majority are, as I hope I've made clear throughout this book, genuinely nice fun-loving people.

They are on the Weekend to participate in what is, when all's said and done, the unique experience of being an integral part of a traditional British whodunnit.

In this respect, the behaviour of the vast majority of guests is as you would expect; they get into the swing of things, play the game to the best of their ability and generally contribute to the fun atmosphere – whether or not they leave the Weekend with a trophy, certificate of merit or just the nagging feeling that if they'd only made the connection between a couple of clues they would have solved the case!

Some guests, however, whether by design or accident, very occasionally leave the actors scratching their collective heads in amazement – and there have been some "memorable guest moments" (sometimes for all the wrong reasons and sometimes for all the right reasons – I'll leave it to your judgement to decide which) that have stuck in my mind. The first of these involved the appearance, on one of the very early Weekends, of Baron Freddie Von Liechtenstein.

By way of background to this story I should add that, right from the start, I've always had journalists contacting me to ask to come on Weekends; my attitude has always been "the more publicity the better" and have always said "yes" if I thought the article they were going to write was likely to bring in more business. Baron Freddie phoned my office one day and explained that he was a British journalist, with foreign relatives (hence his title), writing for the American Press Association. The article he'd like to write about Murder Weekends would be syndicated around the States. I asked him to drop me a line, which he duly did on letterheaded paper, and I invited him to a Weekend at the Prince of Wales hotel in Southport. I made sure he had an excellent room and was well looked after.

As soon as he arrived he came to meet me and my first impressions were of a charming, well dressed and very polite gentleman. We talked a bit about the Weekend and, over the next couple of days, he entered into the spirit of things whole-heartedly and appeared to be having a wonderful time. Everything about the Weekend was going fine until around 12.30am on the Sunday when I took a phone call in my room from Simon, a very perplexed deputy manager, who asked if it was possible to have a quick chat to try to sort out a problem that had arisen.

The problem he explained to me a couple of minutes later, was that two of the guests – an American lady and her daughter – were very upset and he wanted me to put their minds at rest. "Is Freddie Von Liechtenstein," he wanted to know, "a bona fide journalist?". I assured him that he was and explained how he was writing for a syndicate of newspapers in the US – I had letterheads and a business card as proof of his identity. Simon was reassured, but the two American ladies certainly weren't. Ten minutes later I got another phone call from Simon: would I come down to the guests' suite? If it would help ease their fears. I was happy to – and when I got there I found two very hysterical ladies.

Judging by their luggage, clothes and jewellery they were clearly very wealthy and, to cut a long story short the older lady explained, amidst much sobbing and heaving of breasts, that they were taking a long vacation in Europe from their family home in Texas. The reason they were both so upset, she said, was that the man calling himself "Baron Freddie Von Liechtenstein" was not a journalist. The lady was convinced he was stalking them with a view to kidnapping her daughter for a huge ransom.

To say I was a little taken aback is an understatement (incredulous is probably closer to the mark) and I tried to reassure the woman and her daughter that, as far as I was concerned, the Baron was who he said he was and that I was sure they would come to no harm. As we left them in their room and walked along the corridor I said to Simon I thought these ladies had got a little carried away and, possibly caught up in the realism of the acting and plot, had probably overreacted a little. We both agreed there was no need to trouble Freddie at this point, given he was still with the other guests poring over the evidence in the incident room.

If I thought this was the end of the matter I was sadly mistaken; the mother was neither calmed nor reassured by our little talk and demanded that the hotel manager keep guard outside her door throughout the night! The eventual upshot of this was that Simon and I took it in turns to "stand guard" in the corridor outside the bedroom. On my shift I pushed an armchair against the door and dozed fitfully throughout the night while the American lady and her daughter slept on the floor on the other side of the door, presumably on the basis that if "Baron Freddie" managed to force his way past the guard he would be unable to push his way into the room to grab anyone! This, I know, sounds totally bizarre but it is, nonetheless, absolutely true.

The following morning the two American guests checked out of the hotel to catch the first available train to London. They insisted on two conditions for their leaving; firstly, the bleary-eyed hotel manager, who'd stayed up half the night helping to "guard" the two women, had to personally escort them to the station and onto a train. Secondly, I had to stay at the hotel (which, of course, I was going to do anyway because we had to complete the Weekend with the denouement) and ensure that Baron Freddie Von Liechtenstein didn't leave my sight until their train was safely on route to London! I was, I must admit, faintly relieved once the lady and her daughter had left and the Weekend ended. Aside from the fact I thought their behaviour a little strange (paranoid even) I thought no more about it – until a month later when I happened to flick through a Sunday paper and there, staring out from the page at me, was a face I knew well – Baron Freddie Von Liechtenstein!

The Baron, it turns out, had been arrested at the Cowes Regatta on the Isle of Wight. Only this time he wasn't a Baron, but rather a Lord – "Lord Frederick Dalfoyle" to be precise – who, claiming to be a "close friend" of Prince Philip, had managed to find his way, uninvited and under false pretences, into a number of the glitzy and prestigious functions and balls held during Cowes Week. You can probably imagine the "clunk" as my chin hit the floor. And my flush of embarrassment. Unlike the stewards at Cowes I had been completely taken in!

Although I can't remember "Baron Freddie's" real name (I have it in an article somewhere among the thousands of press cuttings I've amassed over the years) it was something very innocuous like "John Brown" and I learned form the newspaper story that he'd been passing himself off as different members of the aristocracy for years. I expect he's out of prison (for now at least) and I sometimes wonder if the two American ladies ever recovered!

If the behaviour of John (or Freddie or whatever name and title he may currently be using) turned out to be, as far as Murder Weekends were concerned, relatively harmless (all he actually did was con a free Weekend from me), there have been times – thankfully rare – when guest behaviour has been altogether more worrying. Just such a time came on a Weekend when I was awakened, in the middle of the night, by the insistent ringing of my bedside telephone. It was the night manager and, if I was barely conscious as I picked up the phone, I was certainly wide awake by the time he'd finished asking if it "was part of the plot that he was to ring for the police and an ambulance?". Incredulous, I thought "No it bloody well isn't!" (or words to that effect) before coming completely to my senses and asking the obvious question: "Why. What's happened?"

As we were speaking there was apparently a terrible row going on in one of the bedrooms; a woman was screaming and there were the sounds of furniture being smashed. Guests near the room had been awoken by the commotion and had called the night manager to complain. I said I'd be right down and that he should definitely call for the police and an ambulance. I threw some clothes on and met him outside the offending room; we banged loudly on the door and it was eventually opened by a very drunk Murder Weekend guest.

The room was in chaos and sitting on the floor in a corner amongst the debris was the guest's wife, also clearly very drunk and nursing a bloody lip. We calmed things down as best we could until the police arrived, whereupon the male guest was promptly arrested. With him out of the way I stayed with the woman for a little while until I was sure she was going to be okay and then I left her to sleep things off.

I later managed to piece together what had happened. After the actors had gone to bed around midnight, a number of guests had stayed drinking in the bar until one of their group, the arrested husband, decided it was time he and his wife went to bed; he was angry at the thought his wife had been flirting with another guest. She left under protest and, once they'd reached their room, the husband in his drunken state had crashed, fully clothed, into bed and fallen fast asleep.

Unfortunately for all concerned he didn't stay asleep for long. He awoke to find his wife wasn't in bed with him. In fact, as he quickly discovered, she wasn't in the room at all. This was because as soon as he'd fallen asleep she decided it would be a good idea to creep back downstairs to continue the party without him. Suspecting what his wife had done the guest stormed downstairs to the bar in, by all accounts, a blind rage. He grabbed his wife roughly and virtually dragged her upstairs, where a heated, very nasty and violent row ensued. After all the trouble it seems that my sympathies with the woman had been misplaced – it was her, not the husband, who'd smashed the furniture in a drunken rage and, in the process, managed to give herself the bloody lip!

Another memorable Weekend, for a rather different reason, took place at a hotel in the presence of 60-odd excited guests. In this particular instance a real life situation got out of hand, so much so that the guests were sure it was all part of the plot much to our embarrassment and, eventually, amusement.

A gentleman in his early 60's (I'll call him "Derek" to protect both his dignity and anonymity) arrived on the Weekend with a very young – and very camp – man called Simon in tow. Before and over dinner on the Friday evening Simon, clearly to Derek's discomfort and annoyance, became progressively more drunk, increasingly flamboyant and decidedly outrageous in his behaviour. Following dinner we'd arranged a trivia quiz for the guests and after they'd all mingled quite happily, trying to answer as many of the questions as they could, Marc Steatham (who was playing the fictional host for the Weekend) got them all together in the restaurant for the answers.

As Marc read each question to the guests before giving them the answer Simon, who by this stage seemed so drunk the actors were surprised he even knew where he was, decided to shout out the wrong answer. After Marc gave the correct answer Simon then insisted on making some comment or other about it – his slurred speech invariably peppered and punctuated with a few choice and very colourful swear words. The other guests were, to be charitable, bemused by this behaviour – at first they thought it amusing but it rapidly became clear Simon was a very irritating individual who didn't know when to keep quiet.

The actors tried their best to (subtly) quieten him down, but to no avail. Deciding to make the best of an embarrassing situation Marc rattled through the answers as quickly as he could and, once he'd finished, had a word with the hotel manager who asked Simon if he would leave the room – which he did under protest, but only to land up in the bar. After the game Derek went upstairs to bed, leaving Simon chatting animatedly, which lead the other guests to think he was one of my actors. This is one of my pet hates because I think my plots are difficult enough without someone trying to muddy the waters unfairly. It also infuriates me that whenever there is someone on a Weekend who is "a little odd" – guests automatically assume it's one of my actors!

Be that as it may, a large group of guests were gathered around Simon, pens and notebooks at the ready, asking the most outrageous questions possible about things like his sexuality, his partner and so forth – and he was giving them equally outrageous answers (which, looking back on it, I think were actually honest ones). Simon was clearly enjoying being the centre of attention and despite the best efforts of various actors to convince the guests that he wasn't actually known to any of them, many told me after the Weekend they were totally convinced he was integral to the plot. After further heavy drinking Simon's behaviour had become so embarrassing that Grant – the actor responsible for actually running the Weekend – decided to go to Derek's room to "have a quiet word" and politely, but firmly, ask him if he could exercise some control over his friend. A few minutes after Grant's request Simon left the bar to go to Derek's room.

A little later – at around 11.30pm – Derek came downstairs in his expensive "Derek Rose" striped pyjamas, walked purposefully into the reception and paid Simon's bill. He then asked that a taxi be ordered "for his friend". At this point Simon suddenly came crashing down the stairs, suitcase in hand and, according to the actors present, "with a face like thunder". He was evidently very, very angry and proceeded to take his revenge on Derek by announcing, at the top of his voice so everyone could hear, that he "was only there because he was a rent boy" and that Derek "had paid for him to come with him to the hotel for sex".

Derek looked mortified. Simon looked victorious and the guests were besides themselves with excitement because they had been so sure this was part of the plot and their first instincts had been correct – they even followed Simon outside as he got into the taxi, firing questions at him until, with a final "Fuck the lot of you", he disappeared into the distance, thankfully never to return. Derek, at this point, returned to his room and we all felt so sorry for him, particularly as the guests were now hounding him with all kinds of questions. It took a lot of effort and persuasion on the part of the actors to finally convince the guests that what had just happened was, in fact, real – and it was nice that, when Derek very bravely arrived for breakfast the following morning, all the other guests were very pleasant to him and never once mentioned the unsavoury incident of the previous night. To his great credit Derek stayed and played the game, thoroughly enjoying the rest of the Weekend. That evening he came to the fancy dress party as a cowboy and told everyone who asked that, "last night he had come with someone else, but now that he'd gone" he was "The Lone Ranger".

Although the majority of guests, unlike the foul-mouthed Simon, behave impeccably on a Weekend, there are some who take their sleuthing to ridiculous lengths. On one Weekend, for example, three guests happened to be passing the hotel housekeeper's office and, seeing the door was open and no one around, went in and stole three staff uniforms and the master pass key to all the rooms.

Suitably attired they then let themselves into an actor's room and proceeded to search for "evidence". We think they found a set of the notes we use to help us plan various bits of action on a Weekend, but whether they couldn't make sense of them or – as I like to think – they felt a bit guilty about what they'd done and decided not to use them as a way of solving the crime they ended up getting their solution hopelessly wrong; which maybe just goes to show that crime doesn't pay after all.

If this sort of behaviour is a little naughty (and ultimately self-defeating), at least it wasn't dangerous – unlike the activities of two guests whose sleuthing instincts obviously got the better of them. Their room was on the third floor of the hotel and just happened to be next door to one of the actors. From their room they heard two actors talking and were convinced that, because on the Weekend these two actors obviously hated each other, they had stumbled across a secret affair that would somehow help them solve the crime. In this situation you'd think that any reasonable person would do something like wait outside the door for the actors to appear or maybe knock on the door to see what, if anything, was happening. But not this couple of dedicated (and, if the truth be told, foolhardy and slightly crazy) sleuths; they had a different idea. They decided to climb out of their bedroom window, crawl along a very thin ledge that connected the two rooms and peek through the window so they could witness, first hand, the couple's supposed "indiscretion" in person.

This was, of course, complete and utter madness; they could easily have been killed but it just goes to show that sometimes guests on a Weekend take complete leave of their senses and become a bit like adults behaving as children, which reminds me of the guest who spent the entire Weekend playing the game like mad, chasing around corridors, following suspects and hiding round corners in the hope of "overhearing something important".

When the Weekend was over and I was laughing with her about her behaviour and how much she'd obviously enjoyed herself her response was: "Thank heavens I didn't bring my children with me this weekend – they would have been so ashamed of me!"

Speaking of overzealous guests, at a Weekend in Farnham some of them got a great deal more than they had bargained for as they chased frantically around the hotel trying to find a murder victim.

I'd arranged the body in a small room at the top of the stairs, the idea being that guests would race up the stairs and see the open door to the room as they turned left into a long corridor. As soon as the body was ready I let out a blood-curdling scream and ducked into the ladies' toilets that were just to the right of the stairs.

Sure enough, I heard a large group clump up the stairs but, once at the top they didn't run left as I'd planned; instead they ran straight ahead along the bedroom corridor. This wasn't a problem, I reasoned, since they would eventually realise their mistake and double back down the corridor to find the body.

I was a bit confused, however, when from my hiding place I heard a scream, loud shrieking and then laughter. I could hear a buzz of excitement coming from the guests somewhere down the corridor and there was a general hubbub going on that intrigued me since I couldn't imagine what was going on. I opened the toilet door and looked down the corridor but couldn't see anyone, so I quickly dashed back to the room where the body was lying to see if it had been found. It hadn't. At this point I decided I'd follow the noise coming from the other end of the corridor and eventually walked slap-bang into a complete bottle-neck – some guests were struggling to get into a bedroom while others were struggling to get out. The situation wasn't helped by the fact that those leaving were almost crying with laughter. It wasn't long before I learned what had happened from someone who'd managed to get in and out of the bedroom.

Having heard my scream the first guests had rushed to the top of the stairs and charged along the corridor until they arrived at a bedroom door propped open with a shoe. They assumed that a body was in the room and just barrelled their way inside. As it turned out they were right – there was a body in the room, just not the "dead body" they were expecting to find. The body in question belonged to a very large (we're talking at least 25 stone) middle-aged gentleman who was lying on his bed watching television. The fact he happened to be stark naked is, I suppose, neither here nor there – it was a very hot night and he'd obviously removed his clothes and propped the door open to try to keep cool.

As those at the head of the crowd burst into the room it was apparently difficult to judge who was more surprised – the large group of guests, cameras at the ready, expecting to find a murder scene or the middle-aged man enjoying what he thought was a relaxing evening in front of the television.

The fact he managed to loudly shout "What the hell do you think you're doing?" did, however, stop the guests dead in their tracks as they realised they were definitely in the wrong place at the wrong time. There must have been 30 or 40 guests crammed into the small bedroom and as they, en masse, turned to leave, they met the remaining 40-odd guests trying to get into the room to see what all the fuss was all about. Chaos ensued as those inside couldn't get out because those outside thought they needed to get in.

Thinking on my feet I shouted "Oh my god. There's a dead body in the room back here," whereupon, almost as one, the guests turned to follow me – allowing those struggling to leave the room to escape from what must have been a highly embarrassing situation for all involved.

My final memory of overzealous guests involves a prank, carried out to great effect, obviously conceived after an evening that involved perhaps just a little too much alcohol. Late on Saturday night the copper came to my room in a mild panic. Someone had stolen the masking tape he used to attach clues to the boards in the incident room and this meant he couldn't put up the final pieces of evidence. He was in a right state about it until I managed to find another roll of tape that sent him happily on his way. I know how this must sound; a copper on the verge of solving one of the most complicated cases in British legal history hadn't got a clue who had nicked his roll of masking tape – but that's Murder Weekends for you!

To be fair to him, the case was cracked the next morning as we all came down to breakfast and couldn't believe what we were seeing – the masking tape had been used to great effect to create the type of "murder scene body outlines" they always show on TV cop shows. Except the imaginative culprit in this case didn't do things by halves. A trail from the reception area to the restaurant led from the outline of a body to that of another body, then the outline of a frog that was followed by a dog which, in turn, led to the outline of a dinosaur and finally, the piece de resistance, the outline of a couple making love! Sean Smith – the masking-tape thief – can't have had much sleep that night, but he got a massive round of applause for his efforts when he arrived for breakfast the next morning.

While some of our guests, as I've suggested, may behave a little outrageously at times when they temporarily get carried away by the excitement of the moment, there have been other times when the behaviour of guests not on the Weekend has been both unexpected and hugely entertaining. We were at the White Hart in Salisbury, for example, on the same weekend as a very glamorous wedding party – to give you some idea it was the type of wedding reception where they have a Scottish piper in attendance and the groom and ushers are dressed in kilts and velvet jackets. The bride looked gorgeous and the bridesmaids, looking both sweet and innocent, were beautifully made up in baby pink dresses. On the Saturday night I was leading the dancing at the fancy dress disco and we were having a fantastic time; the guests had done a great job of creating costumes based around their favourite film – we had everything from Titanic (a man dressed as an iceberg and his wife made-up as the ship) to the Tin Man from the The Wizard of Oz – an exotic ensemble that involved the creative use of yards of tin foil!

The wedding party were in another large room next door to ours and, from the sound of it, were having an equally good time. I was about to start everyone dancing to the Village People's "YMCA" (always a favourite on Murder Weekends) when Linda White, who was playing a quiet and very simple character, sidled up to me and whispered "You've got to come with me".

Since we were due another murder around this time I immediately thought this was her way of saying she'd found the body and started to follow her out of the room. Half the guests then left the dance floor to follow us, sure that something was about to happen. Well it was, but not in the way they or I could have imagined in our wildest dreams.

As I followed Linda she led us in an odd direction; we'd agreed at our meeting where the body was to drop and it certainly wasn't in the ladies' toilet! Linda, very gently, pushed the toilet door open and, putting her finger to her lips in a "shushing" motion, beckoned us with her other hand to follow.

One by one we crept into the toilet, none of us knowing why we were doing so, nor why we were all being as quiet as church mice, until there was quite a crowd in the small space. Apart from us the toilet was empty, but the door to one of the cubicles was shut and we all – men and women alike – were amazed to hear the loud and very physical sounds of passionate love-making coming from the cubicle.

The guests, I'm sure, thought this was part of the plot but Linda and I knew it certainly wasn't. We looked at each other and how we stopped ourselves from giggling I'll never know. After a couple of minutes of much heavy breathing, puffing and panting the noises stopped and I think we must have held our collective breath as we heard the lock being pulled back.

The door opened and out stepped the couple. The look on their faces was priceless – going in an instant from one of grinning satisfaction to absolute horror – as they stepped out to find a huge group of strangers had not only witnessed their clandestine association but then proceeded to break out into spontaneous applause and ribald cheering. It was at this point that the guests realised they'd never seen the couple before – it wasn't actors they were applauding, but complete strangers!

By the time they realised their mistake the "other happy couple" had managed to push their way out of the room and had disappeared into the night.

Chapter 10

Slips of the tongue (right time, wrong place)

As actors performing 'live we're always aware of the danger of saying the "wrong thing" at the "wrong time" to guests and although this normally means having to be careful about how much information we reveal at different times (the way the plots are put together means we're much more likely to admit to something on the Saturday night than we are on the Friday evening) there are times when "saying the wrong thing" is less a matter of revealing something we shouldn't and more a case of saying something we wished we hadn't.

Many is the time, particularly after a furious row or during a bout of ferocious questioning from guests, when I've found myself thinking "Did I really mean to say that?". Getting tongue-tied for example, is an occupational hazard. My personal favourite was the time I managed, during a row with my "husband", to become so angry and frustrated that I blurted out "You've just become so, so. Twitter and Bisted!"

Spoonerisms in the heat of the moment are one thing but Sheila is, without a shadow of a doubt, the expert as far as malapropisms are concerned. Some of the things she's come out with over the years have been so perfectly inappropriate that I've sometimes wondered whether she does it intentionally to corpse the actors. But on the other hand, knowing Sheila as well as I do, I suspect they really were just genuine mistakes, as the next story probably illustrates.

Sheila was playing a grieving mother on the "memorial" Weekend for her "gay son Josh". He had been a successful advertising magnate who's useless live-in lover (played by one of my actors, Chris) had been sponging off him for years. During a very heated discussion about Josh and his will, Sheila was outraged to discover that her "wonderful son" had left the majority of his estate to his lover and, in her blind fury at this unacceptable state of affairs, she accused Chris of exploiting her son's affections and publicly castigated him for "bleeding her son dry". Or, at least, that's what she meant to say. What actually came out of her mouth was the immortal phrase, "Everyone knows you've been sucking him dry for years".

This was one of those moments when everyone did a double-take, unsure about whether she had really meant to say exactly what she'd just said. The consensus of opinion, however, quickly decided that that, whatever the reality, Shelia's double-entendre was actually very funny and everyone, apart from Sheila who kept a perfectly straight face, fell about laughing as the row quickly disintegrated into farce. When she came to my room later Sheila insisted she didn't know why everyone – including Chris – had found her "justifiable accusation" so funny and she's such a great actress that I still don't know whether she was being completely innocent or just being wickedly rude while playing her part to the full!

Another of Sheila's moments came as all the actors and guests were gathered in the incident room late one Saturday night when all the various plot strands were starting to unravel as the police placed more and more information on the evidence boards. This particular plot was extremely complicated and involved a wide variety of different characters. When one of the guests casually asked Sheila who "Samantha" was she replied, in her inimitable way, "Oh she's just a bar floozy". From somewhere to the back of the room we immediately heard a very dejected male voice exclaim "Oh for goodness sake! Not another damn character!". This was followed by a rather more exasperated plea: "Who the bloody hell is Aba Flusi?".

Misunderstandings, as you're probably coming to realise, are an occupational hazard for Murder Weekend actors – although there are times when I wonder whether it's less a case of some actors "misunderstanding" and more a case of them not listening to a word I say! On one Weekend, for example, I bloodied an actor in preparation for his death and left him with Judy Ivor as I went off to run a game. The idea was that Judy would get him into position during the game when everyone was occupied and then, twenty or so minutes later, she would "stumble across him" and alert the guests.

Everything was going to plan when I saw Judy come into the room and start to play the game with the guests – my signal that she'd got the body into position. Twenty minutes later, right on cue, I saw Judy leave the room and I knew that within a couple of minutes the alarm would be raised – or so I thought. In fact, nothing happened. Five minutes went by, then ten – by which time we'd finished the game and Judy still hadn't returned. We were all sitting around relaxing and chatting when, after a further ten minutes (during which I was getting a little frantic about what might have gone wrong) Judy returned looking very confused. I casually went to have a chat with her and the first thing she whispered was "The body's gone!". She'd spent the whole time she'd been away searching to no avail. The actor in question was nowhere to be found.

By this time a few guests had started to notice that "Matthew", the character the actor was playing, hadn't been seen for some time and one or two came up to ask me where he was. "I don't know," was my honest reply (little did they know I really hadn't a clue where he was). Suspicious that something was wrong, a couple of the more adventurous guests suggested we should set up search parties to find him. I thought this was great fun and readily agreed but I was also slightly worried about what we would find when we eventually discovered him. The search parties were duly organised, everyone fanned out around the hotel and several minutes later a shout rang out: "We've found him. He's dead". My immediate thought, as we all rushed to where the actor had secreted himself, was "He soon will be, when I get my hands on him". The actor had decided to dramatically drape himself across a set of stairs that were miles away from where Judy had originally positioned him (no wonder she couldn't find him!).

Once we'd moved the guests away and the body was safely tucked away in his room I asked him what on earth he thought he was doing?

It turned out that, once in position, he'd taken it upon himself to decide that he was lying "out in the open" and he was worried that non Murder Weekend guests might stumble across him – so he decided to up sticks and move. When I pointed out there had been a far greater chance of "ordinary guests" finding him in a public stairwell next to a corridor full of bedrooms, rather than the place we'd originally agreed, the actor in question looked suitably sheepish and mumbled: "You know Joy, on reflection, I think you just might be right."

Another "right time but wrong place" death that got me wondering why we bother to plan everything carefully in advance occurred when Shirley decided, without bothering to tell anyone, that she would make her death "more dramatic". I left Shirley, battered and strangled, on her bedroom floor; because the room wasn't that large it was the best position for the death since it would give the majority of guests the best opportunity of seeing the body.

A little while later the actress playing her daughter started to become hysterical amongst the guests because "her mother was missing" and since there had already been three murder victims that weekend she was fearful her mother might be next. Taking their cue from this everyone followed her to Shirley's room. Frantic knocking brought no response and when the copper eventually unlocked the door and we burst into the room everyone was expecting the worst. Imagine my surprise, therefore, when "the worst" turned out to be the fact there was no body lying on the floor where I had left it not ten minutes earlier! Neither I nor any of the other actors had a clue where Shirley had gone. We surreptitiously threw quizzical looks at each other even as we pretended to reassure the "not quite so distraught as she'd planned" daughter that everything was probably fine and that we'd find her mother "safe and well".

With around 50 guests crammed into the bedroom it took a while to clear the room – it really was an opportunity for the copper to tell people to "move along" because there was, quite literally, "nothing to see here", but thankfully they missed the opportunity because one of the guests heard a noise coming from the large Victorian mahogany wardrobe that stood in one corner of the room. Being naturally inquisitive they decided to open the wardrobe door and, as they did so, several loud and genuine screams suddenly rang out across the room. The unfortunate guests jumped hurriedly backwards as Shirley fell out of the open door and onto the floor at their feet.

It seems that, just after I'd left her, Shirley had decided her death would be much more dramatic if she was found in the wardrobe. This was true – it got a shocked reaction from the guests – but Shirley had forgotten that if she was hidden when everyone came into the room then no one would find her. It was only when she heard the guests start to leave the room that Shirley realised she'd have to do something to save the day – hence the "noise" coming from a wardrobe containing a supposedly battered, strangled and very dead corpse – but if any of the guests thought this a little odd they thankfully kept their thoughts to themselves.

In their defence I should say that at least these "wandering corpses" were found (eventually) by our guests. If it hadn't been for the timely intervention of some helpful members of the general public, however, it's a toss up as to whether the next corpse would have been found before the Weekend was over!

We were at The Green Dragon in Hereford and at our first actors' meeting on Friday afternoon we finalised the details of Marg Hancock's demise. She was going to be found stabbed to death by some rubbish bins at the back of the hotel and to get into her final resting position she would have to walk down the fire escape and walk a few yards by herself until she found the right spot. After the meeting I showed Marg the entrance to the fire escape and we were all set, or so I thought.

Maria Allen was playing a psychic on this plot and after I'd prepared Marg in my room I told her to wait for a couple of minutes until I was safely away and then make her way to the fire escape we'd identified earlier. I then returned to the guests in their function room, which was Maria's cue to start a little bit of business. She started by screaming and then began to have a vision. "I can see Pippa" (Marg's character). She's in some sort of trouble," she began as a way of gaining the interest of the guests. "I think she might be dead!" she suddenly exclaimed. This immediately had the desired effect of working the guests into a frenzy of questions and speculation and, under their prompting, Maria started to sob. "I can see bins," she wailed.

Taking their cue the guests duly dashed outside to find the hotel's rubbish bins and, after a bit of frantic searching they found them. A thorough search of the area revealed precisely nothing. The fact Pippa was no where to be seen didn't deter Maria.

She stuck defiantly to her guns: "I can definitely see bins," she insisted, more in hope than expectation that Pippa's body would mysteriously appear. "Big metal bins," she added as if their size and composition would somehow make a difference. Spurred on by Maria's inaccurate but doggedly persistent visions, the 70 or so guests and actors were searching everywhere; some had even moved out of the courtyard containing "the bins" and were milling around in the small back road that ran alongside the hotel. They were joined by Maria who was, of course, as confused as the guests by Pippa's absence. Unlike them, however, she was pretty certain that "bins" held the key to Marg's whereabouts and, in a strange sort of way, she was absolutely right to continue to flog what the majority of guests were convinced was a dead horse (they were much less convinced about the possibility of a dead body).

"I can see bins. She's dead by the bins," Maria insisted once more, to a frankly sceptical audience, at the same moment three very drunk students lurched down the road. Intrigued by all the activity they stopped to survey the scene and one of them eventually thought to ask "What are you lot doing?". Maria, ever the professional, stepped into the breach and, staying completely in character, screeched: "We're looking for my mother! I think she's dead!" – to which a nearby guest added, deadpan: "By some bins. Apparently". One of the students looked at Maria and said "Well, there's a woman lying on the ground beside some bins by the pub down there". He pointed back down the road in the direction they'd just staggered. "We just thought she was drunk," he added by way of explanation. The assembled guests didn't need any further invitation to investigate and they hurtled down the road for some 300-odd yards until they arrived at the White Hart Pub. And, sure enough, there was Pippa lying dead as a dodo among the bins by the side of the pub.

After the guests had finished inspecting and photographing Pippa's body and the other actors had ushered them back to the hotel I asked Marg what the hell she was doing lying outside the pub when she was supposed to have been at the back of the hotel.

Marg looked at me indignantly. "I did as you said" she replied defiantly. "I went down the fire escape and it went out on to the road. I couldn't see any bins and then I couldn't get back into the hotel because the door had locked, so I wandered down the road for a bit, saw these bins and assumed you must have meant me to die here. I thought it was a bit odd…" "Marg," I said patiently "you may have gone down the fire escape, but it was the wrong fire escape. You walked down the wrong corridor and through the wrong door…" At this the realisation slowly dawned on her that she hadn't really listened properly to what I had told her earlier than day. We both started to laugh at the misunderstanding and I was more than a little relieved that Marg had been found by the friendly drunken students rather than some other more seedy type of individual!

Sometimes, of course, the corpse is meant to move on a Murder Weekend. A staggering body is always a favourite with the guests. But just because a body's "on the move" doesn't necessarily mean nothing can go wrong.

This leads me on to another couple of stories – one of which wasn't the body's fault and the other of which most definitely was.

We were at The Berystede just outside Ascot, a hotel set in large grounds with a small, but reasonably busy, road running a few yards from its front entrance. For the death on Saturday afternoon the plan was that I'd "blood" Jerry Percy in his room, sneak him out of a side fire exit and leave him to make his way around the front of the hotel to the garden where all the guests were playing a game. He would then stagger towards them and fall in a crumpled heap on the ground, a large knife sticking out of his back. I saw him safely down the fire escape and watched as he walked along the footpath to the front of the hotel and a minute or so later I heard a guest scream; the plan had worked beautifully, except for one small detail.

The thought that a car might be passing at the exact moment Jerry was staggering along the footpath was something we'd considered, but the chances of anyone seeing Jerry were remote and, even if they did, it was highly unlikely they would notice anything odd (although, on reflection, the knife in his back and the blood streaming down his face was a bit of a giveaway!).

Well, as you might have guessed a car did pass Jerry and they did notice something was not quite right about him – they obviously decided that, while they weren't going to actually stop the car and get out to help what looked like the victim of an assault, their passenger would use their mobile to call the police! It was only a little later, after I was approached by a very flustered operations manager at the hotel, that I discovered he'd managed to head off a major incident. It seems that the police, thinking that a dangerous individual was on the loose in or around the hotel, had phoned to warn him that there were two squad cars and an ambulance on thier way! It was a good job he had the presence of mind to explain about the Murder Weekend and thereby save a great deal of embarrassment all round!

In terms of the second incident, I think "a great deal of embarrassment all round" probably sums up the whole affair quite neatly. It involved an actress who was about to do a Weekend for the first time; she was down to be a Saturday night death and what I didn't know at the time – but very quickly discovered – was that she was an alcoholic. Her husband, who was also acting on the Weekend, rang me on the Friday evening and told me his wife was unwell; he didn't think she was well enough to do what was, give or take a few hours, a whole Weekend.

At this late stage I told him I was obviously in a fix since it was too late to get another actress to play the part – the best I could do would be to swap the murders around. I told him that if his wife was well enough it would be a great help if she could manage to be a Friday death instead. Thinking on my feet (a vital skill when organising or acting on Murder Weekends) I suggested that, as she was poorly, we could kill her off as soon as possible; instead of going down to dinner she could stay in her room and, once the guests had finished their dinner we'd stage her death. Her husband thought about this for a moment or two and then said he thought that was fine and that his wife would be well enough to carry it through.

During dinner Gemima (the character in question) was nowhere to be seen. Her place was empty and there was lots of speculation among the guests as to where she was. I pretended to be worried and tried to ring her at work and at home – all to no avail, of course, and I felt that something that had so nearly been a disaster was all working out very neatly. Little did I know the horror to come.

Once dinner was over I rushed to Gemima's room and as soon as I saw her I realised she wasn't ill; she was just very, very drunk! With nothing for it but to prepare her as best I could, I managed to apply the dramatic make-up; by the time I'd finished her head was suitably battered, bruised and very bloody.

As I attached the large kitchen knife to her back I gave her very clear and very specific instructions about where she was to stagger and exactly where she was to drop. This was important, as I repeatedly reminded her, because she would have to stoop quite low beneath the height of the restaurant window in order to get herself into the correct position to begin her stagger. If she didn't stoop properly there was a good chance guests might see her before she got to her starting position.

Having satisfied myself Gemima was suitably bloody and that she understood what she had to do I then went back to the restaurant. My arrival was the cue for the other actors to start creating a bit of a buzz about Gemima's absence – they couldn't understand why she hadn't arrived, what could have kept her and such like. One of the actors was loudly disclaiming that he was as perplexed as everyone else and that he couldn't think where Gemima could possibly be when a guest suddenly piped up to say: "You should have a look outside then mate. That's probably her walking past the window smoking with a dirty great knife stuck in her back!"

I thought I was going to have a heart attack. I felt my blood pressure boil to exploding point as I, along with the guests and other actors, watched open-mouthed in amazement as Gemima strolled casually along outside the window, smoking her head off and apparently without a care in the world – and certainly not at all bothered by the extremely large knife protruding from her back! It's a wonder there wasn't steam coming form my ears as, after the initial shock, I rushed out and almost rugby tackled her to the ground and held her down while the guests came to view this most bizarre of bodies. It must have looked dreadful and very amateurish; to say I was not best pleased would be an understatement but thankfully the guests seemed to take it all in good part as just "one of those things". No one mentioned the "Case of the Walking, Smoking Corpse" for the rest of the Weekend (and no one said – at least not within my earshot – that "She must have been dying for a fag!").

Although I said earlier that I suspect some misunderstandings on Weekends stem from actors not always listening closely enough to what's been discussed at our meetings, I would be the first to admit that I'm not perfect – I've certainly made more than my fair share of muck-ups in 25 years. Most of these, as with my actors, have been fairly minor and easily rectified, but I have to say that in a couple of instances my forgetfulness led to an actor spending an uncomfortable hour or two waiting for my return when they should have been relaxing with their feet up.

In the first case Shirley had died in a function room and I told her I would return "in ten minutes" to get her out of the hotel so that she could make her way home, which in this instance happened to be only about 500 yards down the road. Well, one thing led to another; I had to run a game and, once that was finished, got caught up with guests who wanted to interrogate me. The upshot of all this was that I completely forgot about poor Shirley. She couldn't leave the room, or even put the light on, because guests would have seen her. There was no telephone in the room so she couldn't call reception to get them to remind me she was trapped and she certainly couldn't let herself out because the only door opened onto a busy corridor that was in constant use by guests. There was only one thing for her to do and that was to sit tight and wait which, being the consummate professional, is exactly what she did. For two hours.

It was only at the start of our actors' meeting at midnight, when someone innocently enquired if "Shirley had got away alright", that I suddenly shrieked at the realisation I'd completely forgotten her! I rushed down to where she was incarcerated and, as I went into the darkened room, started to laugh and apologise profusely to Shirley for having made her wait so long. She, understandably perhaps, didn't quite see the funny side of the situation and went home to a hot bath and a no doubt well-earned snifter!

If this oversight was bad enough the second was, if anything, even worse for the actor involved. John Shepherd died very dramatically; his hands and feet had been tied to the bedposts and then his body had been tortured – he had been a horrible character and thoroughly deserved it! Again, once the guests had all seen the body I said to him I'd be "back in ten minutes" to untie him and once again I forgot.

It didn't help that he was gagged so he couldn't call for help – not that he would, of course, because, like Shirley, John was always a complete professional on Weekends. He was well aware that if he'd made too much noise the guests might have heard and this would have completely spoiled the illusion we'd created around his death. The fact he was tied very securely (and not for the first time; you may remember he was the one tied up for the voodoo death when I burnt myself trying to rescue him) meant he was completely helpless – a situation made worse by the fact he was desperate to go to the loo. When I eventually remembered, about an hour or so later, that I'd left him tied up in his room he was, as you can imagine, extremely cross. When I walked into the room and saw him still lying where I'd left him on the bed I just had to laugh (I know I shouldn't have) and he did manage to see the funny side of things once I threatened not to remove the gag unless he promised to laugh.

Chapter 11

Friendly fire

If you've ever been on a Murder Weekend you'll know that we invariably stage lots of fights and, as I've said before, I always inform the hotel management about when and where they're going to happen.

This helps us avoid unfortunate incidents like the time two of my actors started an argument on the dance floor and the DJ, who hadn't been told by the hotel manager that they were just acting, waded in to stop the fight (nearly breaking one of the actor's arms into the bargain) with the immortal words "No one fights on my watch!"

Fights are, of course, always carefully planned so as to avoid injury to both the actors involved and any guests unfortunate enough to be in the immediate vicinity when something kicks off. I say "always", but on very rare occasions this isn't necessarily the case.

A few years ago, for example, a regular guest rang me to say that it was his friend's 60th birthday and, as she was a Murder Weekend regular, could I do something to include her? One of my actors Chris suggested we should arrange for a big birthday cake to be brought into the restaurant at the end of dinner, just as two of the actors were starting a fight. One of the actors would then have their head pushed into the cake and this would kick off a massive "cake fight". We all agreed this would be a great bit of action.

I asked chef to prepare something special but when the cake was carried out of the kitchen with candles blazing, I nearly died; it was huge and covered with a very, very thick layer of whipped cream. My heart sank because I feared, rightly as it turned out, that this was going to get very messy indeed – I was particularly concerned because Sheila, our infamous loose cannon, was one of the actors involved in the fight. And I just knew the worst was inevitably going to happen

Just as the cake was being paraded into the room the other actor involved, Stuart Hatcher, started the argument as arranged. Being a very bubbly, cheeky character in real life he was in his element as he scooped up a big handful of the gooey, creamy cake and, very deliberately, took aim at Sheila – it looked hilarious as the creamy mixture slid down her face, but we could all see from the look in her eyes, we were in trouble.

What followed was the biggest cake fight I've ever seen – it was like something straight out of Bugsy Malone (if you've ever seen the cake fight in that film you'll have a rough idea what I'm talking about). Sheila picked up a huge piece of cake and hurled it at Stuart and, one by one, the remaining actors found some excuse to get involved – they were literally picking up handfuls of cake and lobbing it at each other.

My face, so I was later told by guests, was a picture of horror as the cake fight gathered pace. I was so convinced that the hotel management would go berserk at the carnage my actors were busily creating that I dropped to my knees and started desperately trying to clear up the mess.

This, of course, was a completely ridiculous thing to do (I just felt I had to do something, anything!); kneeling on the floor in the middle of the room in the midst of a gigantic cake fight meant I was a sitting duck and my actors didn't disappoint the guests as I was immediately the focus for the action and was duly pelted from all sides. When the actors were eventually separated and things had calmed down I remained on my hands and knees, desperately trying to supervise the cleaning-up process.

The guests, who had all by some miracle avoided being on the receiving end of a misdirected piece of cake, were crying with laughter and I think there was only one person in the room, me included, who didn't find it funny – the copper, played by Chris (whose idea it had been in the first place!). He stomped out of the room towards reception in a very bad mood to arrange to have his suit dry cleaned. Sheila, the most mischievous of actresses, hadn't been able to resist letting the copper have it with both barrels!

Although, at least after the event, I really loved this particular fight (despite all the mess and Chris's tantrum) one of my all-time favourite fights happened one New Year at Whately Hall in Banbury. Maria Allan and I were having the most spectacular of arguments, caused because she discovered I was "sleeping with her husband" if I remember rightly. We were both playing pretty slutty characters and were dressed appallingly. Maria had her hair scraped back across her forehead and was wearing a big, thick false ponytail. All the actors had joked about it during our meeting and we had agreed that, in our fight, it would be both funny and appropriate if I ripped the offending ponytail off her head, threw it triumphantly to the ground and stomped it into the dirt.

So there we were, standing head to head in the garden on the very wet and muddy grass, surrounded by 100-plus guests all egging us on. We started to grapple with each other and fell to the ground; I grabbed Maria's hair but, as hard as I tugged, the wig just wouldn't come off. We were rolling round, churning up the muddy ground as we repeatedly punched and lunged at each other. The fight apparently looked suitably realistic, even though we both started to get a fit of the giggles because, try as I might, I just couldn't pull the wig off Maria's head. Since we couldn't let the guests see us crying with laughter, I buried my head in her chest and she did the same and eventually, with one final mighty tug, the wig came off to much cheering and laughter from the guest. As I held the trophy aloft the coppers arrived to separate us; we were held apart like fighting dogs, snarling and shouting at each other as I taunted Maria with the fact I had managed to remove her ridiculous wig.

One minute I was feeling quite pleased with myself (and not a little exhausted after our frantic efforts) and the next I felt a drip from my nose then another and another. When I looked across at Maria her expression had turned from rage to shock and I realised that blood was pouring from my nose. Everyone went very quiet, obviously thinking that I'd broken my nose, but I just carried on shouting obscenities at my love rival as if nothing had happened. My nose wasn't hurting so

I thought to myself "This must look really good, I'll keep on going". It was Paula who eventually expressed what everyone was probably thinking when she looked at me and softly said: "Do you think you should go to hospital, Tracey?", at which point I started to laugh, as did all of the guests and actors, at the ridiculousness of it all. Everyone, that is, except Maria who was clearly mortified. She kept apologising to me but I just couldn't stop laughing and told her not to worry (it turned out to just be a nosebleed). The guests, however, took lots of photos of my bloodied face so I at least have the evidence to use against her one day, should the occasion arise!

Ending this part of the book on the subject of "fights" is, in a way, appropriate – over the past 25 years I've been battered, bloodied, bruised, had my bones broken and my ego smashed more times than I care to remember – but in many other ways it's not. Over this time I've also met the most amazing people from all walks of life – some of whom have become very good and valued friends – and had so many laughs and experiences that I wouldn't change any of it for a second.

None of what I've written about here would, of course, have been possible without the fantastic people that have worked with and alongside me on the plots I've created; I'd really like to take this opportunity, therefore, to thank all the actors who've worked so hard playing the weird and wacky characters I've created on Murder Weekends and I hope they won't mind too much at the way they've been portrayed! I could, in truth, have written so many more stories but perhaps some are best left untold. There are stories even I would be embarrassed to put down in black and white!

Although this is the end of my tales about Murder Weekends it's not the end of the book. In my introduction I said I would be setting you all a little challenge, in the final part of this book, by way of an unusual and complex "solvable whodunnit", the first of many that will be called 'Absolute Murder'. This first plot is called Love Letters Straight From My Heart. I hope you have as much fun trying to solve it as I had in creating it!

Part Three

Love Letters Straight From My Heart

How to play

On Saturday 16th September 2006 the body of Kevin Doherty was found in the garden of his Ormskirk home. He had been rendered unconscious by a blow to the back of his head before being fatally stabbed by a single knife wound. On closer inspection, police found the letter "G" carved into his left forearm, prompting the start of a murder investigation that was to baffle the best efforts of the Merseyside Police.

Over the next three months the investigating team, led by Detective Chief Superintendent Ian Rutherford, were confronted by further killings, each with the same MO; a series of murders that culminated with the grisly discovery of four victims on the same day – December 16th 2006 – at a reunion for the pupils and staff of Hulme Comprehensive School.

For the past few months Rutherford and his team have been working flat-out on the case (codenamed the "Capital Murders" on account of the single capital letter carved into each body) without success. In desperation Det.Ch.Supt. Rutherford has turned to Greg Sharpe, an old friend and colleague based in the North West with the National Crime Squad – and this is where you come in…

On the following pages you will find the mass of evidence assembled during the murder inquiry giving you the opportunity to follow the investigation, study the evidence and draw your own conclusions about the identity of the killer. I've included some space at the end of the book for you to make notes from the evidence presented.

Deciding which suspect is the murderer is not your only task, you should be able to link all the clues that back up your case. Also what were the other suspects' motives?

Once you have a clear case you can turn to the end of the book for the summation of the case that Assistant Chief Constable Sharpe's has returned to his friend.

This denouement will hopefully confirm your own solution but if it doesn't it will certainly explain where you went wrong! Try not to peek before you've made your decision and detailed the evidence on which it's based – remember the CPS must be satisfied that you've made a convincing case to support a successful proseccution.

And finally…

Also hidden within the clues is another subtle thread of evidence – if you discover it you will be able to enter a draw for some very special prizes. I hope you find the secret and good luck with your entry, which must be submitted before the closing date of 31.12.07.

Prize winners will be personally notified but if you want to know the solution to this hidden competition it will be posted, after the closing date, on our website at "AbsoluteMurder.com" (or you can email joy@thejoyofmurder.com).

I really hope you enjoy solving my first Absolute Murder case.

Good luck,

NB: All characters, locations and events featured in 'Love Letters Straight From My Heart' are fictitious and any resemblance to real persons, living or dead, is purely coincidental.

MEMO

From: Detective Chief Superintendent Ian Rutherford
Merseyside Police
Major Crime Unit

To: Assistant Chief Constable Greg Sharpe
National Crime Squad

13th April 2007

Following our telephone conversation yesterday I know that you are now aware of the complex nature and the circumstances surrounding these deaths.

The enquiries are necessarily complex, protracted and labour intensive.

As you are aware there are several forces and agencies involved, with 8 murders, apparently with a similar M.O.

Although we have several suspects, there is not enough prima facia evidence to support a case to put before the C.P.S. I am not yet in a position to affect any arrests and it is to that end I need your help

Having given detailed consideration as to the nature of the evidence required to support an effective prosecution, and, having considered the most prudent method of obtaining that evidence may I therefore make a formal request to you to provide your assistance and expertise in the collection, collation and presentation of that evidence.

These matters are by their nature very sensitive and I would therefore be grateful if we could discuss this matter further at the earliest opportunity so that I may progress the enquiry in the most expeditious manner possible.

Yours sincerely

Ian Rutherford

Ian Rutherford
Det. Ch. Supt. MCU

VICTIM SHEET	
	Form MG 26
NAME: Faith Cole	

PHOTOGRAPH (IN SITU)	**Circumstances of Death:**
	Faith Cole was found under a desk in one of the classrooms of Hulme Comprehensive. It was the night of the School Reunion, 16th December 2006. All ex-pupils had been at the school most of the day, meeting up, playing games etc. In the evening there was a school disco/dinner. One couple had gone to a classroom for a tryst. They discovered the body. It appeared that she had a single stab wound to her side and a letter (D) had clearly been carved into the skin of her leg.
	Deceased discovered by whom:
	Samantha McKee and Tony Spicer.
	Date and time of discovery
	21.20, Saturday, 16th December 2006.
PHOTOGRAPH OF DECEASED, WHEN ALIVE	**Description:**
	5'3", dark-skinned, dark hair, brown eyes, slim. Single.
	DOB: 13/09.62 (44) **NoK:** Mrs Catherine Cole
	Last known address:
	126 Bayswater Road, London, W8.
	Occupation:
	Although everyone that knew her said that she was doing very well in London, none seemed to know what she actually did. It appears after investigation that she was a high class prostitute, working from a professional address in Dean Street, Soho, W1.

Any other relevant details :
Lead officer – Det.Ch.Supt. Ian Rutherford – who had been involved in the Daniel Fielding Murder Investigation, immediately took lead on this case because of the similarity of the MO. Anthony Milner was again SSU Officer.

MARCH 15

Scored a really good goal — that was the good part of the day

But extra "tuition" with Gregson isn't worth what he makes me do. I know I've got to get my grades up if I'm going to Uni and he will fail me if I told.

;by Herald • Thursday, March 11, 1976

Pet Owners Beware

A series of disappearances of cats and dogs in the Crosby area has prompted the police to warn pet owners to keep their pets in at night. Police believe the animals are being stolen and harmed and are upping night patrols to try and catch the perpetrators.

Monday, December 2, 1963

MURDERER HANGED

At six o'clock this morning, the execution of David Trent was carried out at Walton Prison. The relatives of Minnie Baxter said they were delighted and relieved that justice had finally been served.

David Trent leaves a wife Sylvia and one year old daughter.

Gov, this was a major murder trial in Liverpool in the 60's.

Happy Valentines Day

To the sexiest student alive! I love you more than words can say ?

3Xalady ?!?!

SUSPECT SHEET

Form MG 25

NAME: Charlotte (Lottie) Trent

CURRENT PHOTOGRAPH:

DESCRIPTION:
5'7", slim, olive-skinned, long dark brown hair, brown eyes. Appears very bright and analytical.

DOB: 07/03/62 (45).
Parents: Davey & Sylvia Trent (both d).
No siblings.

Single.

CURRENT ADDRESS:

3 Roe Lane, Didsbury, Manchester.

Did live in Culcheth Street, Waterloo, Merseyside when attended Hulme.

OCCUPATION:

After attending Hulme Comprehensive, Lottie went to Liverpool University where she obtained a first in Psychology. Lottie became a counsellor and now works for the NHS in Manchester, but also privately at her offices in Deansgate, Manchester.

ANY OTHER RELEVANT DETAILS:

Miss Trent does not want to talk about her past and appears to have forged a life in Manchester and was very reluctant to discuss her schooling or parents. She knew many of the other ex-pupils that were at the school reunion, but wasn't that close to them, the impression is that she felt inferior to them and kept her distance. Dated Mal Kane for a short time when at Hulme.

↑

one of the victims

APRIL 30

I can't wait. I'm so excited about the wedding tomorrow. My dress is so beautiful all the flowers in my hair and the bouquet are going to be so beautiful

Mum is so excited, as she's so happy Janet has met Phil - he's lovely.

I don't think I'll be able to sleep tonight, but mum says I must try and get my beauty sleep.

...viviili in good faith, took it to Bonhams auction house.

Double Tragedy

The wife of hanged murderer David Trent was today found dead at her home in Netherton, Liverpool..
A police spokesman said that it appeared she committed suicide on the anniversary of her husband's execution, December 2nd, 1963.
Sylvia Trent leaves a two year old daughter, who is being cared for by her grandmother.

To "Sir"

Very pleased to read about your
Honour, Sir!
But I bet the press would love to know
you're not so honourable
Super "Head" indeed!!
£30,000 should keep me quiet. I'll be
in touch.

Kane M.   B+!!

HULME PRIMARY SCHOOL
Great Crosby, Liverpool

General Report

Name ....JENNIFER WATSON....   Age..10.2   ....WINTER........Term, 1972
Form .....PRIMARY 6.....................

CONDUCT

JENNIFER IS HELPFUL IN THE FORMROOM AND HAS
TAKEN PARTICULAR INTEREST IN ALL ASPECTS OF
PHYSICAL EDUCATION AND ART.
JENNIFER MUST LEARN NOT TO INTERFERE WITH
THE OTHER PUPILS, PARTICULARLY THE BOYS. EVEN AT
SUCH A YOUNG AGE, JENNIFER CAN BE QUITE FLIRTATIOUS.

PROGRESS

GENERAL PROGRESS HAS BEEN ADEQUATE CONSIDERING
JENNIFER'S LEARNING DIFFICULTIES. SHE IS EASILY
DISTRACTED AND MUST TRY TO CONCENTRATE
MORE ON HER STUDIES.

* seems nothing's changed Gov, she
  was flirting with the 'scenes of crimes'
  guys as they were searching the kitchen!!

Next term begins ....JANUARY 5ᵗʰ, 1973   PETER SULLIVAN. Form Master
                                              MISS E. BRASH. Head Mistress

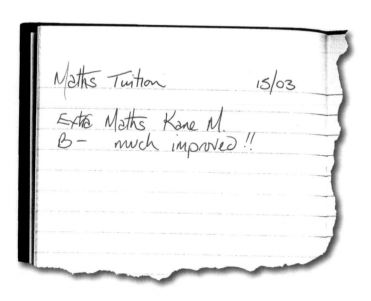

Maths Tuition   15/03

Extra Maths Kane M.
B- much improved !!

Dear Paul
hast wek i had yor baby girl shes very
very pritty and dark like you. i called
her Rosy Jud but i had to giv her away
to some one else cas my Mum sed so
i think yor relly horrid you wodnt marry me
and look after us.
i think you shud giv me some money i
wont to go to Chesta zoo to see the
elefants. i luv elefants but Mum says we
cant aford it.
But if you giv me the money to go
i wont tel thats yor rosys Dady !!
your babys mumy
Jen XX

Day _Munday_ Date_30th May_
_1977_

Bloody hel
up the duff agen

Pauls bin horible said
hes not intrested i
wont to go on the
pill but SHE wont
let me.
it feels diferent this
time i think its a girl
id luv two keep her
and hav some one to luv
me but SHE will say no.
SHE gets the money and
wont giv me any SHE such
a bich.
i want two go to Chesta
zoo but SHE says its
two eespensiv.

Our Festivals
by Paul Judd
(aged 9)

Blackbrooke Home Orphanage
Sycamore St
Waterloo
Liverpool
Lancashire
Tel: Waterloo 1124

27th June 1977

Dear Captain Marshall,

Having received your communication and discussed your proposal with my colleagues, I have, we believe three students that may be of interest to you.

All three boys have the characteristics that you outlined. All are exceptionally bright and are expected to get high grades in all 9 O levels. Although we have tried on several occasions to place them with families, the boys have not easily integrated as they are opinionated, feisty and usually considered unruly, however it is my opinion that they are bored, needing a lot to stimulate their highly developed brains and personalities.

I could make them all available for interview next week in London, as you suggest and look forward to your phone call.

Yours sincerely,

Harold James

Harold James,
Home Principal

VICTIM SHEET		Form MG 26
NAME: Neil Richardson		

PHOTOGRAPH (IN SITU)	**Circumstances of Death:**
	Mr Richardson was found by an SSU officer, on a quiet stairwell leading up to the school library. He was in dinner dress, so clearly had been killed in the evening, but had not been found earlier as the Library was well away from where the dinner and disco were being held. There appeared a single blow to the head, a single stab wound to the chest, and a C had been cut into his arm.
	Deceased discovered by whom: Det.Con. Brad Gerrard, Search Team.
	Date and time of discovery 23.15, Saturday 16th December 2006.

PHOTOGRAPH OF DECEASED, WHEN ALIVE	**Description:** 5'11", slim build, dark hair – thinning. **DOB:** 10/05/62 (44) **NoK:** Mrs Sally Richardson.
	**Last known address:** P O Box 325, Belfast, BT18 5BD.
	Occupation: Detective Chief Inspector, Drugs Squad, Police Service of Northern Ireland (PSNI), working out of Antrim Road Station, Belfast.

Any other relevant details :

Used to be friends with many of the children at Hulme, but has lost touch and only met them again at the reunion. Haven't seen them since he left school after completing A levels and went to Police Training College at Hutton, near Preston.

Everyone we talked to at the re-union said he was "full of beans", "didn't have a care in the world". All who knew him seemed to really like him.

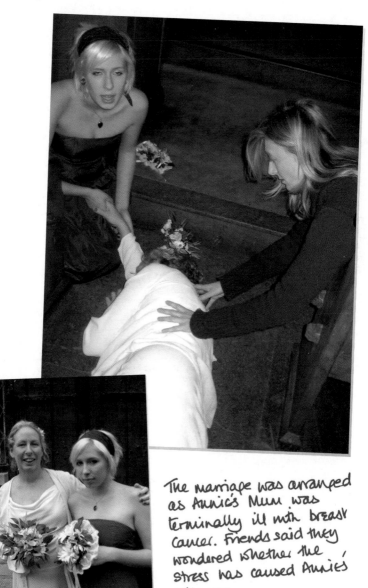

The marriage was arranged as Annie's Mum was terminally ill with breast cancer. Friends said they wondered whether the stress had caused Annie's collapse.

New Message _ ⊡ ✕

Mal Kane
13/11/06
15.34

To: Faith.Cole
Cc:
Bcc:
Subject: Last night
Attach:

Dear Faith,

Just a quick note to say how much I enjoyed our night out (and in!) yesterday.

I really had no idea how accomplished you'd become (or quite how much I'd enjoy being "under the heel" come to that.) It felt great to be in the hands of a Master (or should I say "mistress"!)

I'd really like to get together again sometime – perhaps next time Liverpool are in London? Let me know and I'll book us a table at The Ivy.

Best wishes,

M.

The Childhood Psychopath

Theories of Socio-Psychopathy

as Stephen Lytten (1995) points out, this has not been empirically tested. Further, he argues the socio-psychopathic personality is one established at some point in childhood and is conditioned by both personality-predisposition and socio-spatial contexts (such as the home). Of the factors that differentiate the abnormal personality, Tom Masson (2001) suggests aggressiveness (specifically towards animals and other children) is most significant, while Smith's (2002) analysis of US Police Reports highlights distinctive behavioural patterns involving ritualistic animal experimentation (including death and dissection). Tom Masson estimates the risk of transmitted behaviours from childhood into adulthood at around 75%.

VICTIM SHEET		Form MG 26
NAME: Tracey Tomlinson (nee Green)		

PHOTOGRAPH (IN SITU)	Circumstances of Death:
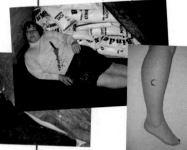	Mrs Tracey Tomlinson was found at the back of the Hulme Comprehensive School Gymnasium. Her body was found underneath some blue tarpaulin that was covering bags of cement. Mrs Tomlinson appears to have been killed by one single stab wound to the chest
	Deceased discovered by whom: Det Serg Ray Walsh, during a detailed search of the school grounds, following the discovery of the bodies of Faith Cole and Neil Richardson earlier that evening.
	Date and time of discovery Found at 01.20 on Sunday, 17th December 2006

PHOTOGRAPH OF DECEASED, WHEN ALIVE	Description: 5'1" – attractive, short dark greying hair, olive-skinned, round features, large blue eyes, plump
	**DOB:** 23/4/62 (44)
	Married to Dr Chris Tomlinson, General Practitioner, she met him when she became a receptionist in his surgery They have three children, Zoe (15), Jamie & Milly (13)
	Last known address: 12 Merrywood Drive Hightown, Merseyside
	Occupation: Housewife and part-time drugs counsellor

Any other relevant details :

Mrs Tomlinson had attended the school reunion without her husband. There are many witnesses that saw and talked to her during the afternoon activities, but no-one remembered seeing her at the evening event. It would appear that she was wearing the same clothes that she was wearing in the afternoon and had therefore been killed before she had time to go home to change for the evening dinner and disco

RREVERENT

SCHOOL FOR 00'S

Ian Fleming had it right when he wrote that James Bond was an orphan handpicked from a Children's Home. It seems that it wasn't just fiction, but that the Government has for years secretly scouted orphanages for highly intelligent, feisty and daring teenagers and sent them to special boarding schools where they were groomed for undercover organisations such as the SAS.

The thinking being that they will not have any identity or family ties to hold them back or that could be used against them. Their loyalty to commanders would be paramount as Bond's was to M.

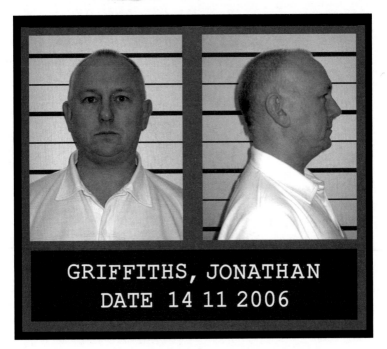

GRIFFITHS, JONATHAN
DATE 14 11 2006

Gov, known drugs dealer in our area, has done time twice.

Outward Bound Course 30th April 1976

Teachers attending: Peter Gregson
Sian Morgan
Philip Watson

Pupils attending:

Paul Bannister	15	Clive Edgington	14	Dianne M'Clean	13
Peter Black	14	Daniel Fielding	14	Sarah M'Clean	15
Carole Brewer	14	Geraldine Francis	13	Neil Richardson	13
Mel Brearley	13	Graham Fuller	14	Chris Spence	14
Steve Butcher	13	Tracey Green	14	Mary Tattersall	15
Mick Chatton	15	Alan Kane	13	Paul Williams	14
Richard Clarke	15	Paul Judd	15	Tony Williams	14
Faith Cole	13	Grace Meade	15		

Arrests have been made since this appeared in the Echo last summer. Still haven't enough evidence against the chief suspects.

OPERATION 'OWNGOAL'

Police Chiefs revealed today they are launching 'Operation Owngoal' across the country to combat the rise of drugs that are being passed to dealers at Premiership Football matches.

Several known dealers have been using matches to pass on drugs from Afghanistan to pushers in Cities with high drug use.

Det Assistant Chief Constable Waterman of Merseyside Police said that they would have undercover officers at every match at Anfield and Goodison.

Faith Cole

III G

Hulme Comprehensive

THE ANFIELD GANG RULE OK !.!.
F.C. M. B. N. R. C.S. P. J. T.W

Faith Cole, Mal Brearley
Chris Spence, Paul Judd,
Neil Richardson. Tony Williams.
WE ARE FAB AND WE
ARE EUROPEAN CHAMPIONS
AND WE ARE LEAGUE CHAMPIONS
AGAIN AND WE ARE THE BEST

13 Williams Drive,
Crosby,
Liverpool,
Lancashire

12th May 1977

Dear Mr Gregson,

We wanted to write to you to thank you for the extra tuition that you have given to Malcolm. His grades are coming up so well now and I think that he will do very well in his exams. Also he has become a lot quieter and seems to be spending a lot more time in his room revising, which is excellent.

I am only sorry that your workload means that you will not be able to give extra tuition to our daughter Annie.

Once again many thanks for all your hard work.

Yours sincerely,

Mrs Patricia Kane

Mrs Patricia Kane

Janet & Philip at their marriage on 19th June 1976.

APRIL 7

I hate Alan so much

He's such a nuesance. Mal asked me to
the pictures but mum said I couldn't
go as Alan has to go for an
appointment and she says I have to
go too

I can't bear it, I'm sure Mal
won't ask me again.

...obligatory in primary schools.

Bowel Cancer Victims angered by ruling

The National Institute for Health and Clinical Excellence (NICE) said that there was insufficient evidence to recommend Avastin and Erbitux, despite the fact that charities say both drugs are the best option for seriously ill patients.

The drugs are widely used in America, forcing sufferers from the UK to mortgage their homes to pay for the life-saving treatment.

Gov, this was sent 14/02/07. Friends said she hadn't been right since the wedding.

My darling Annie,

Another year since we first declared our love for each other. You are my heart and soul. Please don't shut me out – I miss my 'Lady' xxx

Mal

Anniversary

To the oh so high and mighty and very rich school governor,

I watched Saturday's game and I watched you. I know exactly what you're up to.
I would go to the police, I could make you front page of The Echo or... you could give me £30,000 for my silence and the drugs I need to live. It's a small price for your precious reputation. I'll be in touch with my bank account details.

MK

Mr and Mrs Charles Brack

request the pleasure of the company of

Miss Annie Kane

at the marriage of their daughter

Janet Brack

to

Philip Greenwood

on

1st May 1976

at

St Bart's Church, Alessandra Road, Waterloo

at 3.30 p.m.

and afterwards at The Sailing Club, Waterloo

R.S.V.P. to Mrs Charles Brack, 13 Williams Drive, Crosby, Liverpool

This is going to be the best day ever!!

CCF Training   03/02

Boys abseiled & canoed
No accidents this time
Fielding D. A- for effort !!

VICTIM SHEET	Form MG 26

NAME: Malcolm Kane

PHOTOGRAPH (IN SITU)

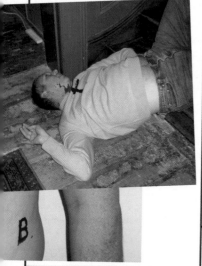

Circumstances of Death:
Annie Kane came home very late from the School Reunion, as everyone present had been questioned about the three murders. Miss Kane said that her partner was meant to be going with her, but went to bed in the afternoon with a bad headache. She went to the school on her own and stayed all evening, not going home to get changed. She arrived home at 2.30 in the morning in a squad car with a WPC, frightened to drive, both because she had been drinking, but was also scared to be on her own. As she walked in the front door, she saw her partner Malcolm at the bottom of the stairs.
He had a wound to the side of the head, a single wound to the chest, and the letter B had been cut in to the left hand side of his stomach

Deceased discovered by whom:
His partner, Annie Kane.

Date and time of discovery
2.30 a.m., Sunday 17th December 2006
DOB: 29/8/62 (44). **NoK:** Annie Kane

PHOTOGRAPH OF DECEASED, WHEN ALIVE

Description:
6'0", medium build, blonde/greying hair, blue eyes.
Ardent Liverpool fan. Popular with colleagues and friends, very witty and good company.
Partner of adoptive sister and father of Katie Kane.

Last known address:

27 Robins Lane, Crosby, Merseyside.

Occupation:
Sports Editor of the Liverpool Echo.

Any other relevant details :
Lead Investigative Officer – Det.Ch.Supt. Ian Rutherford.

27/9/80

Dear Lottie,

I'm sorry to do this in a letter but I think it's best to finish it now before I go to Uni.

Annie and I are getting very close and as we're both going to Manchester, I think something may happen and I'd hate to go behind your back.

Thanks for a great few months.

Take care,
Mal

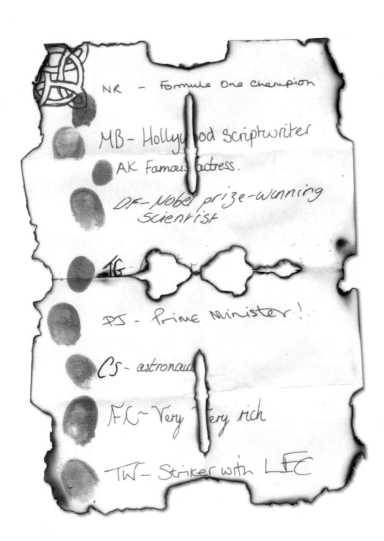

NR - Formula One champion

MB - Hollywood scriptwriter

AK Famous actress.

DF - Nobel prize-winning
scientist

TG -

PJ - Prime Minister !

CS - astronaut

FC - Very Very rich

TW - Striker with LFC

CASE HISTORY

1st Appt Date: 2/10/2006

Therapist: Lottie Trent

Case No: 237

CLIENT NAME: Mal Kane
AGE: 44
Marital Status: Long Term relationship with partner
Children: 1daughter - Katie
Previous Marriage/re'ship: —
Children: —

PARTNER NAME: Annie Kane
AGE: 44
Status: M
Children: Katie
Previous marriage/re'ship —
Children: —

Occupation: Journalist

Occupation: Part-time secretary

Presenting Problem: Severe + sudden relationship + communication difficulties

Clients goal of Therapy: To get relationship back to way it was

Date: 2/10/2006   Session 1   Fee £ ____
Summary:
Mal said that Annie has suddenly became very introverted and melancholy since their wedding day, wants to help her, still loves her.

Date: 12/10/2006   Session 2   Fee £ ____
Summary:
Mal says she will not communicate what problems are, but is very cold towards him, but is same as always to daughter.

Date: 19/10/2006   Session 3   Fee £ ____
Summary:
Mal and I getting much closer. We are probably going to meet for dinner.

Date: 26/10/2006   Session 4   Fee £
Summary:
Doesn't seem to be much improvement with Annie. We're having dinner tomorrow again, I can't wait to talk to him properly + who knows what else! He said he's going to see Faith on Saturday at the match.

Date: 16/11/2006   Session 5   Fee £
Summary:
I can't believe it! - Mal slept with Faith, and said it was great. Betraying lying Bastard + Duty Dirty Whore. I've told him not to come anymore.
Wait till I see them at The Peruvian

Date: Session 6   Fee £
Summary:

Date: Session 7   Fee £
Summary:

Witness Statement

Statement of... Ms Annie Kane

Age if under 18........_____....... (if over18 insert 'over 18')   Occupation... Housewife/ P/T secretary

This statement (consisting of ....3........page(s) each signed by me) is true to the best of my knowledge and belief and I make it knowing that, if it is tendered in evidence, I shall be liable to prosecution if I have wilfully stated in it anything which I know to be false or do not believe to be true.

Dated... 17th December 2006

Signature... *Annie Kane*

Q: Ms Kane we are very sorry for your loss and understand the strain that you are under, but we really appreciate that you have felt able to talk with us this morning. Could you tell us in your own words what happened last night.

A: Firstly can I say that I am very frightened indeed, my husband and three of my friends from school have been killed and I am terrified that I may be next. I am also frightened for my daughter. Is there any way that we could have some sort of protection if we are staying in our house.

Q: Absolutely Ms Kane, please be assured that your safety is paramount to us. So, back to this evening.

A: Well as you know I was partly responsible for arranging this function, in my capacity as school secretary, and working alongside the teaching staff and some old pupils that are involved in organising the whole event. This evening has been so terrible. We had had a lovely afternoon, we had all got together and had a brilliant time reminiscing and we even played an impromptu game of rounders, boys v girls it was hilarious. Then some people went home to get changed and the rest of us just stayed around chatting and drinking. Mal had stayed at home in the afternoon as he said he had a migraine, he has been working so hard lately, he's a sports editor with the Echo you know. Anyway he said if he felt better he would join us in the evening. I had decided I was going to stay at the school all day as I had so much to arrange. Then of course the awful thing happened, a couple of ex-pupils had 'got together' and went to one of the classrooms for a quiet snog and they found poor Faith. Then things just went from bad to worse, when all the police arrived and started to search then they found, well you know what happened. Anyway after we had all spoken to the police and given our statements, then a police officer drove me home, because I was too upset to drive and then when we came in the house then we saw poor Mal, (starts to sob), I'm so relieved that my daughter

Signature... *Annie Kane*   Signature witnessed by... DS Judith Cowan

P.T.O.

HULME COMPREHENSIVE SCHOOL
Great Crosby, Liverpool

Lower Vth Report

Name ...Malcolm Kane...   Age.14:5   ...Spring...Term, 1977

Form .....Fl...............

Average age of Form ....15.1....

Number in Form ......29.........

Subject	Marks Max. 100	No. Examined	Position	Remarks	
English Language	75	29	2	Malcolm's work has been excellent this year. He is perfectly capable of getting a grade 1 in both for levels next year.	MBP.
English Literature	80	29	1	Malcolm is much quieter this year and is clearly concentrating on his studies.	MBP
Maths	65	29	10	Malcolm's work has improved greatly this year. Malcolm should easily attain a good grade at O. level	JMT

In Fondest Memory 10/9/06

I am so sorry for everything.
The adult me is bereft at
what the childhood me
did to you. I'll never
forgive myself or
them.

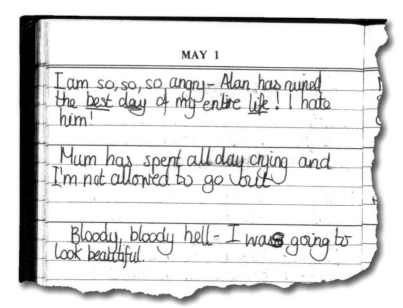

MAY 1

I am so, so, so angry - Alan has ruined the best day of my entire life! I hate him!

Mum has spent all day crying and I'm not allowed to go out

Bloody, bloody hell - I was going to look beautiful.

Crosby Herald • Thursday, Septem

Wedding Hitch

The wedding between Malcolm and Annie Kane, due to take place last Saturday at St Bart's Church, was dramatically halted when the bride collapsed as she walked down the aisle.

Relatives said that Miss Kane was taken to hospital but was released shortly afterwards and was able to join the reception which family had decided should still take place. There will be a small civil service at a later date.

From:	Meredith_judith@ashwood.edu
Sent:	October 26, 2006 12.17
To:	Malcolm.Kane
Subject:	Site generated enquiry

Dear Mr. Kane,

Further to your initial inquiry through our web site, I'm happy to confirm the following:

1. We are able to offer the cancer treatment you require through the agency of the Ashwood Clinic College of Medicine situated at our Westbeach, Arizona, facility.

2. Your treatment would be based primarily around the FDA-approved monoclonal antibodies Avastin and Erbitux and while successful treatment cannot be guaranteed a high percentage of our patients experience a successful conclusion to their course. We would be happy to supply the relevant statistical breakdown should you so desire.

3. A four-week course of treatment, to begin immediately following examination and diagnosis by our medical staff, is currently priced at $60,000. This includes all board and treatments while under the direct care and supervision of our facility staff, although please be aware we cannot guarantee further costs will not be incurred during your treatment. You may also incur ongoing support costs that cannot, at this point in time, be easily quantified.

I trust the above answers your initial questions and, should you wish to take advantage of what our medical facility has to offer, I would be happy to forward the relevant forms to your home address.

Sincerely,

Judith S, Meredith
Administrator,
Ashwood Clinic Corporation

Gov, during the pm it was found Kane was in the latter stages of bowel cancer, probably would have been terminal. His partner didn't appear to know.

SUSPECT SHEET	Form MG 25

NAME: Sir Peter Gregson KBE

CURRENT PHOTOGRAPH:	DESCRIPTION:

DESCRIPTION:

5' 10", slim, athletic build. Balding with grey hair, blue eyes.

DOB: 18/11/41 (65).

Married to Valerie Gregson (59), housewife.

They have two children Christian (37), also a teacher and Emily (35) housewife, has two boys.

CURRENT ADDRESS:

Green Gables, Alt Road, Hightown, Merseyside.

OCCUPATION:
Head Teacher at Hulme Comprehensive School, Crosby.
Illustrious teaching career, having been at Hulme in the 70/80's, as a teacher of Maths and P.E. He moved to London and became a celebrated headmaster in an inner city school. One of the first Head Teachers to be termed a 'Superhead'. Was brought back to Hulme, which was a failing school, in 2003 and has successfully turned it around.

ANY OTHER RELEVANT DETAILS:

Peter Gregson was awarded a Knighthood for his services to Education in the 2006 Birthday Honours list. Although about to retire, he will stay in Education in an advisory capacity.

BRENNANS ANTIQUES — Wayfarers Arcade, Lord Street, Southport

STOLEN ITEM:

Elizabethan Stiletto - gold semi precious stones set into the hilt.

unfortunately this item was new in and hadn't been photographed, so hand drawn estimation attached.
We estimate auction value at £350.00

Signed. *Sue Brennan*

Date 2nd April 1976

PHOTOGRAPH OF ITEM

Roger Brennan was a pupil at HULME. His friends knew his dad owned an antiques business and had access.

256

POLICE CAR REPORT
Officers: P.C. WALTER ROSS
W.P.C. JANE KAY

Car No: 5
Reg No: UML 175N

INCIDENT REPORT

PLACE OF OCCURRENCE: ST BART'S CHURCH, WATERLOO

COMMENTS: WE WERE CALLED TO THE HOME OF
PAT AND DAVE KANE. D.S. RESTON HAD BEEN
THERE TO INFORM THEM OF THE DEATH OF THEIR SON
ALAN.

THEY WERE WAITING AT THE HOUSE AND HADN'T
LEFT FOR THE WEDDING YET AS THEY HAD
RECEIVED A CALL TO SAY THEIR SON WAS MISSING
AND THAT A SEARCH HAD BEEN STARTED.

MR KANE WANTED TO GO AND COLLECT HIS
DAUGHTER ANNIE WHO WAS TO BE BRIDESMAID
AT MRS KANES SISTERS WEDDING. MR KANE SAID HE
WAS TOO UPSET TO DRIVE. D.S. RESTON STAYED WITH
MRS KANE WHO SAID WE SHOULD JUST COLLECT ANNIE
AND NOT TELL HER SISTER AND RUIN HER WEDDING.

WE ARRIVED AT THE CHURCH JUST AS THE WEDDING
PROCESSION HAD BEGUN AND THE ORGANIST WAS
PLAYING THE BRIDAL MARCH. IT WAS HALTED WHILE
WE EXPLAINED TO JANET BRACK THAT MRS KANE WAS
POORLY AND THAT ANNIE WAS NEEDED AT HOME. AS
INSTRUCTED WE TOLD JANET BRACK THAT IT WAS
NOTHING WRONG, BUT SHE INSISTED ON KNOWING.
ONCE TOLD SHE CANCELLED THE WEDDING
WANTING TO BE WITH HER SISTER.

ANNIE KANE BECAME COMPLETELY HYSTERICAL,
SCREAMING AND SHOUTING, APPEARING UPSET
BECAUSE SHE WASN'T GOING TO BE A BRIDESMAID.
ANNIE BECAME SO DISTRESSED THAT SHE HAD A PANIC
ATTACK AND WE HAD TO TAKE HER TO WATERLOO
HOSPITAL.

W.P.C. Jane Kay L2731

Day shitday. Date 16th March 1976

shit
im preggers agen
i havent told Mum
i no shel go mad
but she was OK last
time. As long as i
keep it hiden and
dont tell enyone.

i think its a boy?
but this time its
ok cos i no thats
Mal ♥ luvs me.

X X ☺

maybe well get maried!

Malcolm

No I don't want to
sue him, I've got a good
life and I don't need any
upheavel. All this happened
30 years ago, it's in the past
and that's where it
should stay.—

Dan

September 2006

Thursday 14

Paper reams to order.

Start sending out payment
reminders.

Rounders, netballs to reorder.

[Mr Lewis on holiday]

Friday 15

Trip to Walker Art Gallery.
Check phone contract: review
pricing agreement.

Saturday 16

Sunday 17

September
WK	M	T	W	T	F	S	S
35	28	29	30	31	1	2	3
36	4	5	6	7	8	9	10
37	11	12	13	14	15	16	17
38	18	19	20	21	22	23	24
39	25	26	27	28	29	30	1

Title, Forename, Surname & Address

Malcolm Breasley
Blackbrooke House
Sycamore Street
Waterloo
Liverpool 22

Age if under 12 years

Chemist
Endorsements

Tab Inderal 10 mg
$\bar{1} - \bar{\bar{1}}_1$ tds pm.

(42)

Date
10/10/76

Signature

DR FJ HART
NAPOLEAN SURGERY
NAPOLEAN STREET
WATERLOO
L22

SUSPECT SHEET	Form MG 25

NAME: Annie Kane

CURRENT PHOTOGRAPH:

DESCRIPTION:
5' 8", medium build, blonde, blue eyes.

DOB: 07/02/62 (45)
Parents: Patricia (housewife) and David Kane (Accountant). One brother Alan (d)
Partner of Mal Kane, met when both pupils at Hulme Comprehensive. Malcolm Brearley was adopted by Pat & Dave, aged 14, taking on their name. Became adoptive brother of Annie. They fell in love when at Manchester University together.

One child, Katie (14).
Further details on husband, see Victim Sheet.

CURRENT ADDRESS:

27 Robins Lane, Crosby, Merseyside.

OCCUPATION:
On leaving Manchester University with a degree in English, Miss Kane became a Librarian. She became a stay-at-home mum when her daughter was born, but has since taken a part-time job at Hulme Comprehensive as a secretary

ANY OTHER RELEVANT DETAILS:

Miss Kane, seems hugely protective of her daughter, but is putting on a brave front for Katie's benefit; it would appear she is not only devastated about the death of her husband but also that she is very frightened that she may be next in the slaughter of ex-pupils.

Day **Friday** Date **11th April 1975**

i had a relly good day at scool it wos plum crumbel.

Mum says im geting fat but Tony says i cant be cos it wos the ferst time.

Miss Nellsons sed i wos good at my peg bag in needelwork.

October 2006

Thursday 12

Order re-writeable CD's.
Drawing Pads -
Pen/Pencil order for offices.

Friday 13

All computers to be
serviced. Advise ICT staff.

[Broken window: Classroom 4H
quoted £78 - check invoice.]

Saturday 14

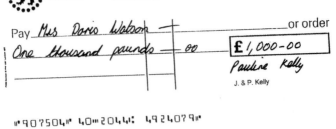

Midland Bank

29th September 19 76

29 HIGH STREET
CAMBERLEY SURREY GU15 3RE

40-20-44

Pay Mrs Doris Watson ————————————— or order

One thousand pounds —— 00   £ 1,000-00

                                  Pauline Kelly
                                  J. & P. Kelly

⑃907504⑃ 40⑈2044: 4924079⑃

To: Mohammad Sharifi

Company: Yalcheri's Carpet Emporium, Kabel

Fax No: +935102095774

MACKEN ANTIQUES
117 Bold Street
Liverpool
L1 4EX

Fax No: 0151-931-5522

From: Charles Macken

Date: 3rd Sept 2006.

Dear Mohammad, As discussed please find to follow the repeat order of Isfahan, Kashan, Kerman, Shiraz & Tabriz carpets. Also, Armoires, Mirror frames, Bidayuh masks and Bactarian idols. Numbers + quantities as listed. Delivery expected early October.

Thanks, regards Charles.

VICTIM SHEET

NAME: Mike Donaldson

PHOTOGRAPH (IN SITU)

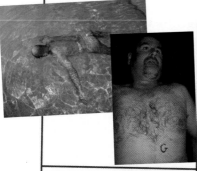

Circumstances of Death:
Mr Donaldson was found floating in his swimming pool, apparently drowned. However when his body was lifted out of the pool there appeared to be a single knife wound to his left side. A G had been cut into his chest. The G was so perfect that it had to have been cut by a very small bladed, very sharp cutter – perhaps some sort of craft knife, as the wound was not very deep, but definitely caused after death.

Deceased discovered by whom:
Mr Donaldson's gardener, Jack Bobson, arrived as usual on Saturday morning; he was tidying the borders around the terrace leading from the pool when he looked in and saw Mr Donaldson's body.

Date and time of discovery
9.45, Monday 27th November 2006.

PHOTOGRAPH OF DECEASED, WHEN ALIVE

Description:
6'4", well-built, very muscley and fit. Dark, very closely shaved hair, blue eyes.
DOB: 28/01/62 (44.) **NoK:** Orphan.

Last known address:
The Larches, Upper Hale Road, Farnham, Surrey.

Occupation:
Like Kevin Doherty, Mike Donaldson worked for a Government agency; we could not get much information, but believe it to be called CRISIS, which stands for Covert Response Investigative Security and Intelligence Service

Any other relevant details :
When we showed the post mortem photo of Mike Donaldson to the pupils at Hulme Comprehensive's Reunion, several of them said that he would have been a pupil called Tony Williams. We later learnt that several of the pupils were good friends and were all members of The Anfield Gang – some of them were still in touch and often met each other for games.
In fact the previous Wednesday, 22nd November, they were all meant to be meeting for the PS Eindhoven Championship League match at Anfield, but Mike Donaldson, as they now all called him, didn't show. They said that this was most unusual; as if he were in the country he would never miss a match. The friends also said that often they wouldn't see Mike for months on end, if he were away on assignment, but that he usually came back for a month or so.

PRESTON (HUTTON) ....Station   2ND MAY 19 76

INTERVIEW OF: PETER GREGSON

Age/Date of birth 34 (18/11/41) .... Occupation TEACHER

Address and Tel. No. 17 SUNNY DRIVE, CROSBY, LIVERPOOL

BY: DETECTIVE SERGEANT THORNTON

AT: 10·30 AM

OTHER PERSONS PRESENT: NONE

TIME INTERVIEW COMMENCED: 10·40 AM   TIME INTERVIEW CONCLUDED: 10·55 AM

MY NAME IS PETER GREGSON AND I WAS THE SUPERVISING TEACHER PG

AT THE OUTWARD BOUND COURSE AT LEIGH VALLEY CENTRE, NR WIGAN. PG

THERE WERE 23 CHILDREN AND I WAS ACCOMPANIED BY MY TWO COLLEAGUES PG

SIAN MORGAN AND PHILIP WATSON. THE CHILDREN ALL WENT TO THEIR PG

TENTS AT 8·00 PM, AFTER A SING SONG ROUND THE CAMPFIRE. THEY WERE PG

ALL TIRED BECAUSE WE'D HAD A FULL DAY OF ACTIVITIES. THERE WAS THE PG

USUAL HOUR OR SO BEFORE EVERYONE HAD SETTLED DOWN. WE STAYED PG

BY THE FIRE SMOKING, DRINKING HOT CHOCOLATE AND CHATTING. WE PG

CHECKED ON THE CHILDREN AT MIDNIGHT WHEN WE WERE GOING TO BED PG

AND BELIEVE ME THEY WERE ALL SOUND ASLEEP WE DID A HEAD COUNT PG

IN THE THREE TENTS AND EVERYONE WAS PRESENT INCLUDING ALAN PG

KANE. INITIALLY HE HAD BEEN RESERVED ABOUT JOINING IN THE PG

ACTIVITIES, HE IS, SORRY WAS, A BIT OF A WHINGER, BUT HE SOON JOINED PG

IN WHEN THE OTHER CHILDREN ENCOURAGED HIM. IT WAS TRACEY GREEN Peter Gregson

Peter Gregson

GOV, NO-ONE WAS ARRESTED FOR THIS MURDER. IT WAS ASSUMED THAT ALAN HAD GOT UP DURING THE NIGHT TO GO FOR A PEE AND THE ASSAILANT WAS HIDING IN THE WOODS. LOCAL PAEDOPHILES WERE QUESTIONED BUT NONE SUSPECTED.

Mal,

In 1963 my Dad killed a prostitute and ruined my life. In 1980 you broke my heart when you finished with me to go out with Annie. I've waited all my life for you & thought This was our time.

Now you have done it again, you led me on & Then broke my heart with that prostitute — one day soon someone is going to break your heart and then you'll know how it feels.

I deserved better Than this for my years of devotion you Bastard.

MAL & ANNIE				09/09/06	
NAME	**accept**	**Coming with**	**Table No**	**Gift**	**Page 2**
Mary & John Albright 27 Poplar Road, Hackney London, N1 6FX	Yes		G	Charity donation	
Faith Cole 126 Bayswater Road, London, W8	Yes *she looked relly ruff and dead taty*	On own	D *and was wearing clothes.*	Painting	
Fred & Mary Cooper 27 Morehouse Drive, Cannock, Staffs, WS12 4DR	Yes		B	Donation	
Kevin Doherty The Barn, Virgins Lane, Ormskirk, Lancs, L39 2AT	Yes, Verbal No reply to invite	Heather Sutton *its relly weerd I no its Paul but Mal called him Kevin dead weerd.*	F	Donation pledge	
Sammy & Len Dowler, 25 Manor Close, Blundellsands, Liverpool, L23 4JX	Yes *Len was relly bald and fat i asced him what went rong in the church and he said Annie painted. Poor Annie im glad i didnt marry Len.*		C	Donation	
Mike Donaldson The Larches, Upper Hale Rd Farnham, Surrey, GU9 7RJ	Yes	If he can find Someone !! *Definitely Tony i dont understand*	F	Donation pledge	
Daniel Fielding 5 Lime Avenue, Blundellsands, Liverpool, 23 5TW	Yes, Verbal, But not Reply to invite	Probably not *Dan remembered me and was nice to me outside the church. I think hes a bit qeer.*	F	Donation pledge	
Janet, Philip, Emma and Tom Greenwood, The Ridings, Green Lane, Ormskirk, Lancs, L39 7BT	Yes		B	Donation	
Simon Johnson 25 Holland Road, Hove, East Sussex, BN3 3WF	Haven't heard *I said to Mal that was looking well but he told*	No *me to piss*		Haven't heard *off Chris*	
Gill & Ken Jones 17 Cambridge Ave Crosby, L23 TBU	Yes	+ daughter Jodie		*off. -Pig !!!*	

2006 November

---

27 Monday Get Miss Johnsons leaving
flowers.
Photocopy mock grades & reports.
Finalise adverts for new staff.
Ray Hopper - mock interview 2.30

---

28 Tuesday

Window cleaning contract up
for renewal: prepare
quotes for discussion.
PTA committee meeting : 7.00pm

---

29 Wednesday

Final numbers for staff
Christmas meal: ring
restaurant
(Get menus in advance.)

Written from hell.
Tuesday.

Dear Mal,

You have broken my heart forever. I know that I will never love anybody like I love you. I know that no-one will ever love you the way I do.

I will wait for you forever. I know Annie is a nice person but she is not the right person for you & when you realise & see sense, I will be here. We are soul-mates, till death do us part.

Lottie.

SUSPECT SHEET	Form MG 25

NAME: Jenny Watson

CURRENT PHOTOGRAPH:	DESCRIPTION: 5'1", round features, brown hair, brown eyes. Plump, very giggly personality and obviously not too intelligent, although very friendly and chatty. DOB: 2/10/62 (44). Parents: Doris Watson – unmarried (d).
	CURRENT ADDRESS: 12b Mount Road, Waterloo, Merseyside.
	OCCUPATION: Left Hulme Comprehensive School with 1 'O' level in Domestic Science; mother, who was a dinner lady at Hulme, gave her a job as a Kitchen Assistant. She has been there ever since. She is now a dinner lady, but works under a Kitchen Manager who is obviously very irritated by her.

ANY OTHER RELEVANT DETAILS:

Single, although seems overly keen to meet the 'man of her dreams'. She chatters constantly and is always bringing conversations back to her non-existent love life. Talks very wistfully about having children.

 Clearly as daft as a brush, but also angry and definitely bearing a grudge against several pupils.

Pauline, Ken + Sam Kelly, Sept '76

Happy Birthday

You're 40 x a lady
to me today
I love you more
than words can say

Mal xxx

PATIENT CASE NOTES

1st **Appointment Date:** 12th Sept 2006   **Case No:** 29 .

Therapist Tracey Tomlinson

CLIENT NAME: Steve Walsh   **D.O.B:** 9/6/81   **AGE:** 25
Marital Status: Single

Occupation: storeman

Drugs of Addiction: Cocaine and marijuana .

Details of notifying Doctor: Dr

Date: 12th September 2006
Session Number: 1
Summary of Session Steve has just got the sack for stealing. He is heavily in debt and has turned to crime both in and outside the workplace. He is desperate (he says) to get off coke but I feel he is only trying to satisfy the court.
Date: 27th September 2006
Session Number: 2
Summary of Session Steve is a bit more relaxed and says he's feeling better. Began to open up. Keen liverpool supporter and very fed up he can't afford to go anymore.
Date: 17th October 2006
Session Number: 3
Summary of Session Missed 3 weeks. Really angry as a friend died two weeks, seems to have shocked him into action. Kept expressing rage at someone called Charles, rich businessman that he blames for his friends death. I think he must be the pusher / supplier .

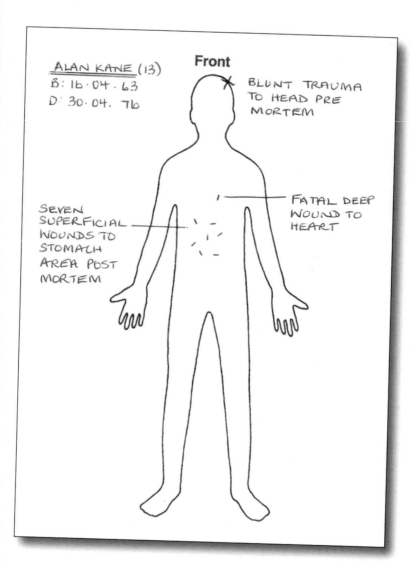

ALAN KANE (13)
B: 16·04·63
D: 30·04·76

Front

BLUNT TRAUMA
TO HEAD PRE
MORTEM

FATAL DEEP
WOUND TO
HEART

SEVEN
SUPERFICIAL
WOUNDS TO
STOMACH
AREA POST
MORTEM

VICTIM SHEET		Form MG 26
NAME: Daniel Fielding		

PHOTOGRAPH (IN SITU)	**Circumstances of Death:**
	Daniel Fielding was found dead in his house (5 Lime Avenue, Blundellsands, Merseyside), 12th October 2006. Neighbours had heard his dog barking for two days and eventually went to investigate. Single wound to the head, one stab wound to the back and the letter C was cut into his left cheek.
	Deceased discovered by whom:
	James Pinnington, next door neighbour, said that the dog barking was 'driving him potty' and he went to tell Mr Fielding to get him to shut it up. He hammered on the door for some time, then went around the back of the house, looking into the drawing room and saw Mr Fielding dead, slumped over a table, apparently having been in the middle of a chess game. James Pinnington did not seem to like Mr Fielding at all.

These initials obviously mean something to someone, or some people, but beats the hell out of us Gov!

	Date and time of discovery 22.55, 12th October 2006.

PHOTOGRAPH OF DECEASED, WHEN ALIVE	**Description:**
	5'11", well built, dark hair, with some grey, brown eyes. Single, homosexual
	DOB: 12/5/61 (45) **NoK:** Mr Charles Fielding.
	Last known address:
	5 Lime Avenue, Blundellsands, Liverpool 23.
	Occupation:
	After leaving Hulme Comp, Mr Fielding went to Goldsmiths in London where he studied Graphic Design. He owned his own Graphics company – Zap that he ran from Albert Dock, city centre.

Any other relevant details :
DCI Farrow was original lead investigating officer, DCS Ian Rutherford then joined the investigation when it became apparent that there were other murders with the same MO. Anthony Milner is chief SSU officer.

Gregson was awarded
an MBE in 1998 for
services to Education
(CCF). Bad call !!!.

• Thursday, June 22nd, 2006

Local Superhead Awarded

Peter Gregson said that he was overwhelmed and extremely proud to be honoured by with a Knighthood from the Queen in her Birthday Honours List.

Mr Gregson was brought back to the failing Hulme Comprehensive three years ago and Inspectors' said that the transformation was remarkable.

Blaze under

Care Order Recommendation Form

Please enter details as accurately and concisely as possible in spaces provided:

Client Name	Paul Judd	Ref. No. 2508	Care Officer	Lesley Wade.

Client Details:	Date of birth: 31/10/60 Age: 10 years 6 Months. Sex: Male Parents: Deceased. Next of Kin: Sarah White (maternal grandmother)

Comments:
Mrs. White has been evaluated as an unsuitable candidate for care responsibilities owing to her advanced years and physical disabilities.

Circumstances of Care Order (use this space to detail any significant background factors).

Paul was recommended to the care of social services following the death of his parents Joseph & Katrina Judd (see attached Police Report No. RP34443). Both parents were known as drug users (although not registered addicts).

Paul currently suffers from repeated nightmares and anxiety attacks that Dr. Kytel (see attached Report P500) attributes to the circumstances of Paul's orphaning. According to the Police Report, both parents died at the scene of a "celebration" in Snickerly Woods, believed by Dr. Kytel to be Pagan in view of the date - 30th April 1971 - and associated evidence, including drug paraphernalia, bonfires, discarded condoms and the presence of several dead animals (including squirrels, several rabbits and a cat).

Paul is believed to have been present, although he is currently refusing or unable to confirm this.

Care Order recommendation?	Yes Yes.	Date: 06/05/71.

Signature of recommending officer	LesleyWade. (Lesley Wade).

VICTIM SHEET	Form MG 26
NAME: Simon Johnson	

PHOTOGRAPH (IN SITU)

Circumstances of Death:
Was found early morning outside his Gym, (LA Fitness, North Road, Brighton) in the back car park, which is not overlooked by the road. It appears that he had tried to get out of his car, a blue convertible Jaguar XKR and fallen out, a lot of blood was in the car and on the grass. There appeared to be a single blow to the head, one stab wound to the stomach and an initial had been carved into his arm – a C. The owner of the gym said that Simon was the last to leave at 23.00 on Monday night, and he waved goodbye, and went to his car at the front of the building, so was the first to drive away and didn't think there was anything wrong.

Deceased discovered by whom:
John Whittacker, deputy manager of the gym who arrived at 6.45 the following morning.

Date and time of discovery
06.45, Tuesday, 26th September 2006.

PHOTOGRAPH OF DECEASED, WHEN ALIVE

Description:
5'9", blonde (dyed hair), stocky build, appeared very fit. Blue Eyes.
DOB: 30/01/62 (44). **NoK:** Orphan.

Last known address:
25 Holland Road, Hove, East Sussex.

Occupation:
Subsequently discovered that like Kevin Doherty and Mike Donaldson, was a member of CRISIS, having been recruited from Blackbrooke Orphanage when they were 16. Their name was changed, but they told their friends that they had been adopted and taken on another name. It appears they were recruited by the government and sent to special schooling, before going to University and then joining up with the above special force.

Any other relevant details : Friends from Hulme Comprehensive identified Simon Johnson as a pupil of Hulme that was called Chris Spence, who they thought had been adopted when 16.

December 2006

Thursday 14

DAY OFF - Final preparations for reunion

Friday 15

Clear all arrangements with Head.

Lunchtime: Go through complete timetable with all

(DON'T PANIC !!.)

Saturday 16

Safety checks on all areas.
Start up heating early: say 11.00
Trim hedges around cricket pitch.
Catering meeting 11.30 Mrs Lowe
School reunion banners.
Wine lists to be printed
Meet caretaker about lighting in hall.
Write blog of events for website. *
Ballroom dancing: PTA
Cath Dale: PTA re decorations
Spreadsheets for years

Sunday 17

Year books on display
Auction display & leaflets (CHASE)
Meeting: Mrs Turner
Pay Disco
Sample menus out @ welcome table
Thank you flowers: Mrs Jolly
All drinks menus out for pre
order on arrival.

December
WK M T W T F S S
48 27 28 29 30 1 2 3
49 4 5 6 7 8 9 10
50 11 12 13 14 15 16 17
51 18 19 20 21 22 23 24
52 25 26 27 28 29 30 31

Definitely not on the school website!

2006 September

25 Monday

INSET DAY: School closed
to pupils

26 Tuesday Richard Hill: interview 3.30.
School break rota spreadsheets.
Enrolment figures to be sent to LEA.
Swimming Gala: 11.00 Leisure Centre
Music stands: send off for cleaning &
maintenance.

27 Wednesday
Gemma Green: Broken Arm (High
Jump) see accident report.

Eve: Governors meeting.
Am. tea/coff.

SUSPECT SHEET	Form MG 25

NAME: Charles Macken

CURRENT PHOTOGRAPH:

DESCRIPTION:
5'11", medium build, blonde hair, blue eyes.

DOB: 14/07/56 (50).
Parents: Patrick & Mary Macken from Belfast.

First wife: Amy, divorced in 1998 – they had three children Tom (12), Molly (10) and Sarah (8).
Second wife: Cassandra (Cassie) married 2000. The children live with Charles Macken, first wife having had a nervous breakdown and unable to cope. Obvious friction between the children and Cassie.

CURRENT ADDRESS:
Originally from Crosby, then moved back to parents' birthplace, (Belfast) when 11. Came back to Southport 10 years ago.

The Grange, Virgins Lane, Birkdale, Southport.

OCCUPATION:
Educated at Hulme Primary, then in Ireland. On return to Southport, set up a successful Import/Export business selling antiquities, (Mackens Emporium). Several shops in the North West.
Charles Macken has recently become a school governor at Hulme Comprehensive, having been approached by Peter Gregson on his return to Hulme.

ANY OTHER RELEVANT DETAILS:

The Macken family are quite well known in Belfast for criminal activities. Several of the extended family have spent time inside. Charles Macken returned to Southport to get away from his family's criminal reputation.
Charles Macken is quite pompous and superior, talking constantly about how well he has done, his beautiful new wife, his children (all at boarding school, not Hulme!) and his social status.

Proposed Order of Service

Music at the Entrance of the Bride
(Bridal March [Lohengrin] - Richard Wagner) is that the right one ? Here Comes the Bride ?

Opening Hymn
Jerusalem (William Blake)

The Introduction

The Marriage

The signing of the Registers
(details of anthem if desired)
Need to choose a hymn / music?

Hymn
The Lord is my Shepherd (Psalm 23:1)

Reading(s) from the Bible and/or other sources - *optional*
Corinthians ?

Vicar's Address

The Prayers
The Lord's Prayer,

Hymn
Make me a Channel of your Peace (Doreen Reynolds)

The Blessing

Music for the exit of Bride and Groom
Three Times a Lady - The Commodores (L. Richie, 1978)

Darling what do you think?
I hope Rev. Humphries lets us have
Lionel Richie — it wouldn't be the same
without our song! I can't wait for the
day — 9 September 2006 — the day you finally
make an honest woman of me!
    I just love you so much!
            XXX

22nd Dec 1977

Dear Mrs Watson,

We can't thank you enough for making us the happiest couple in the world.

Holly is an absolute delight, the quietest happiest baby imaginable. Please pass on this Christmas gift to Jenny with all our love.

David + Alison Oliver.

8.00pm • Saturday 8.30am to

In Memoriam

KANE
Alan

30th April 1976

(30 years gone by, but memories stay, as near and dear as yesterday. Remembering you is easy, we do it every day and missing you is something that will never go away.) — Loving mother and sister Annie.

VICTIM SHEET	Form MG 26
NAME: Kevin Doherty	

PHOTOGRAPH (IN SITU)

Circumstances of Death:
Kevin Doherty was found dead beside the pond in his garden. There appeared to be one stab wound to his back and a letter G had been cut in to his arm.

Deceased discovered by whom:
Heather Sutton was Kevin Doherty's girlfriend, she had a key to his house and had arrived on a Saturday to tidy up his house. According to Miss Sutton, Mr Doherty worked for the government and was away a lot. She had seen him the previous Wednesday, when he was supposed to be abroad for a week. Miss Sutton was extremely distressed.

Date and time of discovery
11.12, Saturday 16th September 2006.

PHOTOGRAPH OF DECEASED, WHEN ALIVE

Description:
5' 10", tanned skin, brown eyes, brown hair slightly greying. Well built, lean and muscled, apparently very fit.
DOB: 31/10/60 (45).   **NoK:** Orphan.

Last known address:
The Barn, Virgins Lane, Ormskirk, Lancs.

Occupation: It would appear that Kevin Doherty was originally called Paul Judd and was a pupil at Hulme Comprehensive.
He works for the government, but we are unable to find out more details at this time as his job is covered by the official secrets act.

Any other relevant details :
DCS Ian Rutherford – lead Investigating Officer. Same MO as Daniel Fielding, so we knew that this could possibly be the work of a serial killer.
Once the murders occurred at Hulme Comprehensive and we questioned pupils we learnt that Paul Judd was a flambuoyant, highly intelligent and adventurous pupil. He left school when he was 16 and who completely lost touch for several years. An avid Liverpool Supporter, he was a member of The Anfield Gang at school. His friends in that gang were surprised when Paul got back in touch with them several years later and told them that his name was now Kevin Doherty. He told them his job was top secret and couldn't tell them what he was doing, but wanted to join them as often as he could in The Cop.

the Womens
hospitel
Wed 22nd Aug 1979

Dear Sally

thank you for the sweats
the nerses are relly nise and
my stiches are heeling nisely
but the docters says i cant
hav any mor babis which
is relly sad and i hate
Neel cos he got me preggers
and his baby made it all
go rong.

See you soon
luv and kisses

Jen

Mr Macken;

I hope that you have a better nature for me to appeal to.

My name is Tracey Tomlinson and when I was at Hulme Comprehensive I was called Green. I vaguely remember you and as I feel that there is perhaps a connection you may listen to me, particularly as you are now a wealthy businessman and more importantly, school governor, responsible for the welfare of our children.

I am a drugs counsellor and over the last few months clients of mine have confided in me and your name has cropped up several times. I did think there must be a coincidence but too many similarities, too many coincidences.

Please stop, surely our children are more important than your now bulging bank account. I am pleading with you before I have to take this matter further.

Tracey Tomlinson.

22.43   07/08/06

Following a dispatch call from H.Q, a request from Richardson, I was sent to the Falls Road to observe Patrick Macken who was, on a tip off, meeting a member of the ILDA to pass some illegal substances.

23.52

As yet there has been no contact. Patrick Macken is still drinking on his own. Macken arrived in his black mercedes convertible, wearing jeans, black shirt and beige overcoat

Notes

TOP SECRET

Detective's Conclusion

Only read this once you have
discovered the identity of the
murderer – NO PEEKING!

You were right Ian – a very complicated and unusual case.
After a few late nights, plenty of caffeine and too much
nicotine I think I have made some sense of the
assembled evidence and have come to the same
conclusions as you – I think there is enough evidence
for you to present to the CPS and I'm sure that a jury
would reach the right decision on this very sad case.
I hope you find my notes of use. Good luck Ian.

Having viewed all the evidence I knew the key to this case was to understand what the letters carved into each dead body symbolised – something I was unable to discover until I'd looked further into the lives of the victims (and the suspects who had been so accurately pin-pointed by your investigation, Ian).

My initial impression was that these murders were purposeful and not random. Victims were targeted with determination and at some considerable risk to the perpetrator. Four victims within the space of 24 hours at the Hulme Comprehensive school reunion suggested to me that the murderer was on a mission and was keen to complete what they started three months earlier.

I began my examination of the evidence by going back, chronologically, to the first murder of Paul Judd – or as he was known at the time of his death, Kevin Doherty. He was killed on the 14th September 2006, beside the pond in his garden and, like most of the subsequent victims, was hit over the back of the head and rendered unconscious before being stabbed and having a letter carved into his left forearm. Being a member of an elite government undercover agency called CRISIS (Covert Response Investigative Security and Intelligence Service) you would think it would be impossible to take this man by surprise and I therefore had to deduce that his killer was known to him and that they were someone with whom he felt comfortable.

Like Kevin Doherty, Mike Donaldson and Simon Johnson (or as they were christened Paul Judd, Tony Williams and Chris Spence) were orphans who originally lived at the Blackbrooke Home in Waterloo, Merseyside. In the course of my review I learnt that in the 60s and 70s extremely intelligent, feisty and daring boys were groomed by a government agency for a life of adventure (and danger) in CRISIS. The government targeted orphans who did not have the responsibility and emotional ties of a family. Paul, Chris and Tony all changed their names and identities and only stayed in touch with a few friends from their school – Hulme Comprehensive in Crosby, a suburb of Liverpool. Although these friends knew Paul, Chris and Tony had been taken to a new and special school, and knew of their change of names and addresses, they never knew of their secret occupation.

It seemed too much of a coincidence that all the apparently random victims were at the same school together and it was at this point that I would have known there was a link, even if the subsequent murders hadn't occurred at the Hulme Comprehensive reunion. The fact all eight victims were pupils at Hulme focused my attention on the people who knew them and I too came up with the same suspect list as you.

The letters were, as I've already said, highly significant – but I wasn't sure whether they represented a secret meaning known only to the murderer or whether the murderer was telling the victims something. I will come back to this later, but first I think it would be useful to review the suspects and evidence and offer my considered conclusions about each.

Although not having had the 'pleasure' of meeting Jenny Watson, I got a distinct impression from your case notes of what this slightly dim, but loveable, woman was like.

Having been brought up by a single mother who didn't seem to like her daughter, Jenny craved love and attention, particularly from boys. At only 12-and-a-half Jenny became pregnant for the first time – and when her mother realised the cause of her daughter's weight gain Mrs Watson encouraged Jenny to hide the pregnancy from her school friends and keep the baby – not out of love and sympathy for her daughter, however, but so that when the baby (a girl) was born, Mrs Watson could sell her to a childless couple for what was then an enormous amount of money; money which clearly never came her daughter's way – in one diary page Jenny mentioned she wanted to go to the zoo, but "Mum said we couldn't afford it".

Interestingly Tony Williams, the teenage father of Jenny's first baby, had the letter "G" carved into his flesh; was that Jenny's handiwork, telling Tony (or Mike as he subsequently became) he had abandoned her and their little Girl?

Her next pregnancy, only a year later, was by Mal (Brearley as he was then before the Kane family adopted him). Jenny loved him and said she thought he would marry her. I believe that was never the case; the boys were only interested in the rampant testosterone that ruled their nether regions at that age and Jenny was an easy target, eager to give away her favours, desperately looking for love. The pregnancy that Mrs Watson encouraged her daughter to hide produced a Boy. Mal had a B carved in his side.

Jenny had a third baby the following year and this time the father was Paul Judd; he had a G carved into his forearm. Her third baby was a Girl.

Jenny became pregnant for a fourth time, this time by Neil Richardson, but sadly the pregnancy went seriously wrong and Jenny had to have a hysterectomy. Knowing that she would never have the baby that she so desperately craved, did Jenny become murderous and kill the fathers of her babies thirty years later?

This initially seemed a fruitful line of enquiry, but a couple of things troubled me: I couldn't understand how Jenny knew who the boys had grown up to be – the two orphans, Tony and Paul, weren't friends with Jenny at school and certainly didn't stay in touch, so how did Jenny discover who they became and, more importantly, where they lived?

It transpires that Jenny was a part-time cleaner for Annie and Mal Kane. Jenny wasn't invited to Mal and Annie's wedding on the 9th September last year, but she did go to watch. The wedding was brought to a sudden halt when Annie Kane was taken ill – but as they were going into the church, did Jenny recognise these men and wondered why their friends were calling them by different names? Did seeing those men from all those years ago set her on a murderous course? We know that Jenny found the wedding invitation list and could therefore have discovered where these men lived.

But if Jenny were our killer why would she have killed Faith Cole, Tracey Tomlinson, Daniel Fielding or Chris Spence, none of whom could have been blamed for Jenny's childless state?

The wedding of Annie and Mal Kane could have been the catalyst for another suspect. Apparently living happily together for 27 years, they had only decided to get married because Annie's mother learned she was terminally ill with breast cancer and said that nothing would make her happier than if her daughter and adopted son would marry and, by so doing, 'legitimise' her granddaughter Katie.

Friends said that both Annie and Mal seemed very happy and excited that they were getting married but it was when Annie was walking down the aisle, with the organ playing 'The Bridal March', that Annie became ill and collapsed at the altar. Annie was taken to hospital and although tests showed nothing was physically wrong with her, Annie's personality appeared to change – so much so her friends were increasingly concerned for her wellbeing. There could have been two reasons for this:

Firstly, during the post-mortem of Mal Kane it was discovered he too was terminally ill with bowel cancer. Annie

Kane denied knowledge of his illness but he had the letter "B" cut into his side and I wondered whether this was significant. Perhaps Annie did know and it was the trauma at the prospect of losing both her partner and her mother that caused her to collapse.

Secondly, evidence showed Mal was having trouble with their relationship; Annie had become very distant since the wedding and Mal had been visiting an old school friend, Lottie Trent – a relationship counsellor who was also an ex-girlfriend and who still carried a torch for him. It appeared innocent enough on Mal's part; he was going to Lottie for advice, but Lottie clearly had other things on her mind; she seemed keen to renew their teenage relationship. There was also an email from Mal to Faith Cole, another ex-pupil of Hulme Comprehensive and someone who was earning a very lucrative income as a dominatrix in London.

Mal and Faith had remained friends from school, as part of the "Anfield Gang" (as they called themselves) – ardent Liverpool supporters, who often met up at matches. It would appear Mal and Faith had struck up a more intimate relationship over the last few months – he had visited her premises and obviously enjoyed her "special services". Had Annie found out and was this a reason for her not wanting to go through with the marriage? Had Faith in fact killed Mal and Faith for their betrayal? This was, I think, a distinct possibility but there doesn't appear to be any evidence this relationship occurred until after the wedding date.

Aside from this, Annie may have had a motive to kill Mal and Faith, but surely she had no motive to kill any of the other victims? From everything I learned about Annie, she didn't seem to be a vicious killer and, certainly before the day of her wedding, she appeared to be a very happy, friendly and popular partner, mother, employee and valued member of the local community.

At this stage my thoughts turned to Lottie Trent, another suspect that you highlighted, who did not appear to be such a happy, well-balanced person. In fact she seemed to have been a troubled soul from a very early age.

Lottie was the only daughter of David and Sylvia Trent and she inherited a label that hung over her head all her life – the daughter of a murderer who was one of the last people to be executed in Britain.

David Trent had killed a prostitute in 1962 and was hanged when his daughter was only a year old. To compound this poor infant's unhappy start in life, on the first anniversary of Mr Trent's execution, Sylvia Trent committed suicide, leaving her daughter to be raised by a violent and embittered grandmother. Lottie's grandmother made her life a living hell and Lottie hated both her parents for, as she saw it, abandoning her to a miserable existence. Lottie grew up with a hatred of prostitutes, blaming them for both her father's execution and her subsequent misery.

Did Lottie kill Mal because she believed he would finally see sense and come back to her now that his 'marriage' appeared to be on the rocks – a dream which was shattered when he let it be known that he only wanted her advice and friendship? Did Lottie kill Faith when she learned Mal had been to visit the dominatrix and that he had, on more than one occasion, spent a very enjoyable night sampling all the delights that Faith could offer?

I do think Lottie – a vindictive and bitter woman – is capable of murder but if she were our murderer I couldn't discover any motive for the other six victims.

Turning now to another of your suspects, the investigation established Charles Macken attended Hulme Primary School several years before the majority of the victims and it seems unlikely he knew any of them during his time as a pupil at Hulme.

Macken lived in Crosby for the first ten years of his life, but left the area to return to Belfast with his Irish-born parents and siblings.

The Mackens had, I believe, originally left Belfast because the police were investigating what amounted to a mafia-style set-up – at that time the Macken family in general were suspected of involvement in both protection racketeering and drug dealing – in addition to many other crimes. When the Mackens returned to Belfast it appears they stayed on just the right side of the law; what I sincerely believe to be their many criminal undertakings were so cleverly concealed that the Northern Irish police were unable to prove any of their many suspicions.

On finishing school in Belfast, Charles Macken joined his father's antiques business, which was ostensibly doing very well and which provided a lucrative living for the family. He married into another wealthy Belfast family and his wife and subsequent children enjoyed a very good lifestyle.

However, the persistence of the Northern Ireland police force meant that Charles, having taken control of the family business, began to feel the heat of a police investigation on his back and he took the decision to return to Merseyside to escape their attentions.

His wife, Amy, wasn't happy in England and although the family business he established in Liverpool (Macken's Emporium in Bold Street) was apparently doing very well, Macken's marriage hit the rocks. He began an affair with a much younger woman that eventually led to both Amy's return to Ireland (where she later suffered a nervous breakdown as a direct result of Macken's adulterous behaviour) and their eventual divorce. Following this Macken married his "trophy wife" Cassandra and, due to his ex-wife's psychological condition, gained custody of their three children (none of whom, it became clear, seemed to like their new mother).

In 2003 Peter Gregson, the "Superhead" who had been brought in to turn the then-failing Hulme Comprehensive around, approached Charles Macken, ex-pupil of Hulme Primary and wealthy local businessman, to become a school governor. Macken readily agreed, believing it would raise his business profile and cement his status as a pillar of the local community. It would also, he believed, provide further cover for what your investigation discovered were his extensive criminal activities. Things were, however, beginning to unravel quickly in Macken's "business" life.

Along with the rugs, furniture and home accessories that were sold in Macken's Emporium Charles had, I am convinced, been importing drugs from Afghanistan. The Merseyside police had been aware that Class A drugs were being pushed at Liverpool's home football matches and they had Macken under observation for some time as they tried to collect evidence to prove their case. A dealer, who had close personal ties to Macken, had been arrested and charged but he was unwilling to broker a deal with the police in return for naming his supplier.

Mal Kane, the Sports Editor at the Liverpool Echo and life-long Liverpool fan, had apparently been involved in a little detective work of his own – initially for the best of motives (he hated the fact his 'beautiful game' was being sullied by the activities of these evil traders) but eventually through naked, if perhaps understandable, self-interest.. Kane had come to the same conclusions as the police – but unlike the police he didn't wait to get the proof; instead he went straight for the jugular and blackmailed Macken. Mal Kane needed money urgently; his cancer was spreading and his only hope of arresting the disease, he believed, was through a course of treatment involving two drugs (Avastin and Erbitux) that had not been cleared for patient use in the UK. Treatment was, however, available in the United States – but at a very high price. Mal knew his only hope of survival was to have private treatment and that Charles Macken could provide the money he desperately needed for a four week course of treatment at a private American clinic.

Tracey Tomlinson (or Green as she was at school), was happily married to a doctor, Chris Tomlinson, with whom she had three children (Zoe, Jamie and Milly). Once her children were at school full-time, Tracey trained as a drugs counsellor, having witnessed the hopelessness of drug addicts when employed as a receptionist at her future husband's surgery. Tracey had been counselling addicts in the Liverpool area for many years and during the course of their sessions, patients would occasionally mention the names of local dealers.

These names, invariably those of petty criminals and addicts like her patients, meant nothing to her – until one day a patient inadvertently revealed the name of Charles Macken as the source of much of the area's crack cocaine. Tracey was appalled that an apparently respectable local businessman – a Governor of the school she had attended and to which she currently sent her own children – was involved in this disgusting trade.

While Tracey's professional code of practice prevented her from passing her suspicions about Macken to the police, she wrote to Charles Macken pleading with him to stop his killer trade. Did Charles Macken meet Tracey Tomlinson at the school reunion and decide to silence the meddling do-gooder before she could deal him and his illegal business a fatal blow? Did Neil Richardson, a detective chief inspector with the Northern Ireland police, arrive at the reunion and immediately recognise Charles Macken, a member of the family the police have been after for so long?

Charles Macken clearly puts his own personal wealth and well-being above the lives of the drug addicts off whom he feeds – were the lives of a reporter, counsellor and police officer no more valuable to a man whose only concern seems to be his own happiness and luxurious lifestyle?

Did Charles Macken arrive for the school reunion and turn it into an opportunity to remove these obstacles to his continued ideal life?

I certainly believe Macken guilty of many crimes (and I believe enough evidence has been amassed by you to warrant his arrest on suspicion of drug dealing); I am also of the opinion that Macken would, under certain circumstances, show little compunction in ordering the murder of those he believed to be a threat – but in this particular case I can find no evidence to connect him to Kevin Doherty, Simon Johnson and Mike Donaldson. I see no reason to suppose he even knew of their existence.

Your final suspect was Sir Peter Gregson KBE, the current headmaster of Hulme Comprehensive and a happily married father and grandfather.

In 1975 Gregson was a Maths and PE teacher at Hulme Comprehensive. He was also in charge of the school's Combined Cadet Force (CCF) and, in this capacity, he frequently oversaw the many outward bound courses organised by the school at this time. In 1976 Peter Gregson was the lead teacher on the disastrous course where a school pupil

(Alan Kane) was murdered, near to the Leigh Valley Centre where the outward bound camp was based. A police investigation concluded that Peter Gregson and his fellow teachers supervising the course were not negligent in any way; the investigation concluded that Alan Kane had got up in the middle of the night to go outside to urinate when an unknown assailant, possibly a paedophile (although no sexual injury was found), abducted and stabbed Kane eight times before leaving Alan's body semi-buried in the nearby woods. No one was ever arrested for this murder.

This tragic occurrence did not seem to damage Peter Gregson's career; he went on to become headmaster in a failing school in London and was eventually awarded an MBE for his services to CCF in 1998. In 2003 Gregson was brought back to the failing Hulme Comprehensive in an attempt to turn the school around, which he did in only two years.

Gregson was made a Knight of the British Empire in the Birthday Honours List, 2006, for his Services to Education. A pillar of the educational community you might think, but it would appear from the evidence you uncovered during this investigation that Peter Gregson had another, much darker and unsuspected side to his personality, that of child abuser.

During at least some part of his teaching career – perhaps under the guise of offering extra tuition and the prospect of improved grades, even to pupils not in his classes – Peter Gregson sexually abused boys that he thought would stay quiet. He would grade their efforts in his 'Little Black Register'. Mal Kane was graded a "B". Was this the key to unlocking the case?

Mal Kane had, as was discovered in a blackmail note to Gregson, decided to get as much money as he possibly could for his cancer treatment – were there other boys at the school who had been abused by Gregson and was he frightened of losing his Knighthood?

Were any of the orphanage boys his victims and did he think he had to silence all the boys who could potentially ruin the life he had worked so hard to create?

That is very possible. Gregson probably could have discovered where the boys had gone – but if Peter Gregson is our killer, what did the initials symbolise – as far as I know "F" is the lowest school grade, but two of the victims had "G" carved into their flesh. In addition, why would he kill Tracey Tomlinson and Faith Cole? Unless one of the boys had told them – and we have no evidence to show they knew about Gregson's vile secret – surely, they could not be a threat to his freedom?

Peter Gregson appeared to have the most to lose in this tangled case. The exposure of his sordid past would surely have led to arrest, conviction and imprisonment – the end of his successful career, the breakdown of his marriage and of his relationship with his children and grandchildren. However, one final piece of evidence led me to dismiss Peter Gregson as our killer. From the original investigation we know that Daniel Fielding was one of Gregson's chosen boys – but as we learned from a letter he wrote to Mal Kane, Daniel did not threaten Gregson. On the contrary, Fielding was quite firm in saying that he wasn't interested in dragging up the past.

Having read my notes of this case it might seem I am no closer to discovering the identity of the "Capital Murderer" than when I began. However, to answer the question of who did commit the "Capital Murders" – and, perhaps more importantly, why they were committed – I believe we need to go back over thirty years to re-examine the death of Alan Kane.

In 1971 a young boy called Paul Judd was present at a pagan festival celebration where his bohemian parents both died from a drug overdose. They had instilled into Paul the belief that these festivities (which, among other things, involved animal sacrifices) were carried out to ensure happiness and success in the future. All of Paul's family and relatives were pagans and they instilled in his impressionable young mind the belief that the Universe would give you anything you wanted; all you had to do was ask and then please the gods with sacrifices.

Paul, an extremely intelligent and wild child, was taken into care believing that "the gods" had taken his parents that night because that was their wish; they had chosen to go on to a 'higher plain' and that through their departure Paul would eventually have the chance of the better life their sacrifice would provide.

Paul, a strong character and a ringleader for some of his fellow pupils at Hulme, had a loyal gang that followed him and believed everything this very strong and persuasive young man told them to believe. He persuaded them they could ask for anything they wanted in later life and that it would be granted them. An aged document showed nine children had written down their ambitions beside their initials and it would appear they had sealed their covenant with bloody thumbprints. One wanted to be an astronaut, another a footballer playing for Liverpool; as with all teenagers, they all had their dreams.

But, unlike most teenagers, I believe they didn't just hope for the best. Influenced and persuaded by Paul they agreed to make the ultimate sacrifice to achieve their goals – a human sacrifice was needed to ensure their ambitions would become a guaranteed reality. A candidate was chosen, a sickly, whiney, child who was disliked by all his peers. They agreed he wouldn't be missed and that the gods would be pleased!

On the 30th April, the eve of Beltane – one of the most important of the pagan festivals and the night Paul's parents died – Alan Kane was murdered. He was stabbed 8 times and the covenant with the gods was made – their childhood fantasies were secure.

The following morning Alan was found to be missing and his body was, after a lengthy search, discovered partially buried in nearby woods. The police were alerted and a squad car was dispatched to inform Alan's parents, Pat and Dave Kane, who were happily getting ready for the wedding that day of Pat's sister, Janet. Annie, their daughter, was staying overnight with Janet at her grandparent's house and was full of excitement that she was going to be the chief bridesmaid at the wedding.

After the Kanes had been informed of the death of their son, Mr Kane said he would have to go to the church to collect their daughter. A police car drove him to the church and they arrived just as the wedding march had struck up and Janet was walking down the aisle, followed by the beautiful bridesmaid Annie Kane.

The wedding was halted and David Kane explained to Janet what had happened. Janet was devastated and immediately decided to postpone the wedding in order to go to her grieving sister. The police drove an hysterical Annie home and the reporting officer noted at the time that he thought it rather strange that the thirteen year old Annie seemed unconcerned that her brother had been found dead – she was hysterical because the wedding had been stopped and this meant she was not going to be a bridesmaid. (The rearranged wedding was a quiet affair at a register office, but Annie did eventually get to wear her dress!).

After a traumatic year, Pat and Dave Kane tried to get their life back on track. Annie seemed to have recovered remarkably well and her teachers commented that her work and demeanour actually improved. Pat and Dave couldn't have any more children due to a complication when she gave birth to her son Alan but decided to give an orphan a second chance at a happy home life and adopted Malcolm Brearley, a boy of a similar age to their dead son and someone they knew was already a great friend of Annie's. The two became inseparable and although both had first loves at school, their affection for each other grew and eventually, when they went to university, they became an item.

Over the last four months 8 ex-pupils have been stabbed and all have had letters carved in their flesh. Alan Kane was stabbed 8 times – and all because Paul Judd persuaded his gang that Alan's murder would bring them everything their hearts desired.

Mal Brearley (MB), Faith Cole (FC), Daniel Fielding (DF), Tracey Green (TG), Paul Judd (PJ), Chris Spence (CS), Tony Williams (TW), Neil Richardson (NR) – all are now dead, stabbed to death as they had stabbed Alan.

But why the letters, not their initials, as they had written on their blood agreement – what could that mean? I believe that it was the wedding of Annie and Mal Kane that set off the sad chain of events that we have witnessed.

As Annie walked down the aisle last September, to the tune of "Here Comes the Bride", it snapped her back 30 years to the marriage of her aunt – to the memory of when she heard that her brother Alan had been murdered. The memory she had suppressed for 30 years came flooding back and at last, after all this time, Annie was finally engulfed by the guilt that she had never felt before.

AK was the 9th set of initials on the document.

Annie Kane knew that her brother was going to be killed that night but she didn't care. She loathed him and had signed her initials on the deed of covenant with the rest of Paul's gang, of which she was an adoring member. AK wanted to be a Famous Actress. Skills I do not believe she will have to use under interrogation, as I suspect she will willingly confess. In fact I believe that Annie Kane is so eager to be caught that she will already have written a confession, which is yet to be found.

Annie has avenged Alan's death and she no doubt feels she has gone some way to right the wrongs done to him all those years ago. Perhaps a long incarceration is what she feels she deserves. I actually believe that she should be put on a suicide watch; with her adored husband gone and her mother dying, Annie Kane may believe that she has nothing left to live for.

And the letters, that so perplexed us throughout this case – D C C B G C C G – the thing that caused Annie to collapse; the thing that brought all those memories flooding back, the day that she was nearly a bridesmaid – snatched away just as she was walking down the aisle; the thing that reminds her that she was too selfish, too bound up in her burning desire to be a bridesmaid to care about her baby brother's murder – when unscrambled to GCCC, GDBC – they become the musical notes that make up the anthem "Here comes the Bride".

Acknowledgements

The production of "Love Letters Straight From My Heart" has involved a lot of help from many people.

I would like to thank Chris Livesey, Donna O'Doherty, Trudy Lowe, Michael Parsons, Martin Payne, Mike Rawling and Damon Smith for their valuable contributions.

I would also like to thank the following people for providing their 'bodies', their thoughts, their handwriting, their images, their houses, their buildings and most of all their valuable time.

Maria Allen; Becky, Paul and Lizzie Benneyworth; Amy Black; Dana, Mark and Benjamin Braithwaite; Geri Brown; Marilyn, Nick and Andrew Catterall; Ron Cook; Brenda Davies; Jayne Domville; Tim Farrow; Sue and John Gerrard; Maria Gowland; Mark Hedges;Chris and Julia Livesey; Em Macer, Barney MacCrudden and Max Macer; Mary-Anne, Paul, Joe, Kitty and Lizzie McKay; Maureen Pinnington; Dave Smith; Paul Stevens; Sue and Tony Swift; Matty Walsh; Marilyn Waring. The Little Chapel at Rodborough Tabernacle.

Also available from Trinity Mirror NW2

Discover Liverpool

Join author Ken Pye on a voyage of discovery around the Capital of Culture.

Where are Liverpool's amazing secret tunnels?
Where is the city's smallest house?
What lies under St George's Hall?
Who was Liverpool's gentle giant?

Discover Liverpool takes you into the heart of the city and out into the suburbs to reveal the historic characters, buildings, myths and legends that have all helped to make this city great.

This full-colour guide book with easy-to-read maps features eight superb driving tours and more than two hours of tour highlights on DVD.

A must for every Merseyphile!

Echoes of Liverpool

Take a journey through the past present and future with Merseyside's much-loved newspaper, the Liverpool Echo.

Echoes of Liverpool revisits some of the great stories that have rocked the city and indeed the world since the Echo first hit the streets in 1879.

See how the Echo reported events such as two world wars, the opening of the Liver Buildings, the first man on the moon, the murder of John Lennon, the Hillsborough disaster and the day Liverpool learned it would become Capital of Culture.

Echoes of Liverpool also takes a trip back in time to see how the paper may have reported the day the city got its Charter from King John. Then travel to the future to see how the Echo might look in 100 years time as the cloned Beatles are front page news.

Read all about it with Echoes of Liverpool.

To order these titles and many more visit www.merseyshop.com or call 0845 143 0001 (Monday to Friday, 9am-5pm)